Hotel Housekeeping Management

Changing Trends and Developments

Jayanti Jayanti

(G) Goodfellow Publishers Ltd

(G) Published by Goodfellow Publishers Limited,
26 Home Close, Wolvercote, Oxford OX2 8PS
http://www.goodfellowpublishers.com

British Library Cataloguing in Publication Data: a catalogue record for this title is available from the British Library.

Library of Congress Catalog Card Number: on file.

ISBN: 978-1-911635-55-0

DOI: 10.23912/9781911635543-5270

Copyright © Jayanti Jayanti, 2023

All rights reserved. The text of this publication, or any part thereof, may not be reproduced or transmitted in any form or by any means, electronic or mechanical, including photocopying, recording, storage in an information retrieval system, or otherwise, without prior permission of the publisher or under licence from the Copyright Licensing Agency Limited. Further details of such licences (for reprographic reproduction) may be obtained from the Copyright Licensing Agency Limited, of Saffron House, 6–10 Kirby Street, London EC1N 8TS.

All trademarks used herein are the property of their repective owners, The use of trademarks or brand names in this text does not imply any affiliation with or endorsement of this book by such owners.

Design and typesetting by P.K. McBride, www.macbride.org.uk

Cover design by Cylinder

Printed by Lightning Source

Contents

Preface — vi
About the author — viii

1: Hospitality, Hotels and Housekeeping — 1
Types of hotels — 1
Hotels and housekeeping — 7
Housekeeping in other establishments — 9

2: Overview of the Housekeeping Department — 15
Housekeeping's coordination with different departments in a hotel — 16
Layout — 20
Housekeeping department responsibilities — 23
Organisation structure — 25

3: Managing Housekeeping Personnel — 29
Introduction — 29
Management functions in housekeeping — 30
Job descriptions and specifications — 31
Attributes of housekeeping staff — 36

4: Contracts and Outsourcing in the Housekeeping Department — 39
What is outsourcing? — 39
Outsourcing costs — 40
Advantages of outsourcing — 42
Disadvantages of outsourcing — 43
Challenges of outsourcing — 45

5: Planning Housekeeping Operations — 51
Operational planning — 51
Performance — 52
Productivity standards — 53
Manpower planning — 55
Covid-19 and its impact on productivity — 57
Staff engagement for enhanced productivity — 61

6: Housekeeping Equipment and Supplies — 73
- Cleaning equipment — 73
- Classification of cleaning equipment — 74
- **Cleaning specification** — 78
- Agents — 79

7: Cleaning Procedure of a Guest Room — 89
- Principle — 89
- Frequency — 90
- Cleaning for health and safety — 92
- Cleaning procedure of rooms post Covid-19 — 94
- Room status — 96
- Cleaning checklists — 98
- Turn down service — 103
- Cleaning of public areas — 104

8: Budgeting for Housekeeping — 109
- Budget cycle — 110
- Budget classification — 111
- Controlling expenses — 112
- Purchasing — 113
- Total Quality Management — 114

9: Linen, Uniform and Laundry Operations — 119
- Linen and its importance — 119
- Laundry operations — 121
- Hotel uniform — 131
- Determining par levels and inventory levels — 133

10: Safety and Security — 139
- Legislation — 141
- Risk and risk assessment stages — 144
- Dealing with emergencies — 147
- Lost and Found — 148
- Pest control — 149

11: Hotel Guest Rooms — 153
- Types — 153
- Design — 155
- Trends — 159
- Guest room amenities — 160

12: Design and Interior Decoration 165
  Design considerations 165
  Colour schemes 168
  Lighting 169
  Flooring 171
  Wall covering 172
  Bathroom 173
  Planning for differently abled guests 175
  Flower arrangements 176

13: Ecotels 181
  Environmental considerations 181
  Ethical sourcing of the uniform 188
  Pro-environmental behaviours 189

14: Changing Trends in Hotel Housekeeping 195
  Design 195
  Amenities 198
  Processes 202
  Ergonomics 207

15: Technology in the Housekeeping Department 213
  Software and apps 213
  Technological solutions 219

Preface

Hotel Housekeeping Management covers the operational and management aspects of housekeeping operations. The housekeeping department is at the core of hotel operations as one cannot attract the prospective customer without a clean, hygienic, luxurious room. This book aims to present a well-rounded picture of the housekeeping department, and students pursuing hospitality degrees must understand its operational and management responsibilities. Housekeeping is one of the largest departments in the hotel operation, and covers various sections which will be discussed in the book.

Although housekeeping is not the major revenue generating department, its role is to offer a clean, immaculate,and pleasant environment to a guest and is vital to meet and exceed the guest experience, which will help to maximise the revenue. The personalisation and customisation that the department brings to each stay is responsible for the customers' satisfaction, experience, and loyalty. Reading through each chapter you will learn the areas of responsibility and the essential attributes of the housekeeper and gain hints of what it takes to be a great housekeeper after you qualify. Housekeeping is a department which entails art as well as science. Art, because of the creativity that one brings to make each guest's stay memorable, and science because you need to understand the chemicals that are used for cleaning the room and the public areas as well those used in the laundry operation and many more.

Passion is the key to success, especially when it comes to hospitality and more specifically to housekeeping. One needs to have that passion for the subject as well as the pride in working and managing the department. If you are seeing yourself as a hotel manager and general manager, you need to understand the nitty gritty of the housekeeping department and therefore each chapter of the book is planned in a simple language to create that understanding. The book covers the trends and developments in housekeeping, making it up to date with the evolving landscape. The housekeeping operation goes back a very long way, and even before the pandemic the rooms were cleaned, maintained, and sanitised, however Covid-19 showed the world the forgotten importance of the department. Suddenly, the focus shifted to the housekeeping department and its staff were mentioned as 'unsung heroes' as the department cyclically regenerated as a phoenix. The book covers the process and product adaptation that happened in the housekeeping operation post Covid-19. The author is grateful to the leading luxury hotels of London and their housekeeping leaders for taking out time and participating in interviews to enrich this book. Its contents have been developed by engaging with the industry and therefore it offers up to date and practical insights.

The book covers the meaning and definition of hotel and housekeeping in the first chapter, and looks at housekeeping roles in other establishments. The second chapter gives a close overview of the housekeeping department, the organisation and coordination with the other departments as well as its responsibilities. The third chapter focuses on the attributes of housekeeping personnel and the management functions of the housekeeping. Chapter 4 discusses outsourcing in housekeeping department and the commonly outsourced activities. Chapter 5 aims to bring the theoretical perspective of the housekeeping department with regards to productivity management and manpower planning, and discusses the shift that has come in the operational planning of the housekeeping department.

Chapters 6 and 7 delve into the selection of cleaning supplies and equipment. The cleaning procedures of the guest room and public areas are covered with appropriate checklists to ensure efficient workflow and quality of the task. The management functions of the housekeeping are covered in the Chapter 8, which discusses budgeting, purchasing, avoiding wastages, and controlling expenses. Chapter 9 covers the linen, uniform and laundry operations and ways to exercise control. Chapter 10 is about safety and security of the staff and the employees, safety legislations and risk assessment and management. Chapter 11 shows the various types of guest rooms, and leads in to Chapter 12 which covers various aspects of design like colour, light, flooring, wallcovering, and considerations when planning the guest room and public area design. It is important to understand that as a housekeeping leader you do wear the hat of the health and safety officers as well as interior designers. So, a good understanding of these concepts helps you to be a more successful housekeeper. Chapter 13 on ecotels and environmental considerations covers pro-environmental behaviours, and green initiatives by the various hotel brands as well as the relevant certifications. The last two chapters of book give an overview of the trends in housekeeping design, process and product, as well as the latest technological solutions in the housekeeping operation. The book offers the latest trends and adaptations that were made in the housekeeping operations post Covid-19 to enhance the operational effectiveness, guest experience and the staff productivity.

I hope you enjoy reading this comprehensive and essential textbook on *Hotel Housekeeping Management* if you are aspiring to be a future hotel manager and leader.

About the author

Jayanti Jayanti, based in London, United Kingdom, has 15+ years of experience in academia and the hospitality industry. She is working as a senior lecturer, course leader and placement leader at London Gellar College of Hospitality and Tourism, University of West London.

She is a Fellow of the Higher Education Academy (UK), associate member of the Institute of Hospitality (UK), member of the United Kingdom Housekeepers Association (UKHA) and a member of the Council for Hospitality Management Education (CHME).

She has a post graduate certificate in Academic Practice (Higher Education) from the University of West London and has completed her graduate programme and post graduate diploma from the Oberoi Centre of Learning and Development, New Delhi. She has a graduate degree in Hotel and Hospitality Administration from the Institute of Hotel Management, India and has also completed her masters in Hotel Management.

She worked in luxury hotels prior to joining academia. She has been in academia for 10+ years and has published multiple articles related to hospitality, customer experience, consumer behaviours and employability.

1: Hospitality, Hotels and Housekeeping

This chapter will help you to:

- Understand the term hospitality, hotels and their types.
- Evaluate the different portfolio of brands under international hotel brands and their unique selling points.
- Review the importance and of housekeeping department in hotel and other sectors.

Introduction: Hospitality and hotels

Hospitality is all about providing welcoming and friendly treatment to a guest or a visitor. The word 'hospitality' is derived from the Latin word '*hospes*' meaning to receive. Therefore, hospitality is mostly the relationship between the host and the guest. Humans have been and will always be inquisitive to travel through the world on business and leisure. Once we are away from home, there is a need to feel safe, welcomed, and comfortable. The hospitality industry refers to the varied range of services for people away from home. These include (but are not limited to) accommodation, food, transportation, tourism, entertainment etc. Accommodation is vital aspects in the hospitality sector and hotels are primarily in the service of this need. Over time, hotels have been able to offer many other services, depending upon the need of the guests, location and culture.

Types of hotels

The biggest challenge for any customer is to find the right accommodation matching their needs and expectations, offers value for money etc. Hotel industry has evolved with time and there are many kinds of accommodation available now-a -day and each may have a unique proposition. A combination of factors including (but not limited to) the demography of the customer, propensity to pay, level of service, purpose of visit and reviews influence the requirement of the guest. Market has tailored offering to satisfy these different needs. There are many ways to classify hotels and they serve specific needs of the guest.

Classification of hotels

Ownership
- Chain hotel
- Independent hotel
- Franchise hotel
- Single owner hotel

Service/star status
- World class hotel (5-star)
- Mid-range (3 & 4 star)
- Budget hotel

No. Of rooms/ size
- Small (up to 200 rooms)
- Mid-sized (up to 400 rooms)
- Large hotel (more than 400 rooms)

Target market
- Business hotels
- Airport hotels
- Suite hotels
- Bed and breakfast (b&b)
- Casino hotels
- Resorts
- Service apartments
- Motels
- Self-catering hotels
- Boutique hotel
- Hostel
- Time share
- MICE (conference and conventions)

> **What is a resort?**
>
> Resorts tend to occupy larger areas and be situated near tourist attraction like a beach, mountains, theme parks, ski area etc. A resort will have a variety of activities as compared to hotels like swimming pool, golf course, spa, etc. Four Seasons Hampshire is an excellent example of resort as it offers a range of activities for the families. Some of the activities include horse riding, tennis, fly-fishing, croquet, clay pigeon shooting, canal walk, seasonal cycling, kids playground, kids swimmimg pool, falconry, highwire, fitness facilities , nature walks etc.
>
> Find out more here: https://www.fourseasons.com/hampshire/

Some of the leading international hotel brands and the portfolio of sub brands are discussed below.

Intercontinental Hotel Group

IHG's impressive portfolio consists of 17 brands with around 6,000 hotels open and a further 1,800 in the pipeline. These new unique hotels brands offer their individuality and memorable experiences, focusing on different age groups, interests and budgets.

Figure 1.1: IHG's key brands.

Accor

Market segmentation is a way for hotel groups to target groups of people at a larger scale. Accor is present in 116 countries with 5,300 hotels and counting. Their massive advantage over most other hotel groups around the world is due to them covering every market segment, with top hotel brands in every segment under their belt. Their properties that range from luxury to premium, midscale as well as economy.

- **Luxury** – Arguably their most popular luxury hotel brand is *Banyan Tree*, with flagship properties in Malaysia, Thailand and Cancun, Banyan tree offers a mental and spiritual renewal, based on traditional Asian healing therapies. The properties' main selling points include garden spas, private pools, and Thai restaurant concepts.
- **Premium** – The *Pullman* hotel group prides itself on innovation and pioneering, bringing today's trends and newest developments to their properties including digitalised room keys and more. Pullman's prime selling points include art, design, fitness, and F&B. Pullman wants their properties to be the main event of their guests' stay.
- **Midscale** – Being a midscale hotel brand, *Mercure* puts its focus on empowering the surrounding areas of their properties, priding themselves on being knowledgeable about the history of the areas, and reflecting that with the décor of their properties. Their goal is for their customers to be 'immersed' in their destination.
- **Economy** – As *IBIS* is an economy hotel brand, they turn to vibrant colours in their properties to make for an inviting environment. They pride themselves on offering 'vibrant places', open to everyone, due to their lower prices compared to their parent companies. Their main selling point is music, with their mission being 'opening peoples mind through music all over the world'. Ibis properties include flagship properties in Spain, Brazil, France, Indonesia and the United Kingdom.

Unique selling points

Unique selling points are used by hotel brands to separate themselves from their competitors – they are what differentiate hotel brands. Unique selling points could be seen as the identity of a hotel brand, it is what they specialise in and is part of the service that they offer their guests. This will vary within segments of the industry. Table 1.1 shows the USPs of three of the brands under ACCOR.

Banyan Tree	Pullman	Mercure
Garden Spa	F&B	Immersing in the destination
Private pools	Art	History
Thai concept restaurant	Fitness	Hotel Décor

Marriott

Marriott's history goes all the way back to 1927, when J Willard Marriott graduated from college, got married and together with his new wife ventured across the country to open a nine-stool root beer stand. Their business evolved into a restaurant company known as the Hot Shoppe food chain. In 1953, they bought a piece of land to build a supply store, but, given the excellent location next to a railroad bridge and highway, they decided to cater to the car driving public and instead opened a motor hotel. In 1957, the Twin Bridges Marriott opened as the largest motor hotel in the world, and that was the moment Marriott entered the hotel business. In March 2012, Arne Sorenson was appointed president and CEO of Marriott International. In 2016, under Arne's leadership. Marriott acquired Starwood Hotels, which offered a complementary array of brands and had a strong history of embracing innovation. Because of this, it made a perfect addition to the Marriott family of hotels. The history of Marriott is summarised in the diagram below:

HISTORY

1927 — THE HOT SHOPPE RESTAURANT OPENED IN WASHINGTON D.C.

1957 — THE TWIN BRIDGES MOTOR HOTEL OPENED IN ARLINGTON, VA

2012 — ARNE SORENSON BECAME PRESIDENT AND CEO OF MARRIOTT INTERNATIONAL

2016 — MARRIOTT INTERNATIONAL MERGED WITH STARWOOD, CREATING THE WORLD'S LARGEST HOTEL COMPANY

- 7,300+ HOTELS
- 30+ BRANDS
- 134+ COUNTRIES & TERRITORIES
- 450,000+ ASSOCIATES
- 85+ LANGUAGES SPOKEN BY ASSOCIATES

Marriott International, Inc.

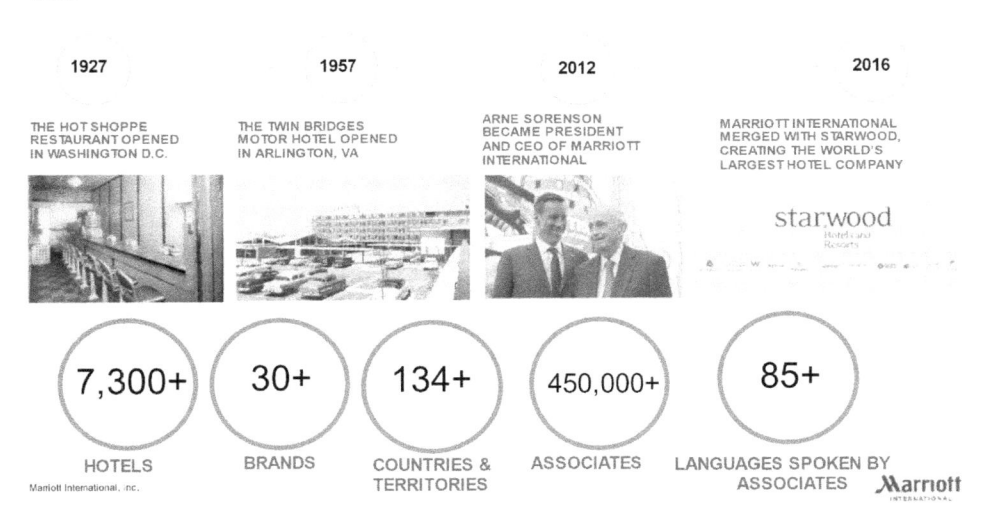

Figure 1.2: Marriot International's timeline. Read more of their story here: https://www.marriott.com/about/culture-and-values/history.mi

With an array of sub brands there's no question Marriott has a brand to appeal to every type of customer in every location for every type of trip. Marriott's collection is divided into two categories: Classic and Distinctive. According to Marriot, brands in the Classic category offer refreshing perspectives on timeless experiences, wherever the guest travels. Brands in the Distinctive category offer remarkable experiences that bring the guest a unique point of view.

The brands are further classified into three segments: Luxury, Premium, and Select, which they describe in this way:

- Luxury brands are extraordinary retreats that elevate every moment of the guest's stay.
- Premium brands offer sophisticated experiences with thoughtful services and amenities to help the guests make the most of their stay.
- Select brands offer simple and convenient experiences that offer exactly what the guest needs, including the extended-stay brands that appeal to the unique needs of the long-term stay guest.

In each category and segment, the brands have similar qualities, but they define their differences through the type of customer they target and the unique experience they deliver.

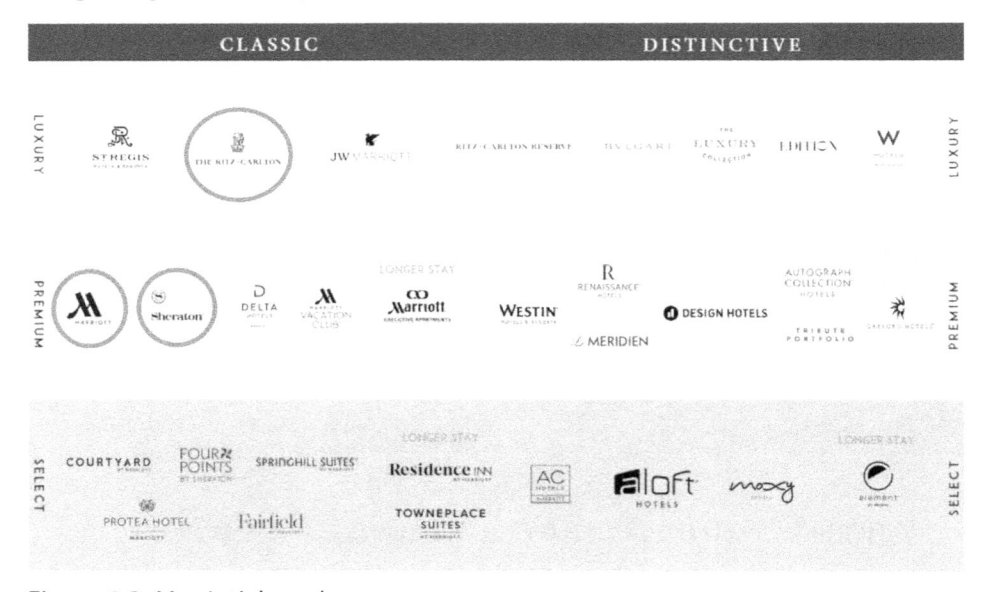

Figure 1.3: Marriot's brands

Hyatt

Hyatt brands offer collection of hotels that are focusing on the designing creative and innovative spaces that is going to inspire and refresh the guests. Miraval and Exhale brands focus on offering overall wellbeing experience for their guests, therefore their line of specialised amenities include meditation and yoga classes, nature walk and fitness equipment. Secrets and Breathless are 'all-adult' getaways, while Dreams and Sunscape focus on the family market.

Figure 1.4: Hyatt brands. Explore them here: https://world.hyatt.com/content/gp/en/landing/brand-explorer-award.html

Hotels and housekeeping

Dictionary defines the word 'housekeeping', in the hotel context, as the management of the guest rooms and public area to provide a safe, clean, aesthetically appealing environment to the guest by managing the set of operations that falls under its purview.

Hotels are an important part of the hospitality industry, and people, irrespective of reason for travel, expect clean, comfortable, and secure places to stay. Hotel housekeeping is one of the vital operational departments in a hotel, responsible for the upkeep of the overall hotel front of the house, back of the house facilities (lobby, guest room, restaurants, offices) as well as the exterior space like periphery, façade, walkways etc.

Importance of housekeeping

According to the Emprise white paper, 97% of travellers say cleanliness is an important factor when booking accommodation. The study also revealed 90% of travellers will avoid booking hotels described as being 'dirty' in a review.

Housekeeping plays a major part in making sure the place of stay and surroundings are living up to the expectations of the guests. It is immensely responsible for meeting guest satisfaction and providing a memorable experience. Imagine yourself walking into a hotel room and the view of crushed linen welcomes you! Cleanliness sets the tone for quality and hygiene of a hotel, which are high on priority list of guests. Poor housekeeping can lead to guest complaints and can be the biggest factor of guest dissatisfaction. In this age of social media interactions, one negative review can cause noticeable damage to revenue of a hotel. Significant study has been done on the impact of negative reviews on hotel revenue.

"Just one negative review can lose hotels around 30 guests, according to an Emprise study. It's not surprising this can have severe consequences in revenue losses" (Walker, 2016)

Not only the rooms, but also the hotel and its surroundings are exposed to the eyes of the guests. They are constantly receiving the feedback of housekeeping efforts. The housekeeping department not only cleans and tidies, but also adds personalised touches to each guest room. They ensure that the surroundings always looks spotless with no trace of dust, dirt, grim. The inviting atmosphere created by housekeeping will lead to converting first-time visitors into loyal customers.

> Rooms revenue averaged 68.1% of total operating revenue in 2015. On average, the profits generated by the rooms department made up 81.7 % of total department profits in 2015. (Walker, 2016)

Many more studies are in line with the above study suggesting that proper investment and focus on the housekeeping resources are key to establishing strict quality standards, which in turn pay dividends with enhanced guest experience, and this translates to a healthy hotel financials.

The housekeeping department is termed as the nerve centre of the hotel business as the success of a hotel is dependent mostly on that department. Therefore, a strong housekeeping operation that constantly evolves its practices, products and technology helps to drive successful hospitality business. A guest makes the first impression of a hotel's operation right from the entrance and observes how clean the walkaway is, whether the glasses are smudge free or not, the floor in the lobby is clean and sparkling, the cloakrooms are clean and fresh, the flower arrangement in the lobby is inviting, the guest room smells fresh, and the atmosphere is warm and welcoming. Huge responsibility of creating guest experience lies on the shoulder of the housekeeping department which we will discuss in the coming chapters. The housekeeping department is not just responsible for creating an unforgettable experience for their guests, but they also need to ensure the employees are safe, everyone is well groomed, in smart uniforms, and the staff facilities are clean and hygienic.

The main responsibilities of the housekeeping department include:

- Achieve the maximum efficiency in ensuring guest care and comfort
- Establish a welcoming atmosphere
- Maintain high standard of cleanliness and upkeep
- Provide linen in all rooms, F&B outlets, health clubs
- Maintain inventory of linen
- Provide and maintain staff uniforms
- Cater to the laundering needs of staff and guests
- Provide and maintain the floral decorations (and gardens)
- Select and manage the right contractors
- Coordinate renovation and refurbishment, in consultation with the general manager and interior decorators
- Purchase and maintain inventories of guest supplies, cleaning agents, equipment, fabrics, carpets, and other items
- Manage guest lost and found
- Provide turn down service
- Ensure training, control, and supervision of staff
- Establish a good working relationship with all departments
- Ensure health and safety regulations are followed
- Oversee supplier relationships
- Prepare the rooms up to required standards.
- Find and apply a technique to the job so it would be fast, productive, and good quality.
- Motivate and train new staff and treating everyone equally. No discrimination on nationality, ability of talking English, speed etc.

Housekeeping in other establishments

Housekeeping is the backbone of all establishments and therefore it is found in most of buildings. As hygiene and cleanliness are the basis of any safe environment, it is essential to have a strong housekeeping service. For example, housekeeping services are essential in the following establishments.

Hospitals

Housekeeper's role is to ensure hospital's ward and other areas are safe, secure, clean and pleasant to offer a feel-good factor for the patients. You will find more information on the NHS website about the skills needed, training required etc. Infection prevention by following the appropriate measures of hygiene and sanitation is essential in a hospital.

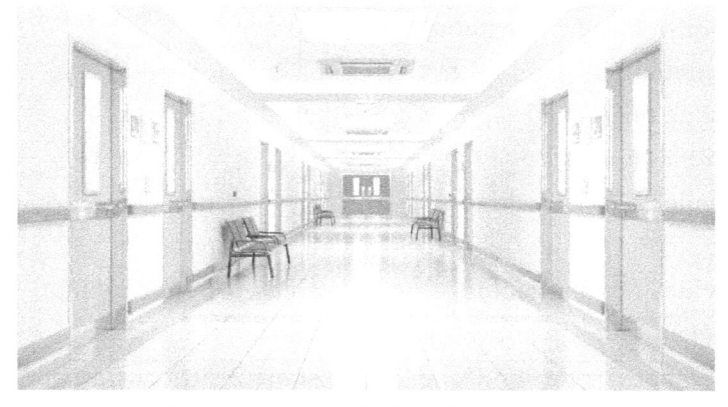

Figure 1.5: High levels of hygiene are vital in hospitals. Photo: Hollywood Building Services (www.hollywoodbuildingservices.com)

Shopping malls

Cleanliness, hygiene and good sanitation is vital for safeguarding the health of the visitors and staff at malls and shopping centres. Every nook and corner of the mall needs to be spotless as it is exposed to the public. Due to the traffic of people visiting each day it is important to keep clean the floor, walls, stairs, washrooms, windows, escalators/elevators, any decorative pieces, waiting sofas and furniture.

Figure 1.6: Professional housekeeping services are needed to keep malls spotless and welcoming. Photo: Hollywood Building Services.

Offices

A clean, pleasant and safe working environment is essential for workers in offices and other premises. It is the responsibility of the employer to safeguard the health of the workers, typically by hiring professional housekeeping services.

Figure 1.7: A clean office creates a better working environment. Photo: Hollywood Building Services.

Universities, schools and other educational facilities

To prevent the spread of the germs, bacteria, and viruses it is important for the educational facilities to hire professional cleaning services. They ensure the safety and hygiene of the premises while the organisation focuses on their core-operation, which is teaching and students' overall development. A consistent and thorough cleaning regime can significantly reduce the spread of the viruses, reducing the sick days for the staff and the students.

Figure 1.8: A thorough cleaning regime can reduce staff and student absences. Photo RapidClean (www.rapidclean.co.uk)

Summary

Hotel housekeeping is a 24/7 operation, with staff working around the clock to ensure that the hotel is always clean and welcoming. Housekeeping managers and supervisors oversee the staff, ensuring that they are working effectively and efficiently. They also manage inventory and budgets, ensuring that the department has the resources it needs to function smoothly. In summary, the hospitality industry relies on hotel housekeeping to provide guests with a clean and comfortable environment. The work of housekeeping staff is critical to maintaining guest satisfaction and ensuring that the hotel runs smoothly.

Activity:

In your working groups:

- Discuss the role of housekeeping in theme parks.
- Have you come across different type of hotels which are unique? List them and note why you feel they are different from others.
- Do you consider visiting review platforms before booking a hotel? How they impact your decision? Discuss the findings in your group.
- Find out what you consider important while rating a hotel for its overall housekeeping. Compare and contrast your results with peer members.

Key terms

- **Hotel**: 'An establishment providing accommodation, meals, and other services for travellers and tourists, by the night' (Oxford English Dictionary)
- **Hospitality**: The act of being friendly and welcoming to the visitors.
- **Housekeeping**: A department of the rooms division, responsible for cleaning the hotel's guestrooms and public areas.
- **Turndown**: This is also termed 'second service', and involves preparing the room for the good night sleep.
- **Lost & Found**: The process of securing the items that are forgotten by gueesst and returning them to the guests safely.
- **Heritage hotels**: Historic buildings, palaces, forts, etc converted into hotels, displaying the cultural heritage – architecture, design and aesthetics.

References and further reading

Chibili, M. , de Bruyn, S., Benhadda, L., Lashley, C., Penninga, S. and Rowson, B. (2019) *Modern Hotel Operations Management*. Taylor and Francis.

Harper, D. (2016) *Hotels and Resorts*. 1st edn. CRC Press.

MacLean, M. A. (2019) *Hospitality*. Society Publishing.

Raghubalan, G. (2015) *Hotel Housekeeping: Operations and management*, 3rd edition. New Delhi : Oxford University Press

Reynolds, D., Rahman, I. & Barrows, C. (2021) *Introduction to Hospitality Management*. Wiley.

Walker, J. R. (2016) *Introduction to Hospitality*, 7th Edition Pearson Education

Wood, R.C. (Ed.) (2017) *Hotel Accommodation Management*. Taylor and Francis.

2: Overview of the Housekeeping Department

This chapter will help you to:

- Understand the role and responsibilities of housekeeping department
- Evaluate the effective coordintion of housekeeping department with other departments
- Review the organisational structure of housekeeping department

The housekeeping department's responsibility lies in ensuring cleanliness, hygiene, comfort, and safety of the customers. Among all the departments in the hotel, the efforts of housekeeping department are most overt. The impact of great housekeeping develops confidence in the customer so that they can check in at the hotel with a positive, stress-free mindset. Witnessing the housekeeping standards of the hotel, a guest decides whether he or she is going to return to there and become a loyal customer, or is going to depart with a negative review.

The housekeeping department is a part of the rooms division department in a hotel. In larger hotels, the rooms division has a front office and a housekeeping department underneath it. However, this may differ from hotel to hotel. The front office department is responsible for maximising the sales of the guest room and therefore needs to use effective pricing policies to attract the customers. The front office works closely with the housekeeping department as the room can only be sold to a prospective customer when it has been made ready for sale by the housekeeping department. Other than the housekeeping and front office department, the concierge, reservation, spa, and security are part of the rooms division. All these departments have specific roles in meeting the guest expectation and creating a positive experience and therefore they work closely with each other. In a large hotel, the rooms division manager (RDM) overlooks the operation and is supported by the front-office manager, revenue manager and executive housekeeper. A RDM reports to the general manager.

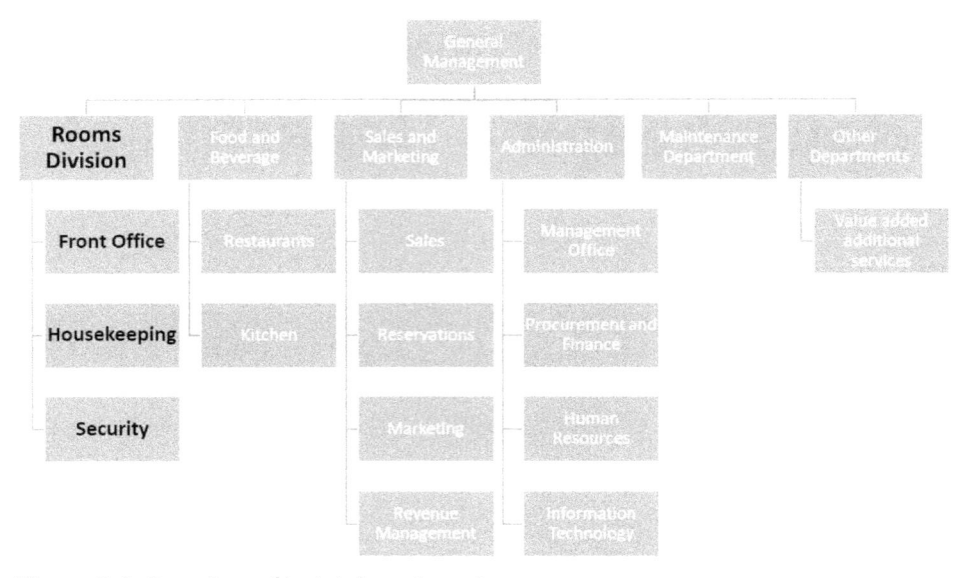

Figure 2.1: Overview of hotel departments

Housekeeping's coordination with different departments in a hotel

The housekeeping department is responsible for maintaining the high standards of hygiene of the rooms and communal areas as well as creating a pleasant environment for the guest, and follows a systematic manner to keep the establishment clean and fresh. The housekeeping department has one of the essential roles, which also requires great level of intercommunication with various other departments for the smooth delivery of services to the guest.

The department's responsibilities are carried out by room attendants. These responsibilities include cleaning the rooms using chemicals, replacing the linen in the guest rooms and bathrooms, and replenishing all supplies daily. This must be done in accordance with the wishes and demands of the guests. It is especially significant and becomes more valued when the guest's room is expensive. For a seamless operation, each department of the hotel needs to coordinate and communicate effectively with every other one. A hospitality operation requires a great deal of teamwork and therefore those hotels where staff are hugely motivated to work with each other and support each other, climbs the ladder of success. The interdepartmental coordination between housekeeping and front office, housekeeping and food & beverage, housekeeping and maintenance, housekeeping and sales and marketing will be discussed below.

Before we discuss that coordination, it is worth understanding the guest cycle and its stages.

Guest cycle

The guest cycle is the sum of the entire experience a guest receives right from the beginning, or the first step, when they decide to stay at the hotel, and research several hotels and brands. The hotel guest cycle is the journey in which a guest meets several touchpoints throughout the process of their stay. The cycle has four main stages: pre-arrival, check-in, in-house (occupancy) and departure.

1. The experience starts in the **pre-arrival stage**, where the first impression is made online, reading travel platforms, such as TripAdvisor.
2. In the arrival stage, guests are **checked in** and registered.
3. **During their stay**, it is important to attend to guest queries when they arise, or to provide information to them that may improve their stay in the city and create memorable experiences that they will cherish throughout their life. For example a leading luxury hotel knew that the guests were coming back to the hotel to celebrate their 10 years anniversary. This information was retrieved from the reservations records as well the guest history. They got married in the hotel. So, they went back to the archive of their banqueting team and recreated their wedding cake and placed in the room on arrival. This gesture created a wonderful experience for the guests and the hotels got their loyal customers for lifetime, for going above and beyond.
4. In the **departure** stage, payment is taken, their luggage may be kept throughout the day, feedback is received, and they are bid farewell.

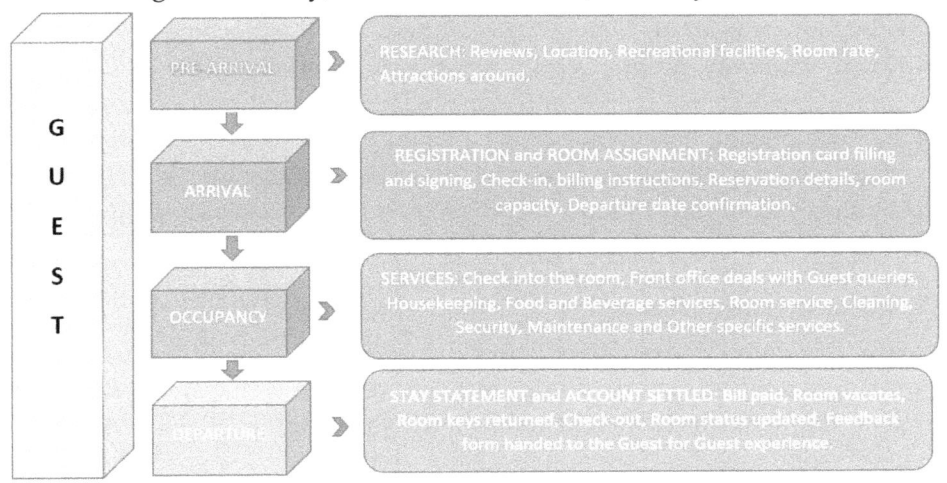

Figure 2.2: The stages of guest cycle and the activities that are carried in each stage

Every stage of the guest cycle is important to the success of a hotel. At any stage of the cycle, something detrimental could go wrong and totally ruin the stay for a guest if effective interdepartmental coordination is disrupted. In each stage, there can be 'moments of truth', where good service quality is found. Within the guest cycle, there are many things that could potentially go wrong and when they do, guests are likely to complain.

Interdepartmental coordination

Front Office

The front office department receives the guest on their arrival. Housekeeping prepares the room between the arrival and departure of guests. The two departments need to communicate effectively and coordinate to ensure the guest rooms are turned around as efficiently as possible, as one of the most disappointing experiences for a guest is to wait for the room, despite guaranteeing the reservation. Therefore, updating the room status on the PMS (Property Management System) will allow sufficient time to the housekeeping department to make the room ready as per the set standards. Additional guest needs communicated to the front office must be serviced by the housekeeping department promptly.

Food and beverage department

The kitchen and the food & beverage service department rely on the housekeeping department for clean uniforms and the linen for the restaurants and banquets. The food and beverage team needs to notify the linen requirements for any special event well in advance, so the housekeeping department gets sufficient time to arrange the linen, to avoid any delay. Few hotels hire their linen from an outsourced company, so this becomes even more critical to communicate the requirement well in advance. The housekeeping department is also responsible for the cleaning and pest control of the kitchen, restaurant, banquets, bar, etc., therefore the two departments need to coordinate this efficiently to ensure its smooth operation. Special flower arrangements and decoration are coordinated by the housekeeping department in a few hotels.

Maintenance department

The maintenance department in a hotel helps in achieving zero defect rooms and public areas for the guests' convenience. The maintenance or engineering department will have, in-house or readily available externally, a whole range of technicians and mechanics who have their specialist role in ensuring smooth hotel operation, like an electrician, plumber, HVAC technician, television and telephone expert etc. The housekeeping staff enter the guest room for cleaning, and after checking the room maintenance as per their checklist, they give feedback on the maintenance needs. The efficient communication and attendance of these maintenance needs (e.g., lighting, plumbing, etc.) result in reduced guest complaints.

Maintenance Order Form

Date: 2/07/2021
Time: 0900 hrs
Room Number: 132
Location: Floor 1 wing C
Reported By: John
Problem:
Entrance Spot light fused.

Assigned To: Shift Engineer/Electrician
Date Completed: 2/07/2021
Time Spent: 10 minutes
Completed By: John
Comments:
Fused bulb replaced and other lights checked.

Shift in Charge: John   Signature: John

Figure 2.3: Maintenance order form

Security department

The hotel security department is responsible for ensuring the safety and security of the hotel guests and employees. They monitor the CCTV cameras, fire alarms, and regularly walk the hotel premises to keep an eye on the overall safety of the hotel. In case of an emergency like fire, bomb threat, death in the room, handling drunken guests, theft, etc they safeguard the hotel building and staff. Housekeeping staff enter the guest rooms frequently for servicing and can report any suspicious guests or items in the room or public area to the security to avoid any mishap occurring in the hotel. Housekeeping will seeks security's help while entering a DND (Do Not Disturb) room if the sign has been there for more than the maximum time set by the hotel, as the reason why the sign has been left out may be more than a member of the housekeeping staff could be expected to handle.

Sales and marketing

The standard and quality of guest room and public area cleaning and hygiene results in repeat business and helps the sales and marketing team in maintaining loyal clients. Sales and marketing communicates any special requirement mentioned by their big corporate clients and businesses to the housekeeping team who must ensure that they show personalisation and care in delivering an unforgettable experience for the guests. The sales team is reliant on housekeeping for clean, fresh uniforms to look professional and smart. The sales and marketing team coordinates with housekeeping to arrange flowers/ bouquet and special gifts (e.g. Christmas/New Year gifts) when they go their sales call to meet the prospective guests, as well as for existing clients, to create a positive impression. Housekeeping prepares the show-around rooms for the familiarisation trips for major sales business.

Sales & Marketing
- Guest Experience
- Value Added Services: Laundry, Tailoring, Show around rooms etc

Front Office
- Status of Rooms
- Additional guest requirements

Food & Beverage
- Uniform & linen
- Pest Control
- Special flower arrangement

Housekeeping

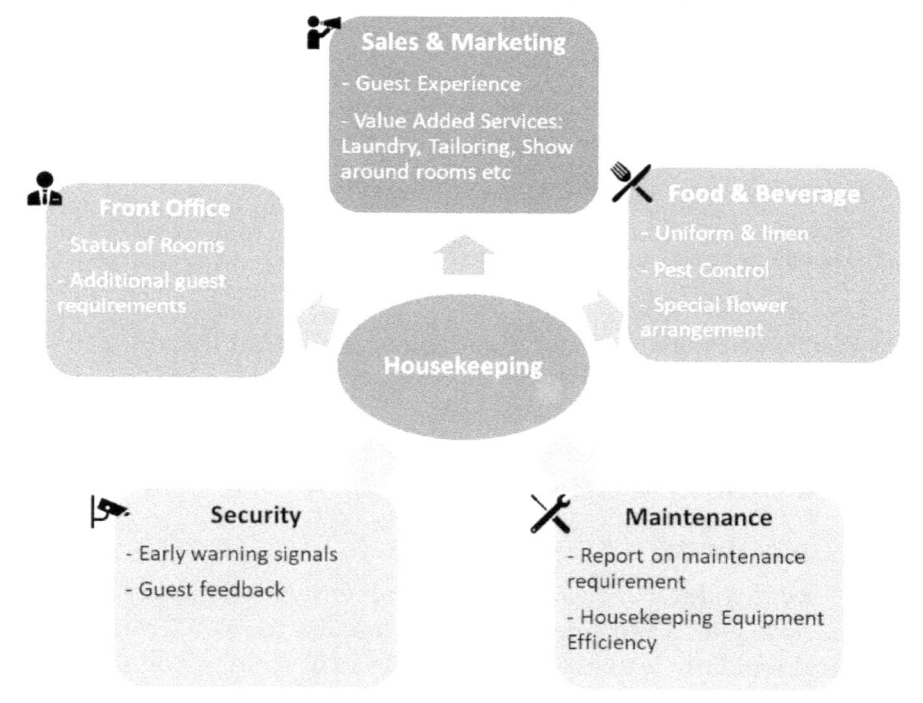

Security
- Early warning signals
- Guest feedback

Maintenance
- Report on maintenance requirement
- Housekeeping Equipment Efficiency

Figure 2.4: Housekeeping department interactions with other departments

Layout

There is no universal layout of housekeeping, and it is dependent on the size and space constraints in the hotel. Based on the level of outsourcing, the layout can look different for hotels with similar sized operations. Space in a hotel is valuable and there is a trade-off between what goes on for revenue generating unit (rooms, restaurants etc.) and what is allocated to non-revenue generating areas, such as housekeeping.

Housekeeper's Office

This is usually a separate office located in a place which can provide a view of movement within the department. Housekeeping is a labour-intensive department for which everyday work needs to be planned. This office is used by the executive housekeeper to plan the work and hold meetings with the staff. The secretary/executive assistant's office is normally located adjacent to the executive housekeeper's cabin to control the movement of staff/other personnel into the housekeeper's cabin.

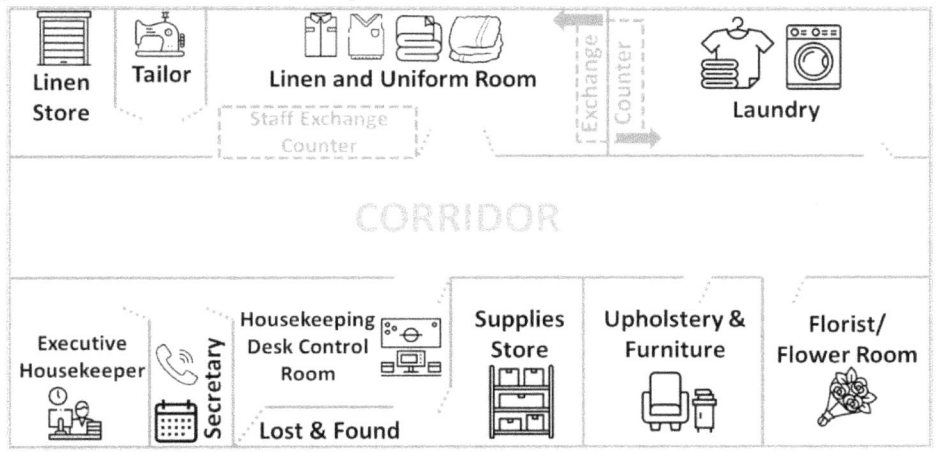

Figure 2.5: Typical layout of a housekeeping department

Housekeeping coordinators' desk

The coordinator's desk is positioned close to the head housekeeper's office and is the central desk to coordinate all the housekeeping activities, like ensuring attendance of staff, job allocation register, handover register or logbook, notice board which has the staff roster and other important information for the staff, section and floor keys cupboard, and lost and found storage. They coordinate the guest request and requests from the other departments from here. They are also responsible for handling the requisition forms and purchase order forms, taking in the completed forms, obtaining signature from the EHK (executive housekeeper), as necessary, then sending them to the store or purchase department for further action.

Laundry

An on-premises laundry has several sections, like linen and uniform sorting, washing, drying, dry cleaning, ironing, folding and stacking section. It also includes a guest laundry section. The laundry will be strategically positioned close to the linen room to deliver fresh linen and uniforms and receive the dirty ones for processing.

Linen storeroom

The laundered room linen, like bedsheets, pillow slips, duvet covers, towels, bath rugs and bathrobes; restaurant linen, like table clothes, runners and napkins; and spa linen, pool towels, etc. are stored here. Different types of linen are recorded, a regular inventory is kept, and stock is administered and issued to the relevant departments as required.

Uniform room

The uniform room is responsible for receiving soiled uniform from the staff and issue them clean uniform, shoes, and name tags, if any, in a timely manner. They stack the appropriate uniform for each staff member in their designated section in the uniform room and issue them as requested. They maintain the records of the employees who have left and new employees and coordinate their uniform request.

Tailoring room

Many hotels have in-house tailors who are responsible for mending and altering staff uniform. Discarded towels and linen are converted into towelling and cotton dusters by the tailors to use them in cleaning the rooms and public area. The tailors cut them into appropriate sizes and add a colouring piping at the end to denote them as dusters. Some hotels get their upholstery, such as cushion covers and curtains, stitched and repaired in house.

Supplies store

The housekeeping department deals with a lot of guest room supplies and amenities which requires up to date stock taking and storage. The store is responsible for ensuring that an effective control procedure is in place to avoid wastage and misuse of the supplies. The housekeeping store coordinates with the main purchase department of the hotel for placing orders and getting approvals from the head housekeeper.

Flower room

The flower room in a hotel is responsible for ordering, storing, and creating the arrangements for different sections of the hotel. The room will be kept at the optimum temperature for efficient storage, and the room design helps the florists to carry out their work effectively by ensuring a proper workstation, sink, storage cupboards for vases, decorative items, and other equipment. Flower arrangements for VIP arrival guest rooms, suites, restaurants, banquets, and the spa are prepared in the flower room.

Lost and found

Househkeeping will maintain a lost and found storage space and keep an up to date Lost and Found register. Any belongings left by guests are stored in that cupboard with a completed form attached to the items for tracking. Details of the lost and found item are passed to the front desk as the guest might inquire with them. Now this communication has become even more quick and efficient with the advent of new technology and software, and the departments can view the log of the lost and found items with a click. Items will be kept for a specific time, perhaps a month, three months, or a year, depending on each hotel's policy and whether the item is valuable or non-valuable. If the items are not reclaimed by the guest within the time, they are disposed of, and in some hotels may be given to the finder.

Housekeeping department responsibilities

Housekeeping is responsible for providing clean, hygienic, and comfortable rooms to the guests. Each room in a hotel is serviced twice: once during morning service and again in the evening to give turndown service. If the guest room is occupied, the housekeeper ensures the room is serviced at a time that is convenient to the guests without intruding in their privacy. Broadly, housekeeping is responsible for three major areas of the hote,l namely rooms, public area and other areas.

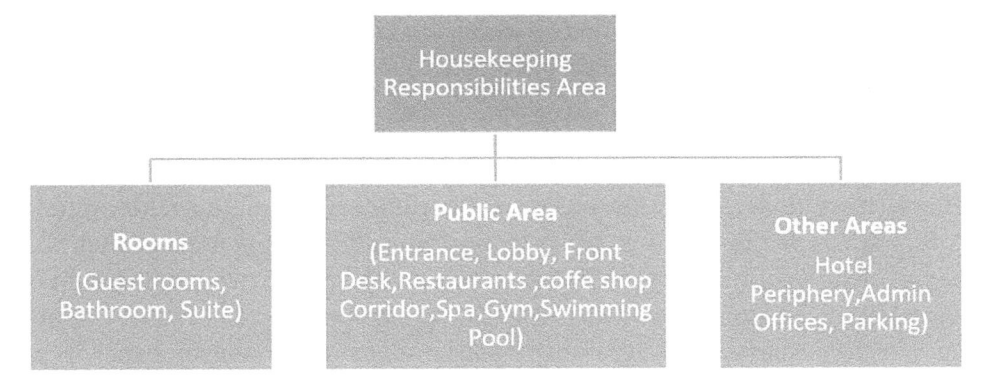

Figure 2.6: Housekeeping responsibilities area

Let us understand the responsibilities area in detail

Guest rooms

Include the maintenance of the floor covering, wall covering, HVAC (heating ventilation and air conditioning) maintenance, lighting fixtures, window cleaning and maintenance, wall painting and colouring, bed, bedside table, and other furniture like a sofa, writing table, coffee table. They are also responsible for the room locking system, telephone and television, and for coordinate the stocking of the minibar in the room.

Guest bathrooms

Housekeeping is responsible for the bathroom fixtures and the units like vanity counter, bathtub, WC (water closet), shower cubicles, and bidet, and for stocking the room with all the necessary bathroom supplies like soap, shampoo, conditioner, dental kit and vanity kit (in luxury hotels), tissue, and toilet roll. They must ensure that the hairdryer and shaving sockets are working, hot and cold water signages are visible, grab bars in the shower and the bathtub are fixed properly, and that the bathroom phone and television are working fine.

Leisure facilities and the public area

These include the guest elevators, staff elevators, main entrance, lobby, reception desk, lobby seating area for the guests, restaurants, bar, coffee shop, banquets, spa, gym, swimming pool, changing rooms, cloakrooms, administrative offices, staff facilities and changing room, staircases, parking space etc.

Hotel periphery and the garden

Large luxury hotels and resorts appoint a horticulturist who has a team of gardeners, and they are responsible for maintaining the landscape and enhancing the appeal of the hotel exterior by taking care of the lawn, trees, shrubs, hedges etc. Some hotels have their own kitchen garden, and grow their herbs and vegetables.

Furniture, fixtures and equipment

Hotels have furniture in the room, in the public area, dining table, lobby sofa, bar stools, lounge furniture etc. and this all requires regular maintenance, cleaning, polishing etc. Fixtures include lighting, artworks, decorative chandeliers. Equipment covers the cleaning equipment as well as in-room devices like television, telephone, I-pad, and in-room control panel in a technologically advanced hotel etc.

Uniform and Linen

The housekeeping department is responsible for maintaining sufficient stock and suitable quality of the room linen, bathroom linen, restaurant linen and staff uniform. There must be regular inventory taking for proper stock control. Housekeeping must ensure that staff members have sufficient sets of uniform for the number of changes required depending on their nature of work. For example, a chef in a live kitchen is required to wear a clean and white chef coat; while cooking, if the chef coat requires a change a clean coat needs to be available.

Pest control

Housekeeping department is responsible for working with a pest control team to identify and control pest infestations.

External contractors

Other than above tasks, the housekeeping department is also responsible for liaison with external companies and contractors offering specialised cleaning and maintenances tasks. Some hotels prefer to outsource their laundry and linen operation instead of having an OPL (on premises laundry) coordinated by the housekeeping department. Thus the housekeeping operation is vast and therefore requires a huge workforce to accomplish the responsibilities that comes under its roof.

Hygiene post-Covid

Most of the luxury hotel chains have appointed, post Covid-19, hygiene officers and health consultants who review the best practices in maintaining the utmost hygiene and sanitation, as well as following government guidelines. Some hotel brands have partnered with the leading healthcare units so they constantly update the protocols and the practices important for maintaining health and safety.

Organisation structure

The largest department in terms of the number of people employed is housekeeping.

"Up to 50% of the hotel employees may work in housekeeping department." (Walker, 2017)

Housekeeping is a labour-intensive department, and the staff can be divided into three broad categories.

Leadership and managerial	Executive housekeeper (EHK), head housekeeper, assistant executive housekeeper (AEHK), deputy housekeeper
Supervisory	Assistant housekeeper, floor housekeeper, linen room supervisor, control desk supervisors
Special skills	Room attendant, public areas attendant, linen/uniform room attendant, laundry staff, porters, tailors, bar attendant, valet etc,

As the operation that comes under the housekeeping department is quite vast, few hotels outsource the entire department. Some outsource the room attendants and cleaning staff, and keep the management team in-house for better control. This business decision varies from hotel to hotel and the location of the hotel. However, luxury hotels prefer to have the complete team in-house to deliver the promised quality and ensure effective control on the processes. Based on business needs, some of the activities may be outsourced and the organisation may vary between hotels.

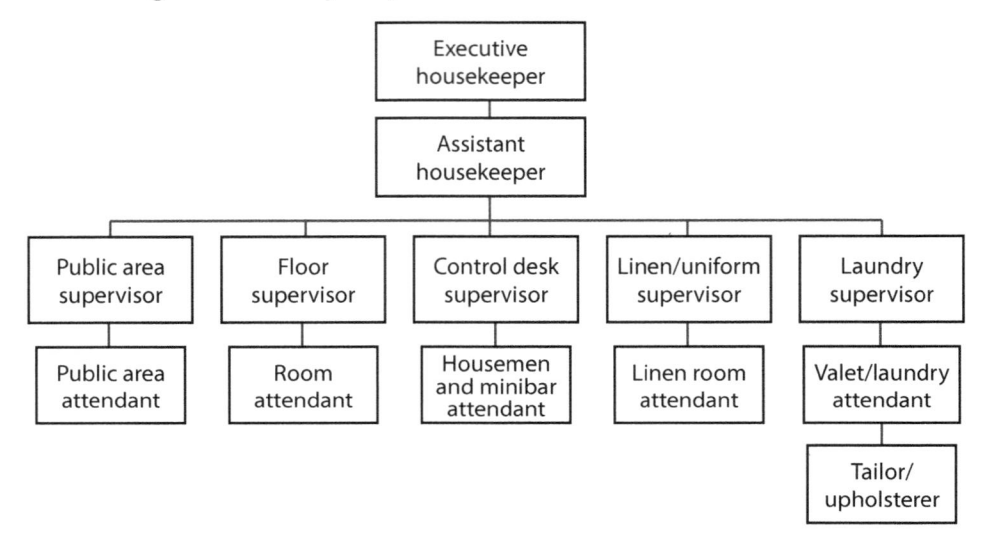

Figure 2.7: Organisation structure of typical housekeeping department

Summary

Effective communication between departments is critical to ensuring that guests have a positive experience. The housekeeping department plays a crucial role in delivering a positive customer experience in a hotel, ensuring guests are likely to return in the future. By maintaining cleanliness and hygiene standards, paying attention to detail, providing guest services, personalizing the experience, and communicating with guests, housekeeping staff can contribute to a memorable and enjoyable stay for guests. It requires a dedicated team of professionals who work around the clock to ensure that the hotel is always clean and welcoming.

Activity

In your working groups:

- Take some examples of hotels and find out which activities are outsourced by the housekeeping department. Discuss some of the common reasons for outsourcing.

- List the consequences of a lack of coordination between housekeeping and the different departments in a hotel.

- Have you faced any issues while staying in a hotel? Can you relate how they connected to housekeeping department?

- Discuss how the housekeeping department can contribute to exceed the guest expectations and experience.

Key terms

- **Occupancy**: The rate of occupation of a hotel's total rooms, at any given time. For example, an occupancy rate of 95 per cent would mean that 95 per cent of a hotel's room inventory is presently occupied.

- **Refurbishment:** The process of restoring, renovating or modernizing a hotels rooms or public areas to bring them up to a certain standard

- **EHK (Executive Housekeeper)**: Responsible for the overall housekeeping department; also termed as Head housekeeper.

- **OPL (On-premises Laundry)** When the entire laundry operation is in house.

References and further reading

Andrews, S. (2013). *Hotel Housekeeping: A training manual*. Tata McGraw-Hill Education.

Devrim Yilmaz, Ö. (2017) An undervalued department or a terra incognita? Hotel housekeeping from the perspectives of executive housekeepers and room attendants, *Tourism*, 65(4), 450–461.

Walker, J. (2017) *Supervision in the Hospitality Industry*. New Jersey: John Wiley & Sons.

3: Managing Housekeeping Personnel

This chapter will help you to:

- Understand the management functions in housekeeping department
- Evaluate the responsibilities and job descriptions of various housekeeping roles.
- Review the attributes of housekeeping staff
- Gain a basic understanding of time and motion study.

Introduction

The housekeeping department is not only responsible for generating most of the revenue, but is also the department which holds most human volume. A room that is not clean and tidy cannot be sold to the guests, therefore the success of the sale depends on the efficiency of the housekeeping department. The work performed by the housekeeping department is very task-oriented and requires rigorous and meticulous effort, hard work and dedication to provide a quality service. In addition to this the housekeepers must deal with lot of time pressure, ensuring that the quality standards and procedures are followed as set by the hotel brand. Housekeeping jobs need training and expertise because housekeeping personnel must deal with:

1. Handling manpower, chemicals, equipment, supplies
2. Learning about technical processes and products utilisation (planning hard and soft furnishings and aesthetic appeal)
3. Time organisation and record keeping (especially when a new hotel prepares to open, as the entire detailed planning list of suppliers needs to be recorded thoroughly for future reference.)
4. Maintaining brand standard operating procedures to meet the expectation of the guests.
5. Cost control and effective waste reduction.

The size of the hotel housekeeping department depends on the size and the structure of the hotel, its star classification and the usage. Housekeeping is the backbone of the hotel operation and is responsible for the upkeep and maintenance of the hotel guest room and public areas. The department is headed by the head housekeeper or an executive housekeeper.

Management functions in housekeeping

Recruitment

As housekeeping is the largest department it needs to employ the right number and calibre of employees to carry out the specific tasks, keeping in mind the recruitment policies of the company. It is one of the most important responsibilities of the department, as manpower is the biggest cost in housekeeping department, therefore planning staffing and recruiting the right number of staff with the right attitude are significant to the hotel's success.

Training

Training staff is crucial to the success of a hotel as high quality and systematic training will develop the skills of the employees, who will then follow the right procedures in completing the set tasks. Investing in training staff will ensure consistency in the service delivery, thus meeting the guest expectation. Evaluation of training is equally important to see if it is effective and is helping to meet the objectives. It is equally important to plan refresher training along with the induction training as reinforcement is the key for success.

Budgeting and cost control

This is the most important management function in housekeeping as the department is responsible for different types of capital and operational expenses and therefore the right planning is the key to successful operation. The budget is based on the forecast and therefore requires a great deal of insight and data to understand the past and likely future occupancy pattern, so that the budget for the supplies and amenities can be set accordingly to avoid wastages and shortages. Budgeting for renovation and refurbishment likewise requires great deal of planning and understanding.

Purchasing

Purchasing decisions determine the quality of the products and services offered to the guests, and the housekeeping department has to deal with a lot of suppliers to procure a wide range of items for the various sections and operations. Therefore they need to review the right quantity, right price and the quality that will be needed. So, they need to decide the purchase specifications, purchase order, terms and conditions of the delivery and contingency planning, etc. to ensure a smooth operation.

Maintaining standards

Housekeeping managers ensure consistency in service delivery to meet the expectations of the customers. Inspections of the guest room and public area using the checklists ensures adherence to standards. Identifying the training needs and planning the training for the staff helps to maintain the standards in the housekeeping operation.

Job descriptions and specifications

Executive Housekeeper (EHK)

An executive housekeeper is responsible for successfully leading the housekeeping department and ensure the successful business, recognition, and reputation of the hotel. In a small or medium sized hotel, an executive housekeeper reports to the general manager, while in big or diversified hotels an executive housekeeper or a housekeeping manager reports to the rooms division manager.

The responsibility of an executive housekeeper is broadly divided into the following categories:

1 Managing operations
2 Managing the departmental costs and budgets
3 Ensuring excellent customer service and managing expectations
4 Participating in the Human Resource activities.

Job specification for an EHK

- A degree in Higher Education
- Management skills (planning/organising/leading and controlling)

Job description of an EHK

- Organise, direct and control the housekeeping operation effectively to deliver the optimum product in line with the business strategy.
- Liaise with the senior management (general/operations manager).
- Be responsible for ensuring the brand standards are maintained, and customer satisfaction is achieved thus contributing to the bottom line of the hotel.
- Ensure staff are trained well to do their job to their best ability.

- Ensure the procurement of goods that meet the required standards while working within the financial targets as well as maintaining an effective and positive relationship with suppliers.
- Be responsible for maintaining an excellent communication channel within the staff by ensuring regular staff briefings and welcoming feedback from the staff.
- Be responsible for planning the departmental budget as well as reducing wastage and controling costs.
- Be knowledgeable about the latest developments and innovations, and achieve technical excellence for their area of the work to enhance the departmental efficiency.
- Ensure legal compliance by undertaking regular risk assessment checks and maintaining the health and safety standards of the department. The EHK is responsible for the safety of staff as well as guests.
- Be responsible for overlooking the performance management of the team, planning successions as well as staff development.

> Read the story of Elinda Keenan, EHK at Hyatt's Andaz London Liverpool Street:
> https://www.housekeepingtodayuk.com/housekeeping-its-simply-the-best/

Job description of an assistant executive housekeeper

In a large hotel an assistant executive housekeeper (AEHK) assists the executive housekeeper in all the roles and responsibilities. In the absence of an executive housekeeper an AEHK leads the department and makes all the decisions.

- Assist the executive housekeeper in formulating and manifesting all the operational and managerial functions.
- Ensure the set standard operating procedures are met in the housekeeping operations by supervising the tasks.
- Coordinate with the floor supervisor, public area supervisor, linen and uniform supervisor, laundry supervisor and schedule their daily activities and any special request.
- Ensure that regular stock is maintained and inventory control is carried out periodically for linen and other housekeeping items.
- Assist the executive housekeeper in the planning renovation and refurbishment of the guest rooms and public areas.
- Ensure all the guest requests and complaints are handled effectively to meet the guest expectation and enhance the guest experience.

- Coordinate the housekeeping staff training with the training department to maximise the productivity of the staff to ensure utmost guest satisfaction.
- Assist the Human Resource Department in the recruitment of staff and setting responsibilities and the specifications for the roles.
- Assist with performance appraisal of all the housekeeping staff and recommends the promotion, transfer and dismissal of the staff as required.

Job description of a floor supervisor

- Be responsible for leading and guiding the room attendants and the housemen/porters.
- Be responsible for assigning work to the room attendants after checking the room occupancy report.
- Check the guest rooms as per the checklist, after they have been prepared and cleaned by the attendants to see the standards are met.
- Meet and interact with the guests on the floor and check if everything is fine in their room and if they need anything specific. This is to ensure a personalised service.
- Coordinate closely with the reception to prioritise the room cleaning and checking depending on the arrival and departure of the guests.
- Plan team building activities to strengthen the group dynamics and to keep the staff motivated.
- Coordinate any defects in the rooms and the corridor with the maintenance department to ensure a zero-defect room to the guest.
- Suggest special cleaning/periodical cleaning to the executive and assistant executive housekeeper, and plan it after checking the occupancy.
- Conduct staff briefing to communicate all the important arrivals and update the staff of any changes in the standards or if any special cleaning is planned for that day.
- Identify the training needs of the room attendants and plan it accordingly to enhance the productivity of the staff.
- Prepare the duty roster of the room attendants and get it approved by the EHK and AEHK.
- Follow the key control procedure as set and ensure that all the keys are returned to the desk at the end of each shift.

Job description of a public area supervisor

- Be responsible for overlooking the cleaning and the maintenance of the public area (includes lobby, rest rooms, restaurants, banquets, meeting rooms, offices, elevators, gym, swimming pool, spa, garden, periphery of the hotel, locker rooms, staircases etc).
- Be responsible for planning and organising the staffing (preparing duty roster as well as assigning duties for each shift) of the public area attendants after checking the planned events and occupancy.
- Inspect the public area cleaning to ensure the highest cleaning standards are maintained to meet and exceed the guest satisfaction.
- Coordinate the public area maintenance with the maintenance department.
- Plan the deep cleaning/periodical cleaning, for example marble polishing, carpet shampooing, façade cleaning, in consultation with the EHK and AEHK.
- Coordinate the pest control for all parts of the public area.
- Coordinate the flower arrangement for the special events and for the lobby with the florists.
- Be responsible for completing the lost and found procedure.
- Carry out preventive maintenance of the equipment, and complete the work order form and take timely stock of the cleaning supplies to ensure smooth operation.
- Conduct timely briefing of the public area attendants and communicate any special cleaning or events planned.
- Inform any health and safety hazards to the assistant executive housekeeper or the head housekeeper.

Job description of a linen and uniform supervisor

- Be responsible for the maintenance and upkeep of the linen, towels, and uniforms.
- Be responsible for the required alteration and maintenance of the quality as per the set standards.
- Plan and execute stock taking and inventory control of the linen and the uniform.
- Supervise the day-to-day operation of the linen and uniform attendants and conduct briefings.
- Ensure smooth flow of linen from the laundry to the various sections and check the proper storage of the linen.

- Ensure the appropriate monogramming of the hotel linen and uniform.
- Be responsible for maintaining and updating the record of the linen and uniform for efficient control and stock check.
- Plan the discard procedure to remove from circulation any linen and uniform that is unfit for use.
- Check the quality of the received linen and uniform and report any discrepancy to the executive housekeeper.
- Prepare a purchase specification for the required linen and uniform for the purchase department of the hotel.
- Ensure the linen and uniform exchange procedure is followed by the staff to keep a control on the inventory. Issue linen as per the requisition forms.
- Inspect the storage of the linen and uniform to maintain the quality and the durability.
- Ensure the linen and uniform required for any special events are ready as requisitioned.
- Check the health and safety of the staff in their area and report any discrepancy to the head housekeeper.

Job description of a laundry manager/ supervisor:

- Be responsible for the overall laundry operation and ensure the washing and cleaning of the linen and uniform as per the standards.
- Oversee guest laundry and ensure guest satisfaction by meeting the standards set by the hotel. Guest laundry needs careful supervision as this is the revenue generating section of the housekeeping operation.
- Oversee the maintenance of the laundry equipment and coordinate the planned maintenance with the maintenance department.
- Prepare the laundry budget and present it to the executive housekeeper.
- To make the laundry operation efficient, explore technically advanced laundry equipment and procedures and make recommendation to the head housekeeper.
- Be responsible for planning the staff roster for the laundry operation.
- Plan the training of the laundry staff to enhance the productivity.

Attributes of housekeeping staff

Keen eye for detail

The housekeepers must ensure that all the areas (rooms as well as the public area) are cleaned immaculately meeting unparalleled standards. The first impression is highly important for the great customer experience.

Highly organized

This is important to meet all the customer's needs and special requests and ensuring customers are having a delightful experience. Learning to prioritise the task by managing the time effectively will lead to meeting guest expectation effectively.

Fit and healthy

The work requires lot of physical effort and stamina, so health and fitness is mandatory for housekeeping staff.

Work under pressure

Housekeeping personnel must be able to work efficiently within changing and conflicting demands.

Communication

It is important for the housekeeping staff to be able to communicate effectively as this will ensure a smooth delivery of the guest expectation.

Creativity

Housekeeping staff are responsible for catering to guests with different needs, for instance the room of a guest travelling with children will need special children's amenities as compared to a business traveller. This is important attribute when it comes to solving problems and complaints.

Excellent team player

The staff should be able to adapt and enjoy working in a multicultural environment with a caring attitude and good cross-cultural sensitivity.

> **Empowered staff are motivated**
>
> An excellent strategy is to allow experienced room attendants to self-inspect their rooms. Empowering staff helps the hotels to manage the workload, enhance productivity and give a feeling of self-pride to the staff. Taking accountability of the job strengthens staff motivation, which is the biggest challenge in the housekeeping department due to the nature of the job and gives an opportunity to hotels to develop the skills of the staff members and prepare them for management roles.

Time and motion study in housekeeping

Time and motion study is a work measurement technique to obtain the productivity standards. Time studies are useful in the hotel industry as most of the work is repetitive and the tasks are controllable, for instance, room cleaning, bed making, laundry, linen room tasks etc. To calculate the average time required to complete a task several employees are observed to complete the same task and their movements and timings are recorded. The results are compared and analysed to derive the average time required to complete a particular task.

Advantages of time and motion study

1. It helps in establishing the employee productivity.
2. It breaks down complex tasks into simpler steps.
3. The steps taken to complete a task are observed carefully to eliminate any wasteful motion and inefficiencies.

Summary

Managing housekeeping personnel requires excellent leadership skills, organisation, communication skills. Hiring staff with a positive attitude and the right skills, and ensuring they receive training and development to improve their efficiency is vital in offering high quality service to the guests.

Time and motion study can contribute to a more efficient and effective housekeeping department. It helps in optimizing housekeeping operations by identifying inefficiencies, improving productivity, reducing costs, and enhancing quality.

> **Activity:**
>
> Imagine you are part of a team opening a new 300 room hotel (you can choose where). Discuss in your group the following:
>
> - What might be the key challenges for the housekeeping department?
> - What will be the key responsibilities?
> - Who coined the term 'Time & Motion'? Read the article on time and Motion in the *Further reading* list to find this out. Summarise some of its key findings.

Key terms

- **Time and motion study**: This is a business efficiency technique, primarily concerned with improving performance by measuring and then minimising the time taken to complete a task without compromising the quality of the service.

- **Productivity**: the ratio of inputs to outputs.

- **Budget**: An estimation of the expenses and revenues over a time period. The process of planning to spend the money and anticipating the sales is termed as budgeting.

- **Standard Operating Procedure (SOP)**: A step by step written set of instructions to complete a task, aiming at achieving maximum efficiency, consistency and quality.

Further reading

Batinić, I. (2015) 'Organization of business in hotel housekeeping', *Journal of Process Management and New Technologies*, 3(1), 51–54.

Chattopadhyay, A. Ghosh, R., Maji, S., Ray, T.G., & Lahiri, S.K. (2012) A time motion study in the immunization clinic of a tertiary care hospital of Kolkata, West Bengal, *Indian Journal of Community Medicine*, 37(1), 30–33. doi:10.4103/0970-0218.94019. 10.4103/0970-0218.94019

Cunha, A. and Oliveira, M. (2021) Human resources in the housekeeping department: A case study, *Proceedings of the International Conference on Tourism Research (ICTR)*, 158–164. doi:10.34190/IRT.21.072.

Jones, P. and Siag, A. (2009) A re-examination of the factors that influence productivity in hotels: A study of the housekeeping function, *Tourism & Hospitality Research*, 9(3), 224–234. doi:10.1057/thr.2009.11.

4: Contracts and Outsourcing in the Housekeeping Department

This chapter will help you to:

- Understand the term outsourcing and its uses in the housekeeping department
- Evaluate the commonly outsourced activities/tasks in the housekeeping department
- Review the advantages and disadvantages of outsourcing in the housekeeping operation.

What is outsourcing?

Outsourcing is a conscious business decision to move internal work to external specialist providers. Hiring skilled and reliable housekeeping personnel requires a detailed hiring function and related managing resources. Using a third party, who can cater to the staffing needs of the business, will save a hotel the time required for recruiting, training, and managing the other human resource related tasks. This will allow the hotel housekeeping management to focus on their core goals and objectives, which are maintaining cleanliness standards, ensuring utmost guest satisfaction by meeting and exceeding guest needs.

In outsourcing, a hotel enters into a contract with a supplier or a service provider in which, as per the terms of the contract, the supplier will provide the agreed services. Outsourcing few specialised services can turn out to be cost effective for hotels as they do not have to spend money on recruitment and training. Additionally it allows hotels to focus on the guests, ensuring they have the best experience and engaging with them to make them loyal, which is a core purpose of hospitality. The money which is saved from outsourcing can be invested in carrying out research and development in services for the guests.

Types of outsourcing options for hotels

- **Complete outsourcing**: When the hotel decides to outsource the entire housekeeping or security department to an external company.
- **Partial outsourcing**: When specific activities are outsourced rather than outsourcing the entire department. For example, a hotel decides to outsource its laundry operations and keep the rest of the tasks in-house.

Outsourcing costs

Outsourcing costs are divided into direct, indirect and hidden costs.

Direct cost is the total cost of the outsourcing specific services and is easier to measure. Administrative fees and other supporting costs like legal fees for contract management, will be classified as **indirect costs** and are difficult to measure. Indirect costs also include the cost that has to be borne by the hotel in case of reassignment and termination of the contract. The **hidden costs** related to the outsourcing include the costs of transition from the previous supplier to the new, costs associated with managing change, costs involving the research, selection, and negotiation of a supplier during the initial stages.

Housekeeping services commonly outsourced by hotels:

The entire housekeeping department

There are pros and cons of outsourcing housekeeping employees and whether this is the best solution depends on the needs of the hotel and its location. For instance, for a resort or any of the seasonal properties where the staffing needs will considerably change over the year, outsourcing staffing may be a better option than having permanent employees.

Laundry

The decision to have an in-house laundry or to outsource depends on cost, quality, and space. To set up their own laundry, hotels would need the space, which can be a huge cost, plus it would need to procure expensive specialised laundry equipment and have the finance to ensure its maintenance. Outsourcing the laundry operation can be the more favourable option as it avoids the challenges of dedicating time and resources. However, the biggest challenge to outsourcing laundry operations is in maintaining the consistent quality standards of the linen.

The contract with the laundry outsourcing partner should clearly cover that inferior quality of laundry items will be rejected without any arguments. The hotel needs to have an employee to check laundry deliveries for the expected level of quality when receiving it from an outsourced agency, for example to see that there are no flatbed iron marks, or dark hairs between the sheets from operatives' hair. Most of the time, as per the contract, the hotel will not pay for rejected linen, thus a thorough checking process enables some cost saving as well maintaining standards.

Combining in-house (OPL – On Premises Laundry) and outsourced laundry is an option preferred by some hotel brands, typically outsourcing the flatware and doing towels, facecloths, and robes in-house. For uniforms and guests' laundry, a collar and cuff machine will cut the drying and finishing time for the shirts.

Due to the technological advancements in the laundry operations, environmental considerations and requirement of specialised training outsourcing laundry operation is preferred by the hotels.

The laundry operation leaves a lasting impression and the aim of any hotel is achieving utmost guest experience. It is important for hotel operators to weigh the pros and cons of both outsourcing and in-house laundry operation, checking the financial capability and professional expertise of the hotel and thus making an informed practical decision.

Other outsourced services

- Linen can be hired from an external agency.
- Specialised cleaning like windows, marble and carpet and upholstery cleaning.
- Pest control: Hotels must be inspected for bed bugs, mould etc periodically and hiring an outsourced agency to do this specialised task ensures they are safe for the guests and helps to avoid any customer complaints, thus maintaining the hotel's reputation.
- Horticulture/florists An art of shaping trees into magnificent designs is termed as arbor sculpture tree art or arbortecture.
- Chandelier cleaning
- Waste disposal

Advantages of outsourcing

- **Employee costs** (reduced hiring and training costs). Hiring cost is greatly reduced as the third party handles all the recruitment jobs like interviewing, assessing the background of the candidate and all the documentation and paper works associated with hiring process. When a third party takes care of the entire housekeeping department, the hiring process and the rest of the human resource activities are greatly reduced, in turn lowering the operational costs. With complete outsourcing of the housekeeping department, the hotel pays the total labour cost as a lump sum amount to the outsourcing company rather than paying each member of staff individually.
- **Improves organisational focus:** Outsourcing allows the hotel to focus on its core competences. In some geographical locations there is a shortage of the required manpower and an outsource company will have better expertise in finding new employees. Training employees is also the responsibility of the third party. Therefore, the hotel can look after the guests with greater focus, offering a more personalised experience.
- **Increases flexibility:** the labour requirement will vary during higher occupancy period and low occupancy period, and the suppliers will be ready to adjust to the needs of the hotels. As the business is impacted by several factors and the plans may change, having a business partner who offers flexible services will be convenient for the hotel operation.
- **Facilitates change**: This is important in the rapidly changing business environment. Process developments, changes in consumer behaviour and technological advancements are shaping the business delivery. In this context it is important to find a business partner or supplier who is constantly upgrading their services and follows innovative processes to keep up with the trend of the business. Generally, the suppliers chosen by the hotel are the specialists in their field, have the expertise and offer excellent output.
- **Cost effective**: The employee salaries and any additional cost or the liability of any aspect of employee benefits and injury are managed by the third party. There can be substantial savings to the hotel as the entire responsibility to administer the employee benefits is the responsibility of the third party. This saves time and resource for the hotel. The savings can be invested in the project to enhance the guest experience and attract more customers.

- **Access to experts** in the specific field, with qualified and experienced personnel enable hotels to complement their resources and services. Hotels receive a bigger pool of specialised type of work which helps them to offer the best to their guest.

Disadvantages of outsourcing

- **Poorly trained staff**: It is vital to hold all the employees to the level of the standards set by the hotel to avoid any customer complaints and dissatisfaction. Emphasising clearly to the third party of the importance of a thorough training programme is essential to ensure that in-house and outsourced employees carry out the goals and mission of the hotels collaboratively. Therefore, planning and adhering to a well-planned training schedule will help to overcome this challenge.
- **Inconsistent staff**: Sourcing the employees outside of the established labour market will bring in challenges of having to recruit people lacking some of the basic prerequisites of the job, for example communication skill. Some hotels have staff who do not speak English and this results in a language barrier between the staff and the guests. Communicating the standards and expectations to the new staff is time consuming too.
- **Poor supervision and a drop in standards**: As all the employee related performance concerns are dealt by the third party, there is a potential issue of varying quality. Hotels set the standards and define the work that they want the third party to accomplish for them, and this is often overseen by a third-party supervisor on the site. If only a portion of the staff is outsourced, then it creates another challenge due to assimilating the two different set of staff to work towards the common goal.
- **Time consuming**: The entire process of getting the contract approved and signed is time-consuming, as the outsourcing company deals with several other hotel brands. It is therefore important to initiate the process in a timely manner and allow sufficient time for this to be put into practice without impacting the guest experience and the service quality.
- **Loss of control over activities**: The outsourcing relationship needs to be managed in an integrated fashion within a framework of trust and cooperation.

Some of the larger outsourcing service providers are mentioned below:

- ISS is a global facility management company and supplies trained staff to the hotels. ISS has the motto "People make places and places make people", and with this they believe they create, manage and maintain high quality environments.
- CLEAN Linen and Workwear are a leading UK's laundry company providing linen and workwear rental services.
- CDC Hospitality is a contract cleaning company based in London with 20 years of experience. They believe that they are strategic business partners collaborating with the hotel general managers to succeed in achieving all the set goals.

Theoretical perspective of outsourcing

The theories of Transaction Cost Economics (TCE) and the Resource Based View (RBV) have been applied to the concept of outsourcing. According to TCE (which emphasises financial efficiency) a firm can benefit from a lower production cost due to the specialism and economies of scale of the external service provider. RBV (which explores the external competencies to maximise the core competencies) emphasises using the concept of outsourcing as the strategic tool to gain competitive advantage by focusing on the core activities and outsourcing the non-core activities.

Outsourcing success is measured by three main factors

- **Strategic performance** is measured by factors such as accessibility of new skills and capabilities by the hotels. The hotel may gain improved focus and more flexibility by contracting an outsourced company.
- **Financial performance** is evaluated by three main factors, and those are the extent by which the outsourcing services have helped to reduce the overall cost and investments, to improve financial results, and to improve the hotel's performance.
- **Overall satisfaction** covers the satisfaction of the seller (outsourced company) and the buyer (the hotel in this case). It is measured as high if the hotel is happy with the overall outsourcing job and is likely to recommend the service to other businesses.

Challenges of outsourcing

There are some challenges associated with the outsourcing as everything has got two sides to it. Hotels find the biggest challenge of outsourcing is maintaining standards and controlling the quality. However, this challenge is overcome by efficient contract management which lists the expected output and the objectives to be met and the consequences associated with failure to meet the standards and the quality.

Other key challenges of outsourcing are:

- Mainting clear lines of communication with the outsourcing company and its staff.
- Possible delayed service as reputable suppliers will have several other hotel partners.
- If the contract between the outsourcing company and the hotel is too tightly written, it might restrict flexibility which is another challenge.
- Instability in the business environment – the outsource company could go out of business, posing a threat to the hotel's operation and cost.
- Change in management in the outsourced company could lead to confusion between the two parties and will require additional time and effort to resolve this.
- Allowing the external company access can result in some additional risk to confidentiality and the security of the hotel building.

Outsourcing of non-core functions in hotels	
Major benefits	**Major challenges and difficulties**
Efficient service delivery Highly specialised workforce Services delivery at a reduced cost Propmptness of delivery Operational flexibility	Risk of losing sensitive data and the loss of confidentiality Losing managment control of business functions Possible delays and inaccuracies in the work output Hidden costs and legal problems may arise Post-contract processes and decision rights not understood Poor mutual understanding of the contract Client retained team lacks required skills Loss of key talent Culture clash between the client and the service provider

Figure 4.2: Benefits, challenges and difficulties of outsourcing non-core functions

Outsourced housekeeping activities and some example suppliers

To give you an idea of the sort of housekeeping activities that can be outsourced, here are some companies and some of the services that they provide.

- **WGC** are a leading facility management company offers services like:
    - Complete outsourced hotel housekeeping services matching the brand standards of the partner hotel.
    - Specialized cleaning along with robotic cleaning and H_3O cleaning (uses ionized, toxin free, water).
    - Disinfection cleaning to restore the confidence of the customers. For this the company uses ozonated water (a safe, effective cleaner and sanitizer that works stronger than bleach and hydrogen peroxide – without the hazardous odors or toxic chemical residues that come with traditional cleaning chemicals).
    - Streak free windows – one of the most essential services as greasy and smudged glass gives an impression of poor housekeeping.
    - Hard floor care solutions tailored to the needs of granite, marble, limestone, and wooden floorings.
    - Services for refurbishment and restoration, using techniques like vitrification, crystallization, diamond polishing, sanding and sealing.
- **Rednum** are specialists in marble and stone polishing. Their services comprise of restoring and maintaining all natural stone surfaces through the traditional method of diamond polishing to remove scratches, stains and etching.
- **Donau Commercial Cleaners** specialise in carpets, curtains and upholstery, with cleaning and stain removal of all fabrics including Damask velvet, leather and antique furniture. They design and make curtains and offer alteration services for net curtains anddrapes, blinds, pelmets, tracks and poles, bedspreads, valances and headboards. Donau also design and fit anti-blast window film and bomb blast net curtains. Installation of security window films offers safety against fractured glass from shattering and provides protection from flying glass in the event of a bomb-blast.
- **V&A Chandeliers** are specialists in the cleaning, restoring and installation of chandeliers. Regular care and cleaning of chandeliers ensures the maintenance of their sparkle and shimmer. They add to the aesthetic appeal of a space whether in the lobby, banquet hall or a guest suite. To maintain the pristine condition of these expensive decorative items, it is necessary to find a trusted partner who can clean, re-wire, re-pin various metal finishes and replace crystals and parts as required.

Figure 4.3: Chandelier cleaning

Load testing is an important service that they provide. This covers the inspection of the structure and the fixing that will be used to hang the chandelier to ensure that they can support the weight of the chandelier. Regular load testing can be scheduled to ensure safety and avoid any accidents in future. Chandelier safe removal, packaging and secure storage services is also provided during renovation, until the task is completed.

Figure 4.4: Chandelier load testing being carried out on site.

- **Axminster Services**, amongst other services they offer night-time cleaning. As a hotel is a 24-hour operation it is important to carry out the deep cleaning at night. Thorough **spa** and **gymnasium** cleaning requires complete sanitisation and electronic infection control, and is best done during the night when these leisure services are closed for the guests.

    Thorough cleaning of the **back of the house** is also best done during the night as there are fewer employees and less activity then. A clean and healthy work environment enhances the productivity and health of the employees.

    Other specialised services they offer include chewing gum and graffiti removal, building façade/cladding cleaning, and repair/maintenance of cleaning equipment.

Outsourcing insights from luxury hotel housekeepers

Each hotel has a different take in terms of outsourcing, and some luxury hotels are not outsourcing labour and specialised cleaning from agencies. The common reason for this being to maintain standards and consistency and thus enabling good control. Other luxury hotels have realised that manpower is the biggest cost in housekeeping and recruiting permanent staff is expensive, especially after Covid-19, when hotels are in the recovery stage. It is better to work with several agencies who can supply trained staff when the occupancy goes high. As the demand fluctuates, a hotel can ask agencies for staff during busy period or during group arrivals, train them for a week and put them to work as porters, room attendants or even floor supervisors.

The agencies have a contract with the hotels that if they would like to hire any staff from them, they would need to pay them a fee else the agency will terminate their contract. Some staff prefer to work for agencies as it allows them flexibility, they get to work for different hotels and if they are good in their job, they get an opportunity to join hotels as permanent staff.

Summary

The decisions on resourcing comes down to whether the hotel has the internal capability, appetite, and financial ability to recruit, train and develop their own in-house team. If not, then an agency will act as an extension for the business. The outsourcing decision can be economical in the context of fluctuating demand in the industry and allows the hotel to outsource when there is the need, rather than employing the staff all year round without sufficient tasks for them. Outsourcing offers flexibility in terms of hiring staff, especially for hotel having set seasonal patterns.

Outsourcing gives access to the most innovative products and processes as the specialist companies invest in the research in their specific field to offer the best and stay competitive. As the staff is hired and trained by the outsourcing companies the liability of hotels is reduced and the outsourcing company takes care of the insurance for the tasks that involve high risk, for example window cleaning of high-rise buildings. Outsourcing also reduces the need for capital expenditure as the contracted company uses their specialist product and equipment so a hotel gets to explore the efficiency of the process and product before deciding to invest into it.

In conclusion whether the hotels contract their staff out or employ directly, the most important factor is to meet and exceed the customer expectation by proving magical service and consistent cleanliness. The contribution of the housekeeping department to the growth of the business is undeniable. The hotel industry is witnessing massive transformation and rapid technological advancements. However, the fundamentals of hotel housekeeping remain unchangeable, which is our customers are looking forward to crisp linen, immaculate rooms and quality mattresses for a good night's sleep.

Activities

1. Look at your organisation or place of work and find out if the entire department is outsourced or if there are specific activities which are outsourced.

2. What are the considerations a hotel manager needs to take into account when making possible outsourcing decisions?

3. Summarise the challenges and benefits of outsourcing the housekeeping operation.

4. Consider yourself as a head housekeeper of a luxury hotel, what services and operations will you outsource and why?

Key terms

- **Supplier identification:** This is the process of finding potential suppliers and looks at the legal background checks, quality and the guaranteed certificate, company criteria, etc..

- **Supplier selection:** The key criteria for selecting a supplier include effectiveness, efficiency and expertise, as well as – of course – cost.

- **Supplier relationship management:** The communication, evaluation and the relationship building efforts between the supplier and the buyer.

- **Downtime:** This is how long it takes for the maintenance contractors to repair the broken-down machines.

- **Lead time:** The interval between the initiation and the completion of a contract or project.

References and further reading

Hiamey, S.E. and Hiamey, G.A. (2020) Supplier selection and management in hotel outsourcing: an exploratory study in Ghana, *Anatolia: An International Journal of Tourism & Hospitality Research*, 31(1), 62–75. doi:10.1080/13032917.2019.1697938.

Jenkins, L. (2012) Hotel laundry in house or outsourced?, *Caterer & Hotelkeeper*, 202(4711), 38–40.

Lai, P.-C., Soltani, E. & Baum, T. (2008) Distancing flexibility in the hotel industry: the role of employment agencies as labour suppliers, *International Journal of Human Resource Management*, 19(1), 132–152. doi:10.1080/09585190701764048.

Housekeeping Today (n.d.) https://www.housekeepingtodayuk.com/outsourcing-the-perfect-balancing-act/

5: Planning Housekeeping Operations

This chapter will help you to:

- Understand the terms 'operational planning' and 'measuring performance' in housekeeping.
- Evaluate productivity standards and how productivity can be maximised in the housekeeping operation.
- Review the impact of Covid-19 on operational planning and the ways to mitigate those challenges.
- Learn about the LQA standards and their application in housekeeping processes.

Operational planning

Operational planning is a detailed plan which clearly defines what everyone in a team or department needs to do to achieve the strategic goals of the organization. This includes things like which tasks and strategies need to be completed, who is responsible for completing the tasks, when they need to be completed, and how much they will cost. One challenge of operational planning is effective communication. Making sure communication is consistent and effective can be difficult for anyone within an organization. However, for day-to-day operations to run smoothly it is vital to master written, oral, and non-verbal communication. Well-communicated expectations and tasks are more likely to motivate staff and ensure targets are met through high productivity. Good communication also builds employee moral, which is essential for maximizing productivity and deepens employee trust with management. On the other hand, it is important to make sure effective communication doesn't turn into information overload. This is because when there is too much information for individuals to manage, they will simply start to ignore and discard information, which will not ensure productivity maximization.

Performance

Performance in housekeeping operations is defined as the ability of the team members to attain the highest standards set by the hotel. Performance is the output expected from each employee with regards to their specific task. To achieve the maximum efficiency each task has its set principles and specifications which, when followed, generate the expected results. Time and motion studies help the housekeeping department to determine the average time required to finish each task.

The role of the housekeeping department in attaining the overall guest satisfaction and having a positive impact on the bottom line is vital. For a hotel to achieve a promising RevPAR (Revenue Per Available Room) and a higher guest satisfaction score it is important to evaluate the performance of the housekeeping department. Measuring performance of the housekeeping department is crucial as it is one of the most labour-intensive departments and is responsible to provide a high level of quality service by adding value to the guest experience and must adjust to the varying demands of the hotel. Therefore, to evaluate the performance of the team members it is important to set he KPI (Key performance Indicator).

Performance and productivity standard varies as they depend on the size of the hotel. The KPIs (key performance indicators) must be relevant to the core activity. When setting the KPI for a task, is important to analyse the trends and foresee the challenges coming to determine the strategic changes required. It also helps to support the staff members who are unable to meet the expected performance standards by planning required training. Once the KPIs are set, they are evaluated by carrying out regular inspections and audits, and this planned systematic approach helps to utilise the management time in an effective manner.

The KPI can be identified by breaking down the housekeeping task into three categories using the framework:

1. Input which includes the preparation stage
2. Process includes the actual delivery
3. Output includes the result

Scheduling time for the managers and supervisors to focus on the individual performance of the team members by identifying the training needs and guiding mentoring accordingly will ensure a consistent and quality service.

Performance standards can be set by working on the following factors:

- Required level of performance
- What must be done?
- How it must be done?
- The standards should be developed with the participation of the room attendants or the relevant team member.
- The standards should be communicated through training.
- Endure conformity through inspection

Productivity standards

Productivity is defined as the efficiency, effectiveness, and quality of the operation, and it signifies the relationship between input and output. Due to the intangible, heterogenous and perishable nature of the hospitality industry, productivity management and measurement is challenging. Evaluation of performance is essential to ensure the consistency and is central to quality management. If productivity problems are identified, it is important to follow the Systems Model to approach the solution.

1 The first step to this approach is to set the output – That is what we want to achieve. This might be how many rooms the hotel expects a room attendant to clean in the morning shift.

2 Once the output is set it is important to evaluate the symptoms that indicate something is wrong. For instance, the number and type of complaints regarding room cleaning.

3 Once the symptoms are evaluated it is important to verify them through interview or observation to find the root cause of the problem. For instance, in case of complaint about the room cleaning the problem could be the benchmark of the housekeeping inspector is too high, which is causing unrealistically poor ratings.

4 Next step is to identify the trends, the critical areas and issues, for example with the room cleaning the problem may be arising from the poor quality of the cleaning products or poor manpower planning or insufficient training etc.

5 Once the critical issues are identified, the planned output and actual result should be compared to arrive at the solution to correct the deficiencies. For example, if the complaint concerning the room cleaning is arising on weekends, the probable reasons could be understaffing or insufficient supervision on weekends.

6 Then the proposed solution is pilot tested before full implementation to check the impact of the change on the overall operation.

7 Thereafter, evaluation is ongoing to ensure the set output and objectives are met.

Maximising productivity through workplace and job design

- Well planned layout of the workplace areas will maximise the use of the equipment and labour.

- Employee scheduling and task planning, termed as *work schedules* and *job planning* helps the employees to use their hours more effectively by guiding them on their allotted tasks and duties during their shift.

- Motivating the employees by focusing on an organisational culture (developing a productive company culture) and climate which is based on high standards, clarity, commitment, teamwork, responsibility and recognition, and which is embraced by the workers in the workplace.

- Establishing procedures, termed as *Standard Operating Procedures*, to meet the productivity standards which aid in imparting effective training to the staff as well as standardising the tasks to enable consistency in the operation.

Some of the below mentioned points aid in standardising productivity when planned efficiently:

- Monitoring the unrelated tasks consuming employee's time. Can any tasks be eliminated without impacting the result?
- Combining tasks.
- Unnecessary delays resulting in slow down, for example insufficient supplies while cleaning a guest room.
- Matching employees to tasks, ensuring that employees know the best procedure to do a task.
- Entrusting the room attendants to check and release their own rooms and thus empowering them.
- Carrying out random inspections and audit to ensure the standards are followed and documenting the same. The documented quality check audit results will enable the management to reward the high performing staff members and plan training for the members of the staff struggling to meet the standards.
- Making a cleaning checklist for the crew

- Improving the working connection between cleaning and maintenance personnel; collaboration will increase overall productivity.
- Ensuring that cleaning inspections and quality checks are not skipped, as one minor flaw that goes unchecked might lead to a slew of problems. Furthermore, it degrades the quality of cleanliness.

Manpower planning

The housekeeping department is the largest department and thus employs the biggest number of workers, so consideration needs to be made to ensure the effective manpower planning. This will differ from hotel to hotel, however there are some approaches which will remain common in all the hotels irrespective of their differences. As the manpower is the biggest operating expense made by the hotels it is important to consider the following points while determining the staffing for the housekeeping department:

- **Size of the hotel** – number of rooms.
- **Expanse of the public area** and the landscaped area.
- **Type of hotel**, for example a luxury hotel/a resort will need more detailed cleaning schedule as compared to a city centre business hotel.
- **Occupancy rate** of the hotel and whether the hotel enjoys a consistent occupancy throughout the year, or it has seasonal demands.
- **Location** of the hotel to see if the staff can be hired from the local labour market and what skills are available.
- **Policies** of the hotel, for example what are the quality standards, and the frequency schedules
- **Area inventory list**, this comprises all the items in an area that require attention (cleaning and maintenance). Each guest room and the public area will need an area inventory list to ensure none of the items in it are missed while cleaning.
- **Frequency Schedule** indicates how often an item in an area inventory list needs attention. Some items need cleaning daily, other weekly, monthly, periodically or even annually.

Setting productivity standards

For manpower planning of the housekeeping department, it is essential to set the productivity standards of the hotel, as this determines the amount of work which needs to be done by the housekeeping staff. How many rooms a room attendant can clean depends on several factors like: standard of service, size of the room, and the nature of the fixtures in the room, for example if there are frosted glass, silver or brass fixtures that require polishing a room attendant will need additional time to clean the room.

As a rule of thumb, a hotel can plan the number of room attendants required to service the total guest rooms by following these steps:

Step 1:
Determine how long it should take to clean one hotel room according to the department's performance standards
   Assumption: 27 minutes

Step 2:
Determine the total shift time in minutes.
   8 hours shift × 60 minutes = 480 minutes

Step 3:
Determine the time available for hotel room cleaning.

Total shift time	480 minutes
Less:	
Beginning of Shift duties	20 minutes
Break	30 minutes
End of shift duties	20 minutes
Time avaijable for hotel room cleaning	410 minutes

Step 4:
Determine the productivity standard by dividing the result of Step 3 by that of Step 1

The result indicates that one room attendant can clean 15.2 hotel rooms in an 8-hour shift.

Assume that a 456-bedrom hotal has an occupancy of 80%. How many room attendants need to be scheduled to clean the hotel roms?

   0.80 × 456 hotel rooms = 365 hotel rooms need to be cleaned

365 hotel rooms divided by 15.2 results in the need to secure 24 room attendants to be able to clean the hotel rooms with the given productivity.

Figure 5.1: Sample productivity standard calculation (based on Chibili et al., 2019)

Time & Motion Study

For calculating the staffing needs of a hotel, time and motion studies help to determine the standard performance of an employee by calculating the average time taken to complete a particular task, and thus guides the hotel to plan their manpower effectively.

Planning the duty roster

A duty roster aids in planning the staffing for the department and ensures that the correct number of staff are present at any given point of time to maintain the set work schedules.

Points to consider while planning the duty roster:

- Ascertain the forecast occupancy of the hotel weekly, if planning the weekly roster, as well as checking the planned events before scheduling the room attendants and public area attendants.
- Coordinate with the front office department to take into account the occupancy levels of the hotel, before approving staff annual leaves/holidays.
- Evaluate the operational hours of the department as well as the required full time/part time or agency staff.
- Calculate the total number of hours per week ascribed to the staff.
- Do not forget to consider the time for meal breaks.
- Look at the expected productivity and workload calculated for the staff in each specific area.
- Plan reliefs for each shift to cover last-minute sickness and absence.
- Plan weekly days off and bank holidays for the employees, to offer the required rest. Ensuring the reliefs are available to cover the scheduled work.
- Schedule spring cleaning or any special cleaning regimes

> **Work schedules** should be adjusted according to the occupancy schedule, and feedback should be provided. Be receptive to criticism, suggestions, and issues. Make a cleaning checklist for the crew. Improve the working connection between cleaning and maintenance personnel; collaboration will increase overall productivity. Work schedules should be adjusted according to the occupancy schedule, and feedback should be provided.

Covid-19 and its impact on productivity

Operational plans are normally short term – they run for a year or less and are monitored frequently for progress. The unforeseen Covid-19 pandemic in 2020, which has proven to be one of the most disruptive events in recent decades, has led to a lot of changes in the procedures and operational organisation of housekeeping department, as well as in the customers' expectations and needs. Hotels have had to make changes to the way they operate which means they either must make a new operational plan or update the previous one to make it relevant to handle the situation at hand.

Before the pandemic, guests had already ranked hotels' cleanliness and hygiene as one of the most important factors when choosing a hotel. However, after the pandemic it has gained more of an importance to all individuals. Based on this, hotels are challenged with adding extra precautions to the housekeeping department. This had massive implication on the costs as the hotel needed to invest in higher level cleaning products and equipment to ensure customer safety and trust, and further disinfect their premises. For example, prior to the Covid-19 pandemic, a room attendant at a well-reputed hotel was required to do 16 rooms in eight-hour shift, so half an hour for each room. At another well-reputed brand, a room was expected to be cleaned in 25 minutes, increasing the number cleaned to 20 in an eight-hour shift, spending 14 minutes for stay-over cleanings without linen change and 17 minutes for stay-over cleaning including linen change. With the new guidelines and the enhanced cleanliness to stop spreading the virus, the time needed to deep clean and sanitise a room has increased to 1 to 1.5 hours, dramatically decreasing the number of rooms that can be cleaned within a shift. This is challenging the productivity and the organisations of all cleaning times and schedules, along with the number of staff required.

While interviewing the executive housekeeper of a leading luxury hotel it was found that, on average, a room attendant in a luxury hotel was supposed to be doing 8.7 credits (the number of rooms) that is approximately 9 rooms per room attendant. However in the wake of Covid-19, as the cleaning time has increased, most of the hotels have reduced the allocation by one room making approximately 8 credits per room attendant. Some hotels in central London are smaller, with sma;ller rooms, so an attendant can easily do 10 credits. These expectations are communicated to a room attendant, and they are provided sufficient training to ensure meeting the productivity standards. A suite room will have two credits, for obvious reasons, as it is a bigger space.

Housekeepers and attendants are exposed to the virus; best practices include allocating one attendant per floor to reduce cross-contamination. Another challenge relates to the introduction of new products and protocols, hence the introduction of new trainings, pivotal for both customer and staff safety. The implementation of all those changes has led to extra costs for the businesses, which are trying to reduce some other expenses through outsourced labour for a portion of their staffing needs.

Challenges in operational planning

Some of the challenges in operational planning faced within the housekeeping department that impacted the productivity and customer expectation are discussed below.

Managing daily housekeeping targets

The time between reporting and meeting the housekeeping targets is crucial to ensure the quality and speed of maintenance. However, in the case of the Covid-19 pandemic, there has been an irregular influx of tourists to hotels, which could not be tracked down by the housekeeping departments. With the stringent cleaning and sanitising sessions, the task could be delayed or even missed by the housekeeping staff on account of too many influxes of tourists into the hotel. It must be noted that the Covid-19 guidelines require thorough and frequent cleaning measures, which could double or triple when there are more guests in a hotel. Failure to execute the cleaning and sanitising tasks could pose a significant operational challenge for the housekeeping staff, and undermine the ability to meet the customers' expectations.

High operating costs in the housekeeping department

High operating costs have been an overwhelming challenge to the operational planning of the hotel industry, with the focus on the role of the housekeeping department. It must be noted that with stringent cleaning protocols, the department must procure additional stocks of cleaning materials, equipment, facial masks and PPE kits, which have added greatly to the costs. However, the housekeeping department has been finding it difficult to identify cost reduction strategies that do not compromise the safety of the housekeeping staff. Hence, the operational cost increase could not be curtailed by the housekeeping departments, leading to channeling funds from other housekeeping activities, which creates an imbalance in the operating planning and reduces the productivity of the organisation.

Stringent cleaning and documentation requirements

In the wake of the Covid-19 pandemic, there was a significant increase in the demand from guests for stringent and high-standard cleaning. This in turn placed an additional burden on the housekeeping department to continuously document and track cleaning records – another factor in the rise in the workload of housekeeping staff post-Covid-19 pandemic. The state and national standard guidelines imposed additional work pressure on housekeeping staff to follow mandated cleaning requirements along with reporting and documenting daily tasks. The increase in the workload of housekeeping staff post Covid-19 pandemic has increased mental stress and degraded physical wellbeing, in the effort to deliver a high level of cleaning to guests and document daily cleaning practices. This has affected hotels' customer service.

How technological advancements came as a boon and helped to support this increased expectation will be discussed in later chapters.

Outsourcing to cleaning agencies

One solution to coping with the increased workload of the housekeeping department, especially during the post-Covid-19 pandemic, has been for the housekeeping management in the hotel to outsource cleaning and documentation activities to specialised cleaning agencies. The role of these agencies would be to oversee and document all cleaning activities of the hotel, using staffs with multi-tasking skills to reduce the additional work pressure on the in-house staff. This approach reduced mental and physical stress, and allowed the housekeeping staff to focus on improving customer service.

Incentives and pay rises

Housekeeping departments have considered improving incentives and pay scales to reflect the hard work of housekeeping staff post-Covid-19 pandemic. Housekeeping management teams in hotels have rolled out new rewards and recognition plans, such as points-based recognition, and tuition reimbursement, to boost the morale and confidence of staff to carry out duties efficiently and thus to improve customer service. Point-based recognition systems would allow housekeeping staff to redeem points collected on every service done outstandingly in the hotel, to purchase merchandise and gift cards based on their personal need and preferences. Offering tuition reimbursement has also proved to be effective in retaining housekeeping staff as they feel supported in achieving their educational goal and career advancement in near future. Some of these strategies helped housekeeping management to overcome the issue of employee turnover.

Sourcing cleaning materials and PPE from local suppliers

Higher operational costs have been incurred by housekeeping departments post-pandemic, and hotels have looked for ways to reduce these. The housekeeping department cannot compromise the safety of its staff, but may be able to procure cleaning materials and PPE kit from local suppliers at lower cost. This can help the operational costs to balance without compromising staff safety, and can improve productivity.

Staff engagement for enhanced productivity

Staff engagement is the relationship between the staff and the company, and an engaged staff will actively work to benefit the organisation. An engaged staff results in higher productivity as they enjoy their work and therefore add creativity and enthusiasm to it, resulting in improved guest relations, a higher customer satisfaction index and higher retention rates. An engaged staff will act as an advocate of the organisation and promote the business generously. A disengaged staff will cost the business, eroding a company's profit margin.

One of the most important strategies to boost employee engagement is strengthening the internal communication between the staff and the management. Therefore, some hotels have sought to create internal communications platforms to connect their team using an app. A leading example of such app is *Beekeeper*. These apps allow staff to connect with staff from other departments, thus enabling smoother interdepartmental communication and collaboration. They enable the management to send out notifications, inform the team of any new developments, share company values, source opinions, and encourage the staff. The apps also include engagement features like in-app feedback, surveys, and quizzes leading to better staff involvement. The analytics dashboards of the apps provide insights about the internal communications app usage, attendance, performance records, work records and notes. Therefore, the early signs of disengagement and low morale can be addressed before it is too late using the insights provided.

The app *Beekeeper* is used by some luxury hotels to strengthen the communication between the team and share some of the good practices, and positive guest reviews. The app has similar features of like, share and comment, as are found on any other social media platforms. Staff recognition is also a great way to motivate and engage the team and the app allows them to recognise and appreciate in a timely, genuine, specific manner. The app allows the team members to secure the communication and they can choose to chat in the public news feed as well as the private chat mode. The app is mobile friendly, and has the feature of attaching pictures and files, as well as choosing an alternative language option. Find out more about Beekeeper here: https://www.beekeeper.io

Some leading luxury hotels encourage and empower their staff to create WOW moments for their guests, anticipating their needs by careful listening and observation, and the employees are encouraged to share the same on the app, thus encouraging other staff members to go above and beyond to exceed the customer expectations and delight the customers. Sharing creativity and appreciating each other generates a healthy work environment where the staff feels motivated, and engaged. During the Covid-19 pandemic, the app helped to digitise the information flow, checklists, forms etc, and the social distancing protocols were adhered as there was no need to gather the staff for meetings in a closed space. The physical meetings were replaced by bulletin board, posts, chats and push notifications features. The app was used to share videos of the changed protocols allowing staff training on new operating procedures.

> **Accor's Peopleology**
>
> Accor hotel believes that it's all about people. Human connection is valuable to enhance the productivity of the staff which in turn enhances the profit of the business. So, they came up with concept called 'Peopleology' to make everyone feel valued and welcomed. There is a full training programme behind this, but there is also an app which employees are encouraged to download on their mobile. Through the app, staff are sent activities, videos and challenges, with a focus on the issues that can arise from emotional labour. The strategies support the employees to manage their stress and boost their emotional intelligence, which is significant for their wellbeing as well as for the business. As it is rightly said, a happy employee makes a happy customer. Another big benefit of the app is it helps to impart training. Engaging with the staff and training them as per their needs, reduces their job ambiguity, reduces the staff turnover and offers job satisfaction.
>
> 100% OF CUSTOMERS ARE PEOPLE.
> 100% OF EMPLOYEES ARE PEOPLE.
> IF YOU DON'T UNDERSTAND PEOPLE, YOU DON'T UNDERSTAND BUSINESS.
>
> **Figure 5.2:** The 'Heartist' symbol at the centre of Accor's Peopleology

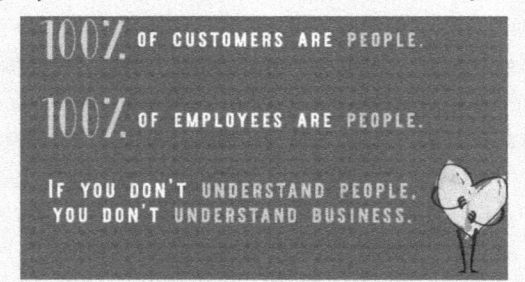

LQA audits

Leading Quality Assurance, famous as LQA, offers an anonymous three days, two nights assessments of standards and processes, and works in partnership with the leading luxury hotel chains to optimise guest satisfaction and experience. LQA audits follow a unique approach; they audit each department of the hotel following the international standard benchmarks, and emotional intelligence as well as the set brand standards. After the audit they give the hotels a detailed narrative of their service standards as well as clear recommendations on how to improve them through their actionable insights and analytics. LQA offers customised training modules with assisted tools to work on the areas that need improvement during the quality assurance assessments.

Once the assessment is done LQA offers a five-step tool.

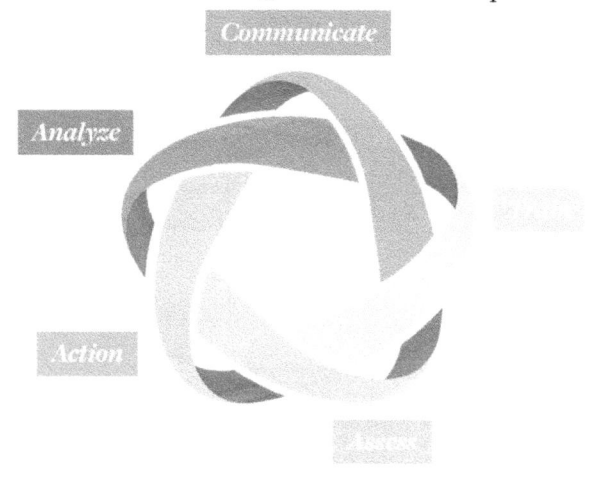

Figure 5.3: The LQA five-step approach

1 The first step is to *Communicate* the international standard benchmarks to all the employees and the information is available in different languages.

2 The next step is *Training* in which each department is trained, based on their identified needs. The training modules are created by the experts of the LQA, and the videos are shared with the team. These can be viewed by the staff as many times as they need to full understand them, and are followed by a set of multiple-choice question to evaluate the training.

3 Once the team has undergone training it is good to carry out an internal *assessment* to see if the staff has got complete understanding of the highest possible standards to be followed.

4 In the *Analyze* step the LQA website offers tools that analyses the assessment data and presents this to the hotel in a dashboard, and most importantly gives actionable insights for the hotel and brand.

5 Finally, the hotels are provided with an *Action* plan to be followed to meet and exceed the customer experience in the future.

Some of the LQA checklists for housekeeping processes are shown below.

HOUSEKEEPING ARRIVAL DATE AND TIME:		LQA Score	0.0%		
	STANDARD	PERFORMANCE CLASSIFICATION	MET	BELOW	N/A
	BEDROOM				
1	Were the carpet/tiles/wood flooring clean and free of stains/dust?	CLEANLINESS			
2	Were all walls, doors, baseboards clean and free of marks/dirt/smudges/dust?	CLEANLINESS			
3	Were ceilings, vents, smoke detectors and sprinklers clean and free of any dust?	CLEANLINESS			
4	Was the room at a comfortable temperature on arrival and free of odour?	CLEANLINESS			
5	Was the bed neatly made with clean linen, which was free of stains and tears and was the bed valance/skirting (if applicable) clean and neatly arranged?	CLEANLINESS			
6	Was the headboard in good condition and if applicable, were the bedspread/blankets/scatter cushions/bolsters clean?	CLEANLINESS			
7	Was all upholstered furniture clean and free of stains?	CLEANLINESS			
8	Were all the furniture surfaces clean and dust/smear free?	CLEANLINESS			
9	Were all the picture/door/mirror frames clean and dust free?	CLEANLINESS			
10	Were all the windows/mirrors/chrome/metal surfaces clean and free of smears?	CLEANLINESS			
11	Were the curtains/voiles/shutters/blinds clean and properly fitted?	CLEANLINESS			
12	Was the wastepaper bin clean and in excellent condition?	CLEANLINESS			
13	Was a notepad, pen/pencil available next to each telephone in the room?	CLEANLINESS			
14	Was all in-room collateral clean and in excellent condition?	CLEANLINESS			
15	Were the wardrobes/drawers clean and free of any scuffs, dust or debris?	CLEANLINESS			
16	Was the television clean and correctly tuned in?	CLEANLINESS			
17	If there were clocks in the room did, they all display the correct time and were they synchronized within 2 minutes of each other and were all alarm clocks reset to no alarm?	CLEANLINESS			

18	Were all light fixtures in the bathroom and bedroom working properly and were they clean and dust free?	CLEANLINESS			
19	Was the balcony clean, swept and all balcony furniture clean and set up (weather permitting)?	CLEANLINESS			
20	Were any pre-arrival requests/personal preferences in place on arrival (e.g. non allergic pillows, baby cot, etc.)?	CLEANLINESS			
BATHROOM					
21	Was the bathroom completely mold free?	CLEANLINESS			
22	Were the floor, walls, doors and ceiling clean?	CLEANLINESS			
23	Were the shower, bath, sink and toilet clean?	CLEANLINESS			
24	Were the showerhead and bath/sink taps polished and free of lime scale?	CLEANLINESS			
25	Was the shower screen/door clean?	CLEANLINESS			
26	Were all counters, shelves and soap dishes clean and dry?	CLEANLINESS			
27	Was the wastepaper bin clean and in excellent condition?	CLEANLINESS			
28	Was a complete set of unused amenities present on arrival?	SERVICE			
29	Was there a full box of tissues, a well presented toilet roll and a spare toilet roll available?	CLEANLINESS			
30	Were there 2 x clean drinking water glasses or similar present?	CLEANLINESS			
31	Were all towels clean, unstained and in excellent repair?	CLEANLINESS			
32	Were bathrobes and slippers present on arrival and were they clean and in excellent repair?	CLEANLINESS			
BRAND SIGNATURE					
33	Was a welcome amenity provided (e.g. fruit, chocolates, etc.)?	PRODUCT			
34	In the case of a special occasion (i.e. anniversary, birthday, etc.) was a special amenity provided to acknowledge this (i.e. small appropriate gift)?	SERVICE			
	TOTAL NO. OF STANDARDS		MET	BELOW	N/A
	34				

TURNDOWN		LQA Score	0.0%		
DATE :					
STANDARD	PERFORMANCE CLASSIFICATION	MET	BELOW	N/A	
BEDROOM					
1	Was a turndown service provided between 18h00 and 21h30?	SERVICE			
2	Did the employee knock on the door/ring the doorbell and if required wait 10 seconds, and then knock on the door/ring the doorbell again and announce their department before asking to enter the room?	SERVICE			
3	If a 'privacy' sign/light was present was a calling card/doorknob card left under/on the door or a silent message left on the telephone?	SERVICE			
4	If the employee was encountered was he/she well-presented and did they greet the guest with a smile?	SERVICE			
5	If guest was present in the room during turndown, did the employee arrange to return at a later convenient time when the guest was out of the room?	SERVICE			
6	Were the scatter cushions removed and the bedspread either folded back or removed and if removed, were they not placed directly on to the floor?	SERVICE			
7	Did employee fold back sheets neatly and adjust pillows accordingly whilst respecting the guest's preference (i.e., bed turned down on the correct side of bed based on previous evening)?	SERVICE			
8	Were bedside slippers laid out next to the bed (bedside mat optional)?	SERVICE			
9	Did employee draw curtains/blinds/shutters fully and neatly, unless purposely left open due to view/seasonality?	SERVICE			
10	Did employee turn bedside lamp/s on and in the case of key activated lighting had the lighting been adjusted accordingly when the key card was inserted?	SERVICE			
11	Was complimentary bottled/filtered drinking water provided?	SERVICE			
12	Did employee empty waste bins and ashtrays?	CLEANLINESS			
13	Was the room tidied with all hotel amenities returned to their original locations (i.e. hairdryer, ironing board, etc.)?	CLEANLINESS			
14	Were the guest's clothes tidied and his/her shoes paired, with all items left in view?	SERVICE			

15	Was the stationery/amenities replenished where required (i.e. when all of one type of stationery was missing)?	SERVICE			
16	Were any used glasses or room service soiled plates and cutlery removed from room and replaced (where required)?	CLEANLINESS			
17	Was the television remote control placed on bedside table?	SERVICE			
18	Did turndown include any additional personalized touch (e.g. amenity, bookmark, etc.)?	SERVICE			
	BATHROOM				
19	Did the employee replace any used towels with clean ones and were they in excellent condition (mark n/a if green housekeeping option was chosen)?	CLEANLINESS			
20	Where a Green housekeeping option was present for sheets/towels, was it clearly stated and did employee adhere to what the guest had requested?	SERVICE			
21	Was a bathmat laid out in front of the sink and available at the bathtub and shower?	SERVICE			
22	Were all empty or almost empty amenities replaced/re-stocked (i.e. if less than 1/3 full)?	SERVICE			
23	Were the shower/bath/sink/toilet and floor wiped clean?	CLEANLINESS			
24	Were the bathroom water glasses cleaned and/or replaced?	CLEANLINESS			
25	Did the employee tidy guest's personal toiletries (i.e. replace lids, neatly arrange and/or place items on to a washcloth/linen cloth)?	SERVICE			
	BRAND CORE				
26	Did employees take ownership of guest requests and effectively communicate them to other departments where necessary (i.e. guest does not need to repeat request)?	SERVICE			
27	Did employees acknowledge guests in passing, using their name if known?	SERVICE			
28	Did employees show a genuine sense of care during interactions by smiling, making eye contact, and using positive body language?	SERVICE			
29	Were all written communications to guests (i.e. notes, email, etc.) on hotel branded stationery, personally addressed where applicable (i.e. use of guest name) and signed by a named individual?	SERVICE			
30	If the guest was staying for a special occasion, did the employee show recognition of this?	SERVICE			

	BRAND SIGNATURE				
31	Was a complimentary bottle of water on a tray or coaster placed out for each guest at turndown?	PRODUCT			
32	Were all small items/amenities requested from housekeeping presented in a branded linen/cloth drawstring bag?	EFFICIENCY			
33	Did employee offer to set up any large items/amenities requested from housekeeping as required (e.g. iron and board) and agree a suitable collection time to retrieve these after use?	SERVICE			
	TOTAL NO. OF STANDARDS		MET	BELOW	N/A
	33				

SERVICING			LQA Score	0.0%	
DATE:					
	STANDARD	PERFORMANCE CLASSIFICATION	MET	BELOW	N/A
	BEDROOM				
1	Was servicing completed by 15h00 each day or within 1 hour of hanging/activating the 'service room' sign/light?	SERVICE			
2	Did the employee knock on the door/ring the doorbell and if required wait 10 seconds, and then knock on the door/ring the doorbell again and announce their department before asking to enter the room?	SERVICE			
3	If a 'privacy' sign/light was present was a calling card/door knob card left under/on the door or a silent message left on the telephone?	SERVICE			
4	If the employee was encountered was he/she well presented and did they greet the guest with a smile?	SERVICE			
5	If guest was present in the room during servicing, did the employee arrange to return at a later convenient time when the guest was out of the room?	SERVICE			
6	Was the carpet/tiles/wood flooring freshly vacuumed/mopped and free of any debris?	CLEANLINESS			
7	Was the bed neatly made with clean linen which was free of stains or tears and were the bedspread/throw and decorative cushions replaced, if applicable?	CLEANLINESS			
8	Did the employee open the blackout curtains fully and neatly with sheer curtains opened or closed depending on the heat/temperature?	SERVICE			

9	Did the employee empty the waste bins and ashtrays?	CLEANLINESS			
10	Was the room tidied with all hotel amenities returned to their original locations (i.e. hairdryer, ironing board, etc.)?	CLEANLINESS			
11	Were the guest's clothes tidied and his/her shoes paired, with all items left in view?	SERVICE			
12	Was the stationery/amenities replenished where required (i.e. when all of one type of stationery was missing)?	SERVICE			
13	Were any used glasses or room service soiled plates and cutlery removed from room and replaced (where required)?	CLEANLINESS			
14	Were any used laundry bags/lists replaced (if all bags/lists were removed)?	SERVICE			
15	Were any complimentary food and beverage amenities tidily arranged and partially eaten fruit removed as required?	SERVICE			
16	If a bottle of wine/beverage was presented in an ice bucket on arrival, was the ice bucket either emptied and cleaned or refreshed during servicing?	SERVICE			
17	Were any blown light bulbs replaced?	SERVICE			
	BATHROOM				
18	Did the employee replace any used towels with clean ones and were they in excellent condition (mark n/a if green housekeeping option was chosen)?	CLEANLINESS			
19	Where a Green housekeeping option was present for sheets/towels, was it clearly stated and did employee adhere to what the guest had requested?	SERVICE			
20	Were all empty or almost empty amenities replaced/re-stocked (i.e. if less than 1/3 full)?	SERVICE			
21	Were the shower/bath/sink/toilet and floor wiped clean?	CLEANLINESS			
22	Were all bath/shower and sink controls polished and was bathroom counter clean, dry and free of any debris?	CLEANLINESS			
23	Were all mirrors clean and free of smears and was the shower curtain/door clean?	CLEANLINESS			
24	Were the bathroom water glasses cleaned and/or replaced?	CLEANLINESS			
25	Did the employee tidy the guest's personal toiletries (i.e., replace lids, neatly arrange and/or place items on to a washcloth/linen cloth)?	SERVICE			

	BRAND CORE				
26	Did employees take ownership of guest requests and effectively communicate them to other departments where necessary (i.e., guest does not need to repeat request)?	SERVICE			
27	Did employees acknowledge guests in passing, using their name if known?	SERVICE			
28	Did employees show a genuine sense of care during interactions by smiling, making eye contact, and using positive body language?	SERVICE			
29	Were all written communications to guests (i.e. notes, email, etc.) on hotel branded stationery, personally addressed where applicable (i.e. use of guest name) and signed by a named individual?	SERVICE			
30	Were service times coordinated with the guest's schedule, when known?	SERVICE			
	BRAND SIGNATURE				
31	If an employee was servicing the room, was the door closed and a sign present advising servicing was taking place?	EFFICIENCY			
32	During servicing, was a note left in the room describing a current event in London?	PRODUCT			
33	Were all small items/amenities requested from housekeeping presented in a branded linen/cloth drawstring bag?	EFFICIENCY			
34	Did employee offer to set up any large items/amenities requested from housekeeping as required (e.g. iron and board) and agree a suitable collection time to retrieve these after use?	SERVICE			
	TOTAL NO. OF STANDARDS		MET	BELOW	N/A
	34				

Summary

An effective and excellent operational plan for the housekeeping operation will involve determining the scope of the work by devising checklists, prioritising the tasks, establishing standards and developing the work schedules, training manuals, standard operating procedures for specific tasks. Efficient allocation of resources and monitoring the tasks and the performance of the staff is imperative in maintaining the standards and offering a clean and organised environment to guests. Adapting to changing circumstances, prioritising the quality standards by regular inspection and audits, embracing technology, software and automated tools to streamline communication will enhance the quality standards and productivity thus adding to the profitability of the hotel business.

> **Activities**
>
> - How can hotel operators achieve good housekeeping?
>
> - In your groups, can you identify some of the challenges of the housekeeping department.
>
> - What are the factors that need to be considered to maintain standards and meet the customer needs?
>
> - Read this article https://www.researchgate.net/publication/348153625 on 'The role of management in the hospitality industry during Covid-19 outbreak' and summarise the findings about the housekeeping department in 500 words.

Key terms

- **Performance standards** indicate what must be cleaned in a particular area and how the job must be done. Performance standards establish the expected (minimum) quality of the work to be done.

- **Standard Operating procedures (SOPs)**: Provide instructions on how all housekeeping activities should be carried out within the hotel.

- **Standardised and repetitive tasks**: Housekeeping work is repetitive in nature with tasks being standardised and routinised to maintain consistency and standard of service.

References

Chela-Alvarez, X., Bulilete, O., García-Buades, M. E., Ferrer-Perez, V. A., & Llobera-Canaves, J. (2020) Perceived factors of stress and its outcomes among hotel housekeepers in the Balearic Islands: A qualitative approach from a gender perspective, *International Journal of Environmental Research and Public Health*, 18(1), 52. doi:10.3390/ijerph18010052.

Chibili, M., de Bruyn, S., Benhadda, L., Lashley, C., Penninga, S. & Rowson, B. (2019) *Modern Hotel Operations Management*. Taylor and Francis.

Hasnat, Q. (2021) *An exploration of employee engagement and employee commitment in the London hotel sector: the perspectives of migrant housekeeping workers and their managers*. Doctoral thesis, University of Brighton.

Jones, P. & Siag, A. (2009) A re-examination of the factors that influence productivity in hotels: A study of the housekeeping function, *Tourism and Hospitality Research*, 9(3), 224–234.

Shahane, R. & Fernandes, M. (2021) To study the training program implemented by the housekeeping department for onboarding staff in a post pandemic world and its impact on employee motivation', *Atithya: A Journal of Hospitality*, 7(2), 39–43.

6: Housekeeping Equipment and Supplies

This chapter will help you to:

- Understand the various types of cleaning equipment and supplies in housekeeping.
- Evaluate the factors that need to be considered while selecting cleaning equipment and cleaning agents.
- Review the safety considerations while handling and storing cleaning chemicals.
- Learn about the impact of Covid-19 on cleaning and the cleaning chemicals used.

The biggest factor contributing to guest satisfaction is hotel cleanliness, and good housekeeping results in maintaining customer loyalty, thus ensuring repeat purchase. A clean and hygienic guest room is the basic amenity. That is why it is pivotal to procure high quality and efficient equipment and cleaning supplies to ensure hygienic and safe guest rooms and public areas.

Cleaning equipment

Selecting the most suitable and efficient cleaning equipment is essential to meet and maximise the productivity standards.

Points to consider while selecting cleaning equipment:
- The cleaning equipment selected must be suitable for the type of the area and surface, and should be versatile, so that it can be used for general as well as for tougher cleaning purposes.
- The selected piece of equipment should be easy to handle and store, and be portable (e.g. has wheels and detachable parts) as the housekeeping staff will need to carry it on floors as well as in various public areas.

- The equipment should have an excellent manoeuvrability, so that it is able to clean every nook and corner as well as high areas.
- The equipment should be safe to use, with no sharp edges to avoid injuries, and employees should not have to overstrain while using it. Thus, enhancing the productivity and reducing the accidents.
- The selected equipment should be durable, and spare parts should be easily available. The maintenance of the equipment should be easy. The long term operating and maintenance costs need to be taken into account at the time of purchase.
- It is equally important to check the noise level of the equipment, as the guests should not be disturbed and have cause for complaint.

Classification of cleaning equipment

Cleaning equipment are broadly classified into two categories: manual and mechanical equipment.

Manual equipment

Manual equipment uses the manual energy of the employee and therefore while selecting, care must be given to ensure they will not cause fatigue. If they are efficient an employee's dependency on mechanical equipment will be less.

Some of the examples of manual equipment are:

1 **Brooms** can be *hard* (bristles of coconut fibre), or *soft* (bristles of corn/grass fibres); *wall brooms* have long handles and are used to remove cobwebs from ceilings.
2 **Brushes**: Used to remove dust and dirt from the surfaces. They have non-slip handles and the bristles attached to clean the surfaces. Examples: Carpet brush, feather brush, toilet brush,
3 **Mops**: There are *dry* mops (dust control mops) and *wet/damp* mops (used with a bucket to remove dirt from surfaces). *Cotton* mops have high absorbing ability but need more maintenance and care as compared to synthetic mops. *Mop wringler trolleys* are used to squeeze the excess water from the wet mops.
4 **Dusting cloth**: Soft microfibre cloths used for wiping the surfaces and removing the settled dust. Various types of dusters include *swabs/wipes* (loosely woven cotton absorbent material used for bathtub and washbasin) and *floor cloths* (big and thick coarse knitted cotton).

5 **Containers**: Used for carrying or storing chemicals and cleaning agents. For example, buckets, spray bottles, sani- bins, hand caddy etc.

6 **Trolleys**: A *room attendant's* trolley is used to carry all the required supplies, linen, and cleaning agents to service a guest room. Should be sturdy and movable. A *janitorial* trolley is used by the public area attendants to carry the cleaning agents; a *linen* trolley is used for transferring linen from laundry to floors and vice versa.

7 **Mechanical box sweeper**: The attached brush sweeps the floor when pushed and removes the dirt and crumbs in the dust collector pan.

8 **Scrim cloths** are lint free clothe used for mirror and glass cleaning.

9 **Chamois leathers** are used for glass/window/mirror cleaning and to polish silver. The leather is from the chamois goat.

10 **Druggets** are made of linen or canvas and are used on the floors on the doorway to absorb excess dirt produced due to bad weather or during renovation.

11 Swiffer dusters, fat microfibre mops, brushes, lint rollers help to remove hair from bathroom floors and from linen before cleaning.

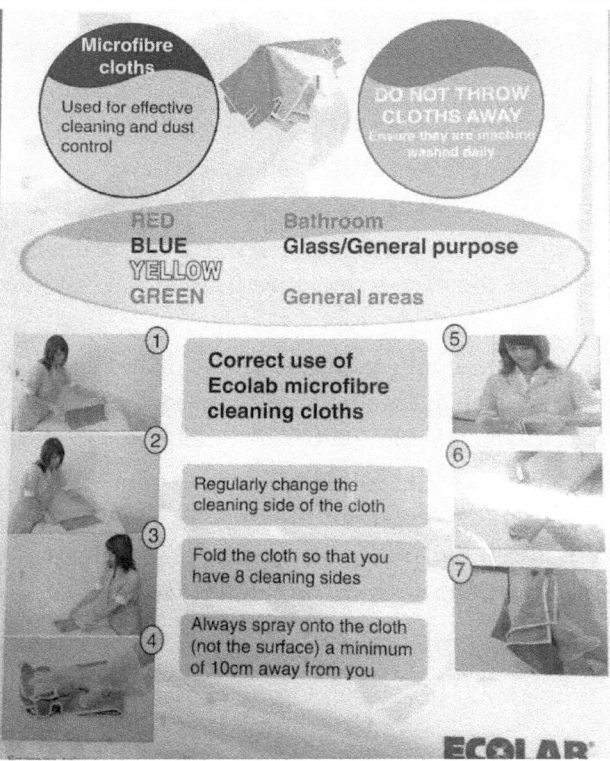

Figure 6.1: An information sheet produced by Ecolab to show the correct use of their microfibre cloths.

Mechanical equipment

Mechanical equipment is powered by electricity and care needs to be taken that the staff are well trained in its to ensure efficient cleaning and to avoid any safety hazards. Some of the examples of mechanical equipment are:

Vacuum cleaners

Vacuum cleaners are the most common mechanical equipment and work on suction power. They suck up dirt, dust and debris by creating a pressure difference. Vacuum cleaners are of different types depending on the shape (cylindrical/upright) and the function (dry/wet). Some of the common types of vacuum cleaners used are:

- **Cylindrical vacuum cleaners**: Used for cleaning guest rooms and can carry out light duty suction cleaning. They have different attachments to clean a variety of areas, for example upholstery, corners, floors etc.
- **Upright vacuum cleaners**: Used for cleaning large, carpeted areas like banquet halls. They have rotating brush attached to dislodge heavy dirt from the carpet pile, thus enabling the deep cleaning of the carpets.
- **Backpack vacuum cleaners**: These, as the name suggests, are carried on the back of the operator, and are small, lightweight and battery operated. They are generally used for cleaning high wall fixtures and fittings, curtains, staircases etc.
- **Dustettes**: These are handheld battery-operated lightweight vacuum cleaners used for cleaning the upholstery, mattresses, carpet edges etc.
- **Wet pick-up vacuum cleaners**: These have a squeeze head and are used to remove the excess moisture from surfaces after carpet shampooing or floor scrubbing.
- **Large dry & wet vacuum cleaners**: These are heavy industrial vacuum cleaners, fitted with a large tank and can pick up water as well as dry dirt. Used for large cleaning areas like lobbies.
- **Pile lifters**: These are not for daily use, and generally only used before shampooing carpets to groom the pile. With constant use, the carpet pile flattens and these are used to restore the vertical orientation of the pile, to facilitate deep shampooing of the carpets.

Floor maintenance machines

These are multifunctional floor cleaning machines which can scrub, polish, and buff the floors. They have rotating discs, with different coloured nylon pads for specific tasks, e.g. a black pad for scrubbing, a red pad for polishing, and white pads for buffing, which restores the lustre of the floor.

Hot water extraction machines

These machines are used for deep cleaning of the carpet and carry a tank filled with hot water and cleaning detergent. The high-pressure spray nozzle of the machine sprays the hot water and the cleaning agent, and the suction nozzle removes the soiled solution from the surfaces. These are efficient in removing the deeply embedded dirt which is not removed by suction cleaning.

Shampooing machines

These are also used to deep clean carpets and release the embed dirt. Nylon brushes are attached and there is a pressure tank along with the foam generator that produces the foam in the dry form. This ensures the carpet does not get too wet.

Scarifying machines

These machines are used when scrubbing is not effective and the surface has got thick dirt and grease deposition, or to remove the floor seals and renovate old floors. They have a wire brush cutting tool which performs a chisel-like action to cut the dirt.

Considerations while choosing vacuum cleaners

- Minimal intrusive noise
- Fast, efficient, thorough, and unobtrusive.
- Width – a too wide machine will not get between furnishings in a room and a small one will not be able to cover large areas with ease and speed
- Quality and ergonomic design

Sebo Dart (top) is a popular vacuum cleaner used by luxury hotels for guest rooms as they are lightweight, and the head can be changed to convert it to a floor polisher. It has an integral hose for cleaning upholstery and curtains.

Dyson cordless vacuum cleaners make it easy to clean all around the area with 60-120 minutes of powerful suction and the extra battery and filter for convenience. It can be transformed easily into a handheld cleaner by a click of a button. The versatility allows this vacuum cleaner to be used in multiple working environments.

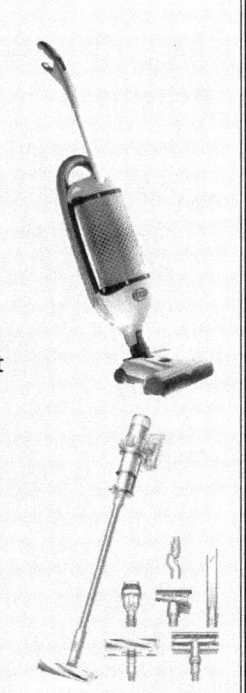

Cleaning specification

A cleaning specification refers to a set of guidelines and instructions for a specific cleaning task. It includes the techniques required to clean a particular surface or area, and the equipment, chemicals, or agents needed. It sets a benchmark for the cleaning tasks and helps in maintaining the standards, ensureing safety while cleaning and achieving consistency in the task.

Preparing a cleaning specification

Cleaning specification of cleaning a small table

Steps	Health and Safety Tips
1.Take away all objects on small table	Place objects in a safe place where people cannot trip over them
2. Dust with a clean, slightly damp cloth followed by a dry cloth. Dust natural finished wood surfaces with only a dry cloth unless otherwise instructed. If you use a polish, dust first then apply about one capful per small table 500 x 500. Clean all over the top, legs, and underneath	Do not use a chemical cleaner, glass cleaner, brass polish or cleaner, or furniture polish unless told to do so.
3. Put all objects back onto small table	
4. Check positioning.	Time to do: 1-2min Material cost: £1.00 Labour cost: £2.00

Activities

1. Explain the importance of cleaning. Discuss in your groups.
2. Outline the basic principles of cleaning. What are the main stages?
3. Give examples of some of the factors you would need to consider when cleaning different areas within a commercial establishment. Consider timing of cleaning, use of chemicals, etc.
4. Draw a rough plan of a hotel bedroom
   - Make a list of furniture, fixtures, and equipment
   - Suggest which order you would clean things in and how often would this be done
5. As the knife is to the chef, the vacuum cleaner is to the _____
6. *Individual exercise*: Prepare a cleaning specification for any surface or object in the guest room. Outline each step in the process. Explain how each action is to be carried out and what equipment/chemicals are needed. Highlight any health and safety points that must be considered.

Agents

Cleanliness and hygiene are the most important factors when it comes to guest satisfaction. The selection of cleaning agents and supplies play a crucial role in ensuring that the hotel can provide a safe, clean, hygienic, and welcoming atmosphere to its guests. The moment a guest enters a hotel lobby they make their first impression of the hotel. Witnessing the sparkling floor and the fresh fragrance of the air enables a positive aura of the hotel in the mind of the customer. This is all achieved by the tireless efforts made by the housekeeping department. Therefore, choosing the right cleaning agents, and equipping your staff with the right tools are paramount in achieving a lasting impression.

Factors responsible for effective cleaning

- **Time**: The time allowed for the chemical reaction between the surface and the cleaning agent decides the effectiveness of the cleaning. Incorrect disinfection time will lead to compromising the safety of the surface or the areas. It is advisable to read the instructions on the label and advise the staff using the same.
- **Temperature**: It is important to check the temperature of the water if used for dilution to ensure the appropriate cleaning. Some surfaces may be damaged if the correct temperature is not maintained.
- **Mechanical action**: The right amount of physical action (wiping/scrubbing), using manual or mechanical equipment, will aid in desired cleaning. Care needs to be taken, as too much pressure or mechanical action might damage the surface.
- **Chemical reaction**: Using the correct product and accurate dilution will result in effective cleaning. It is important to understand the chemical constitution of the product. Care needs to be given to check the alkalinity, pH level/hardness, chlorine, and iron content.
- **Procedures**: For achieving an enhanced user experience and optimal product effectiveness, it is critical to follow the prescribed steps of cleaning. Regular staff training and guidance will ensure the correct procedures are being followed and the desired results are obtained.
- **Clean in phases**: Allow time for cleaning agents to work. Sweep or vacuum before mopping; dust before sweeping or vacuuming. Thoroughly spray the chemicals in the bathroom first, allowing the chemicals to disinfect and remove any stains, then strip the linen, clear the garbage, finish the room cleaning and finally clean the bathroom.

Factors to consider while selecting cleaning agents or chemicals

- **The strength of the cleaning agent**: The different areas of a hotel need cleaning products of different strengths, which is advised on the description of the products on their labels. For example, a toilet will need harsher products compared to the offices and the rooms.
- **Type/area for cleaning**: Consideration must be given to which area needs to be cleaned, for example floors, furniture tops, glasses, bathtub etc. Select the right type of product for the specific area.
- **Safety of the cleaning agents/chemicals**: As some of the cleaning agents are strong and are designed to clean harsh surfaces, check that the chemicals are safe for the type of environment in which they are going to be used, so they do not create any health concerns.
- **Environment-friendly cleaning chemicals**: While choosing the cleaning agents it is good to check that the chemicals are not posing any threat to the safety of the environment witihin and beyond the hotel.

Points to consider while safely storing and using chemical agents

- Read the labels carefully before using them as chemicals can cause harm to people and the environment, for eample causing irritation and skin allergies.
- Staff must be trained to read the labelling instructions on the chemical and be aware that a particular cleaning agent can be inflammable, toxic, corrosive etc.
- While using strong chemicals, the area should be well ventilated to prevent breathing in fumes.
- The chemicals at no point should be mixed and the original container should not be changed, if possible. If decanting, care must be taken that the decanting container is clean, safe, and clearly labelled, identifying the hazards of the substances. It is vital to avoid any confusion about the contents.
- While storing chemicals, care must be taken to store them, in a locked space, away from sunlight, heat and food items. Any spillages should be responsibly cleaned up immediately.
- Employees have a duty of care for themselves and others who may be affected by their actions, and therefore must comply by the safety procedures.
- Regular training and supervision are necessary to ensure that the employees understand the hazards and the measures needed to control any risks.

> **ECOLAB**
>
> **SAFETY DATA SHEET** according to Regulation (EC) No. 1907/2006
>
> Taxat supra Gran.
>
> **Section: 1. IDENTIFICATION OF THE SUBSTANCE/MIXTURE AND OF THE COMPANY/UNDERTAKING**
>
> **1.1 Product identifier**
>
> | | |
> |---|---|
> | Product name | : Taxat supra Gran. |
> | Product code | : 101107E |
> | Use of the Substance/Mixture | : Laundry product |
> | Substance type: | : Mixture |
> | | For professional users only. |
> | Product dilution information | : No dilution information provided. |
>
> **1.2 Relevant identified uses of the substance or mixture and uses advised against**
>
> | | |
> |---|---|
> | Identified uses | : Laundry detergent. Semi automatic process |
> | Recommended restrictions on use | : Reserved for industrial and professional use. |
>
> **1.3 Details of the supplier of the safety data sheet**
>
> Company : Ecolab Ltd.
> PO Box 11; Winnington Avenue
> Northwich, Cheshire, United Kingdom CW8 4DX
> + 44 (0)1606 74488
> ccs@ecolab.com
>
> **1.4 Emergency telephone number**
>
> Emergency telephone number : +441618841235
> +32-(0)3-575-5555 Trans-European
>
> Date of Compilation/Revision : 22.03.2018
> Version : 1.0
>
> **Section: 2. HAZARDS IDENTIFICATION**
>
> **2.1 Classification of the substance or mixture**
>
> Classification (REGULATION (EC) No 1272/2008)
>
> Eye irritation, Category 2   H319
>
> The classification of this product is based on toxicological assessment.
>
> **2.2 Label elements**
>
> Labelling (REGULATION (EC) No 1272/2008)
>
> 101107E   1 / 14

Figure 6.2: Sample safety data sheet – page 1 of 14. (To see the full sheet, go to https://documents.alliancenational.co.uk/Products/celab912.pdf)

- It is advisable to have an alternative arrangement for employees if English is not their first language. Ensuring the staff understands the MSDS (Material Safety Data Sheet). Pictures and infographics can be used to remind the staff about the safety measures.

- Appropriate protective equipment and gear, like masks, gloves and visors must be provided to employees while using the cleaning agents.
- Staff should be encouraged to share the feedback about the usage of the cleaning agent and immediately inform their supervisor if any cleaning agent is causing irritation and breathing issues.
- Appropriate first-aid provision should be available, and staff must be trained in first aid actions in case of an accident or emergency.
- Supervisors and managers must carry out random inspections to check the safety guidelines are being followed, and if staff are using worn out gloves or safety gear, immediate replacement must be requested.
- While diluting, the cleaning concentrate should be added to water and not vice-versa.

COSHH

COSHH stands for Control of Substances Hazardous to Health. The law states that employers and businesses must prevent or reduce workers' exposure to hazardous substances like chemicals, gases, fumes, dust, and biological agents like germs. COSHH sets out the basic advice in the form of the factsheets called control guidance sheets.

Figure 6.3: COSHH Symbol Identification sheet (RB Health and Safety Solutions)

6: Housekeeping Equipment and Supplies

Ecolab is a major supplier of chemicals to th luxury hotels and has a wide range of chemicals. They also impart COSHH and other relevant training for staff. They offer a partnership scheme in which they cover the supply of chemicals, setting up the chemical stations which ensures appropriate dilution and refilling of the spray cans, annual maintenance of the stations as well as training on site and online for the staff to handle the chemicals safely and effectively. An experienced consultant from the company can inspect a hotel prior to opening or when renovation is planned, noting the surfaces and materials in the guest rooms and the public area that will need cleaning, and will suggest appropriate cleaning agents. Selecting the right chemicals is essential to achieve the expected quality and standards of cleaning.

Figure 6.4: Ecolab's cleaning agents

Picture	Name of the product	Price (GBP)
	Evans Hi-Phos Toilet Cleaner & Descaler 5ltr x2	£ 32.3
	Evans EC9 Washroom Bactericidal Cleaner & Descaler 5ltr x2	£ 47.0
	Jangro Floral Disinfectant 5ltr	£ 3.5
	Ecolab Pro Shine Special Furniture Polish 500ml (Case of 6)	£ 46.0
	Peek Premium Metal Polish Paste 1ltr	£ 19.0
	Suma Silver Dip 5ltr (2x1)	£ 42.7
	Ecolab Oasis Pro Glass Cleaner 2ltr (2)	£ 184.0
	Evans EC8 Air Freshener & Fabric Deodoriser 1ltr (Case of 6)	£ 129.0
	Diversey DI Oxivir Plus 5ltr (Case of 2)	£ 85.2
	Jangro Concentrated Multipurpose Cleaner 5ltr	£ 9.0
	Jangro Premium Floor Undercoat Sealer 5ltr	£ 23.0
	Jangro Premium Wood Floor Seal 5ltr	£ 47.0
	Total cost per month	£ 667.7

Figure 6.5: Ecolab's prices

Supplies

The different types of cleaning supplies used in the hotels are classified into:

- **Detergents**: contain soap/surfactants and phosphorus which is toxic, so care needs to be taken to check that the product is used correctly. Most all-purpose cleaners contain detergents.
- **Degreasers**: are used for removing heavy duty grease, dirt, grime from the heavily soiled hard floors. As degreasers are highly alkaline, they can cause chemical burns to the skin. Therefore, they should be used in a well-ventilated area and protective gear should be worn. Instructions on the label should be read carefully before using them to avoid damaging the floors as degreasers are corrosive.
- **Abrasives**: are cleaning agents that remove the dirt by scratching action and therefore have some coarse particles like chalk (gilder's whiting) in silver polish, calcite, quartz, silica, feldspar, calcium carbonate, aluminium oxide etc. Care needs to be taken that those abrasives are used on the right surfaces and excessive use can gradually scratch the finish of the surface. Mostly used on the bath, sink etc. Some abrasives also contain chemical or organic disinfectants and come with antimicrobial properties which should be checked on the labels. A small quantity of abrasive must be first tested on small inconspicuous areas to confirm its usage.
- **Acid cleaning agents**: Extreme care needs to be taken while handling these as they are highly concentrated and therefore dangerous and corrosive in nature. Mostly used for descaling, tough stains, moulds, for cleaning bathroom tiles etc. Examples of mild acids are vinegar and lemon juice, which are organic acids and mostly used for removing hard water deposits from glasses. Strong acids include oxalic acids, hydrochloric acids and sulphuric acids, and are mostly used to clean the toilet bowls and for removing rust marks.

Housekeeping supplies: Sybron

Sybron supplies cleaning products (sanitizer and disinfectants, multipurpose all surface cleaner, odour neutralizer, glass and metal cleaners and polish, laundry chemicals etc). Sybron also supplies janitorial equipment like vacuum cleaners, mops, buckets, colour coded cleaning cloths, multipurpose gloves, dustpan, bin liners, washroom paper consumables, facial tissues and hand rolls, wiper rolls, personal hygiene and safety products, first aid supplies, guest amenities, headwear and face masks and safety signages. Find out more about their range at https://www.sybron.co.uk

Cleaning Post Covid-19

The housekeeping department has adapted its practices in cleaning and sterilising of hotels due to Covid-19. All hotels have had to adopt strict clinical procedures to comply with new government health and safety guidelines, to safeguard staff, guests, and contractors. New and improved sanitisation kits were introduced, for example, commercial-scale air-purifiers & sterilisers, automated sanitisation mist walk-throughs, touch-free sanitiser dispenser. Although the chemicals used previously served the cleaning purposes, an extra touch was needed to help disinfect and sanitise. The chemicals companies adapted by making products effective for multiple surfaces to meet required criteria, for example Oxivir, a highly effective but non-hazardous anti-virus chemical.

As a result of the Covid-19 pandemic, innovative new housekeeping products have emerged including electrochemically activated solution disinfection (ECAS) which can remove a variety of pathogens such as bacteria and viruses, quickly and effectively, since they remain active on the surface longer than traditional disinfectants. Tools such as *Room to Breathe* which transforms indoor environments into hypoallergenic spaces (https://www.roomtobreatheuk.co.uk); disinfectant dispensers; hygienic solutions for toilets such as motion sensors to detect movement that regulate the flow of water; air purifiers adapted to guest rooms to offer additional safety.

A new technique for the housekeeping department is steam sterilisation. The hotels equip the housekeeping departments with steam mops because they kill the bacteria, and surfaces dry faster due to lower water usage. Surprisingly, the steam mop is non-toxic and cheap. The advantage of this innovation is that it ensures the health and safety of the room attendants when using it, and complies with Covid-19 cleaning procedures.

Summary

The housekeeping department uses a range of manual and mechanical equipment, and od cleaning agents. Selecting the right equipment and cleaning agents are central to achieving high standards of cleaning and high productivity. Some cleaning agents can be hazardous to health and to the environment and must be handled correctly and stored safely. The housekeeping management should prepare cleaning specifications for all areas and surface to ensure consistency of standards. The Covid-19 pandemic had a major impact on hotels' cleaning practices and led to the development of new products and tools.

Activity: Case study analysis

Workers at a company premises in Bristol were exposed to hazardous chemicals over a four-year period leading to the onset of a disease called 'allergic contact dermatitis.' One employee suffered four years of his skin blistering, cracking, splitting, and weeping because of this allergic dermatitis.

Two other employees also suffered the symptoms of allergic dermatitis, including fingers and hands becoming so badly swollen and blistered that one could not do up his shirt buttons without his fingers splitting open. All three employees had been working with photographic chemicals.

The company was fined a total of £100,000 and ordered to pay £30,000 costs. They were fined £30,000 for breaching The Health and Safety at Work Act 1974, and £10,000 for 6 separate breaches of the Control of Substances Hazardous to Health (COSHH) Regulations for not making adequate risk assessments, not preventing, or controlling exposure of employees to chemicals, and for not providing any 'health surveillance' of employees at-risk. They were also fined £10,000 for not reporting a case of allergic contact dermatitis.

After reading the above case study answer the following questions:

1. How this situation could have been avoided?
2. Can you summarise the points to be considered before selecting a chemical for cleaning?

Key terms

- **COSHH**: stands for Control of Substances Hazardous to Health. It is legislation that covers the safe use of potentially hazardous chemicals. https://www.hse.gov.uk/coshh/
- **CSSA**: The Cleaning and Support Services Association in the United Kingdom that serves the cleaning industry. https://www.cssa-uk.co.uk/
- **BICSc**: The British Institute of Cleaning Science https://www.bics.org.uk/membership/
- **COPC**: The Cleaning Operators Proficiency Certificate produced by BICSc. https://www.bics.org.uk/training/
- **Dilution**: The ratio of the chemical cleaning agents to water.

References

Almanza, B.A., Kirsch, K., Kline, S.F., Sirsat, S., Stroia, O., Choi, J.K., & Neal, J. (2015) How clean are hotel rooms? Part I: Visual observations vs. microbiological contamination, *Journal of Environmental Health*, 78(1), 8–13.

Brunet, R. (2014) Achieving the extraordinary, *Western Hotelier*, 38(3), 57–63.

Neog, R. (2021) New hotel cleaning procedures after COVID-19: A study of new housekeeping practices in hotels, *Atithya: A Journal of Hospitality*, 7(2), 1–7.

Sheelam, H. & Goud, M.M. (2019) Cleaning chemicals usage for house keeping with special reference to hospitality industry: A study, *Journal of Hospitality Application & Research*, 14(2), 41–57.

7: Cleaning Procedure of a Guest Room

This chapter will help you to:

- Understand the cleaning procedure and the principles of cleaning.
- Evaluate the frequency of cleaning and their types, understanding the differences between them.
- Review the selection and trends in guest room cleaning post Covid-19, understanding cleaning for safety.
- Learn about the application of cleaning checklists.

Cleaning is the basic requirement of a hotel guest. A clean, hygienic room and bathroom leads to the customer satisfaction and therefore hotels need to ensure that they use the right cleaning products and equipment, train their staff in cleaning and supervise efficiently to reduce customer complaints.

Cleaning is defined as the process of the removal of dirt from things and surfaces, typically using water and detergents.

Principle

Some of the basic principles of cleaning that should be followed by staff to get consistency in the cleaning are:

- While cleaning the effort should be made to extract all the dust and dirt from the surfaces ensuring no damage to the surface is made.
- The order of cleaning needs to be strictly maintained, for example sweeping and dusting before mopping.
- Effort should be made to use mild cleaning solutions and restore the appearance of the surfaces.
- Cleaning must be carried out from high to low to achieve the maximum efficiency.

- Cleaning should start with complete planning and organisation, ensuring one has all the required cleaning agents and equipment to avoid the wastage of time.
- Clean the less soiled areas first, and then move to the more heavily soiled areas. For example, while cleaning a guest room an attendant must clean the room first and then the bathroom.
- Housekeeping staff must consider the safety while cleaning and equip themselves with all the necessary safety gear.
- While mopping, staff should move backwards from the surface that is mopped to avoid the soiling of the surface with footmarks. Clean the farthermost area first and then move to the exit while cleaning.
- After the cleaning is over, all the equipment needs to be cleaned and stored for next use. For example, the vacuum cleaner's dust bag should be emptied, the dusters should be sent for washing, etc.
- The housekeeping trolley, while working, must be parked so that it does not obstruct the way, and needs to be sufficiently stocked but not over-stocked.
- Cleaning agents should be replenished from the store before the end or at the start of the shift. Never begin cleaning without checking the cleaning caddy and ensuring you have all you need for the cleaning.

Frequency

The frequency of cleaning sets the repetition of the task at a configured time and interval. As the housekeeping department is responsible for cleaning all the hotel guest rooms and public area, it is important to schedule periodic cleaning tasks. Therefore, the housekeeping department prepares a cleaning schedule which includes the frequency (number of times) at which a particular surface and area requires cleaning. The frequency depends on the amount of traffic in an area, level of soiling, and the cleaning standards set by the hotel. The cleaning schedule needs to be given to the housekeeping attendants to follow and should be pasted in the floor pantry and the public area pantry for the staff to refer and follow.

Frequency of cleaning are of two types:
- **Daily** includes cleaning and servicing of the items like the guest rooms, bathrooms, cleaning floors etc.
- **Periodical** cleaning is carried out weekly, monthly, once in six months, or annually. It complements the daily cleaning and is often planned by

the supervisor in advance, looking at the occupancy percentage. This is done less frequently, and on the days when the hotel is not too busy, for example, floor polishing, polishing chrome fixtures, deep cleaning telephones by opening the mouthpiece and earpiece and thoroughly disinfecting, etc. Such thorough and deep cleaning is not possible to be carried out daily, however is important to maintain the appeal of the surface and the building.

- Examples of **weekly cleaning** will include high level dusting, polishing brassware, scrubbing tiles and terraces, balconies.
- Examples of **monthly/quarterly/half annually/annually** tasks include carpet shampooing, chandelier cleaning, marble polishing, façade cleaning etc.

Daily cleaning	Periodical cleaning	Annual cleaning
Bed/bedlinen/towels	Vacuuming under heavy furniture/bed	Chandelier polishing
Vacuuming/dusting/disinfecting	Polishing brassware/marble	Carpet wash
Polishing furniture	Cleaning drawers/wardrobe	Steam clean armhcairs
Bathroom cleaning	Scrubbing bathroom tiles/shower head/WC	Clean grout around tiles
Mopping	Mattress rotation/maintenance	Mattress bed bugs fumigation
Turndown service	High dusting/chandelier/lamps/curtains	Steam clean curtains
Replenish guest amenities	Cleaning the windows and ledges	Walls/doors/baseboards

Spring cleaning

This is also called as the deep cleaning of the hotel guest room and is carried out to ensure that no corner of the room is left uncleaned. Spring cleaning of the room is done periodically, when the hotel is not too busy. It involves moving the furniture to reach the areas which are not easily accessed.

Sample of spring-cleaning plan of a guest room and bathroom

STEAMING ROOM TASK LIST		
Name: Date: Room Number		
TASKS	COMPLETED	COMMENTS
Bedroom		
High dusting throughout the bedroom and living room (Pictures, wall lights, top of wardrobes, art decor)		
Steam throughout fireplace		
Remove headboards and clean behind it		
Steam all skirting boards and walls remove all black marks including inside cupboards and white doors		
Clean all air vents		
Remove TV cabinet and clean under it and behind		
Steam heavy curtains including pelmet and all upholstery		
Clean all window frames and sills (remove all the black marks)		
Steam carpet & remove stains if possible		
Steam metal threshold		
Bathroom		
Descale shower heads and taps		
Steam all the marble décor		
Clean air vents		
Steam all tiles and remove all black marks (mould)		
Steam all taps including bidet and the shower shoulder		
Clean the sink plug hole and remove all grease		
Steam behind the radiator and between panels		

Cleaning for health and safety

Switching to scientific cleaning

The need of cleaning has shifted from creating aesthetically clean premises to creating a clinically clean environment. To gain the confidence of customers and employees it is important to choose cleaning products that can destroy the pathogens that cause influenza, norovirus, SARS Covid-19 and rhinovirus etc.

Different types of cleaning to ensure safety

- **Physical cleaning**: This includes manual and routine tasks to remove the visible dust on a surface like mopping, sweeping, and dusting.
- **Chemical cleaning**: Use of chemicals while cleaning either manually or using a machine.
- **Bacteriological cleaning**: The purpose is to remove the bacteria and viruses using manual and chemical cleaning processes.

Using products correctly

It is important to adhere to the guidance stated on the product label to ensure the cleaning is effective. Using the right product on the right surfaces, following the cleaning protocols and the processes will help to achieve the operational efficiencies. This will require partnership with the chemical supplying companies. Collaborating with the chemical suppliers to provide the training and understanding of using the right products in the right manner, which will drive consistent results and help in meeting the customers' expectations and maintaining the brand standards.

Training

Reinforcing the training and re-examining the supplemental staff training and learning resources offered by leading chemical vendors will help to meet the increasing cleaning needs of the staff. Exhaustive training should be provided by the housekeeping department during initial onboarding of staff, however this needs to be refreshed with time. Ecolab assists hotels by offering, as part of the contract, on-site and on-line training for the staff to enhance their efficiency.

To meet the overall purpose of the cleaning and disinfection and offer a clean and safe environment to the customers it is important to make the housekeeping staff understand the processes and the expectations from the cleaning. For example, it is essential that staff are trained in the accurate dilution of the disinfectant and cleaning agents; in the duration of the contact between the surface and the cleaning agent necessary for the best results; in difference between normal cleaning and the upgraded cleaning processes; in the use of colour coded microfibre cloths; and in understanding ways to avoid cross contamination and ensuring everyone's safety. All staffs should be retrained about the new service protocols and essential new way of working and maintain safe distance (with colleagues and customers) before sending them back to operation.

There should be mandatory health and safety training for all staff members, and not just the housekeeping staff. To optimise the training efforts, it is important to ensure the housekeeping staff are properly trained and therefore auditing and evaluating staff performance is a key aspect. Training leads to reduced waste of material, improved safety, and fewer accidents and injuries. Creating video tutorials is a good idea and is quick and efficient way to train the new staff as well as to provide refresher training to the existing staff. Training the staff to use the housekeeping software as well as the apps and the tools, in addition to training about cleaning techniques and the desired results, leads to higher productivity and job satisfaction from the staff's point of view.

Well trained and mentored staff possess higher motivation to work and aim to exceed the customer expectations.

New products

It is good practice to keep a constant watch for innovative and unique cleaning products that will help the staff to obtain the rigorous cleaning requirements more efficiently. For instance, using products that have combined cleaning and disinfecting properties will save time for the staff as both tasks can be done in one step.

Cleaning procedure of rooms post Covid-19

Sanitising requirements, post Covid-19, have greatly increased the cleaning times of rooms. Cleaning times, which were previously 30 to 40 minutes, now range between 1 to 1.5 hours per room or suite to allow for a deep clean. As staff time is limited, but rooms must be vacated by guests before any cleaning can commence, some hotels are already using motion sensors to detect when rooms are vacant and work can commence.

The new procedures as set out by the WHO (World Health Organization) must be frequently evaluated to enable managers to identify if they are effective, and if they do locate gaps where improvements are required, they can then make the necessary adjustments.

New cleaning techniques

- **Ultraviolet light** is a new type of cleaning that has been proven to be up to 99.9% effective.
- An alternative way to disinfect soft surfaces is to use a **hydrogen peroxide** vapor system. These systems bio-decontaminate a space by creating a uniform layer of hydrogen peroxide vapor on all surfaces. When the vapor completes its task, it decomposes into oxygen and water vapor, without leaving any traces

Microbiological decontamination using hydrogen peroxide

Hydrogen peroxide is a highly effective anti-bacterial and anti-viral decontaminant, delivered either by spraying or by a vapourisation machine. The solution is ionised and works by stealing electrons from the bacterial cell walls, destroying them. After use it breaks down into water and oxygen, leaving no toxic resdues or fumes, so that the room can be reused almost immediately. Steps in using it are as follows:

1. Prepare the room for decontamination by removing all the linen and any other absorbent material. The HVAC needs to be off and all vents closed.

2. After preparing the room place the system and the aeration unit in the room and make sure the door is closed and sealed.

3. The dimensions of the room and the other details will have been entered into the system or automated vaporisation will ensure the vapour is homogeneously distributed throughout the selected area through the purpose designed nozzles.

4. A safety check is important once the vaporisation begins to see if there are any leaks. These can be detected by a handheld monitor. The system is not a pressurised one, so that leaks, however it is worth covering the door gaps with adhesive tape.

5. It is important to allow the correct contact time to kill the tough pathogens and bacteria and ensure efficacy.

6. The final step is the aeration of the room using the catalytic aeration or other aeration unit to break down the hydrogen peroxide gas into water vapour and oxygen.

7. Once the air levels have been measured and found to be safe, the room is ready for reoccupation.

(This can be used for removing heavy smoke smell from a room and thorough disinfection as it is quick and efficient. Through this innovation rooms do not need to be out of use for days, thus preventing loss of revenue.)

- The **electrostatic sprayers** provide disinfectant for all surfaces in a consistent manner. Surfaces that are easy to lose or difficult for cleaners to properly soak in more traditional ways are sprayed by the systems. According to the manufacturers, it protects a surface for up to 90 days.

> **Virucidal disinfection treatment by Ecolab**
>
> The disinfection treatment uses electrostatic spraying technology, combined with Ecolab's proprietary Desguard 20 disinfectant, is proving to be a effective targeted method of application. Desguard 20 is a bactericidal and virucidal product which is highly effective against enveloped viruses such as Covid-19.

Swab tests

Housekeeping supervisors and managers should carry out random swab tests in the rooms after cleaning to ensure the surfaces and high touch points (remote controls, door handles, light switches) have been thoroughly cleaned and disinfected.

UV lights

UV torch lights can be used for spot checks and inspection. Problems that are not visible with normal lights stands out in these lights. Room attendants and supervisors can use a blue UV light to highlight any stains. In the bathroom areas they will spot any organic matter or any traces of soaps in the vanity counter. If the curtains are closed, when the light is flashed the dust becomes more visible.

Steam cleaning and disinfecting

Saturated and dry steam, superheated to 180°C, effortlessly removes all the dirt and grim, and can be used to disinfect, to sterilise guest luggage and to kill bedbugs. It has minimum environmental impact, and does not require insecticides or toxic chemicals. Steam can easily reach into the nesting areas and can kill 99.99% of the bugs and their eggs. We will look in more depth at steam cleaning in Chapter 14.

> The Polti Sani System is one of the leaders in this field. Find out more at: https://www.polti.co.uk/polti-sani-system

Room status

Room status is defined as the condition of the guest room (vacant, occupied, dirty), and signifies its cleaning as well as its occupancy status. Each guest room goes through the different stages and to complete one cycle, as shown in Figure 7.1. Room status needs to be coordinated by both front office and housekeeping department. While planning the cleaning of the guest room it is important to check the status of each room.

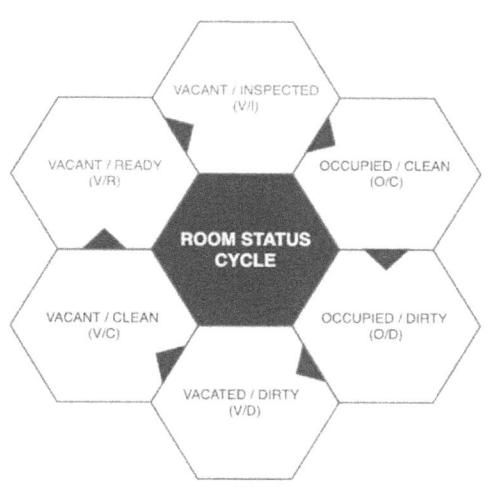

Figure 7.1: The room status cycle

Stages in the room status cycle

- **Occupied Room (OCC)**: These rooms have guests staying in them and will need to be cleaned. If an occupied room is cleaned it is **Clean OCC** and if the room has not been serviced, it is **Dirty OCC**. The cleaning of an occupied room takes approximately 30-35 minutes. As the guest is still in the room care must be taken while cleaning not to disturb the placement of the items in the rooms and to respect guest privacy.

- **Departure Room (DEP)** or **Vacant Dirty(V/D)**: There are rooms where the guest has checked out. They need to be thoroughly cleaned, and replenished with new items and amenities for a new arrival/new guest. The thorough cleaning of a departure room takes 45 minutes to one hour.

- **Vacant Ready (V/R)**: These are rooms which are cleaned and serviced by the housekeeping assistant, and need to be inspected by the housekeeping supervisor before assigning to a new guest. If the room was cleaned on a previous day, then on the next day to make it ready for an arrival it needs a quick freshen up and replenishing the amenities and the supplies. So, servicing a vacant ready room will not take more than 15-20 minutes.

- **Vacant Inspected (V/I)**: The vacant ready room is checked by the housekeeping supervisor or a manager and is ready to be assigned to a new arrival. Vacant inspected rooms are communicated to the front desk, and they assign only inspected rooms to the guests.

- **Out Of Order Rooms (OOO)**: These rooms are unfit for sale as they have some maintenance issue or repair required. OOO rooms are not available to the front desk for assignment, and it reduces the total number of rooms available in a hotel.

- **Out Of Service Rooms (OS)**: These rooms have minor maintenance issues like a fused light bulb or the amenities to be replenished. These rooms are not taken out of inventory. Sometimes during low occupancy, a hotel may keep certain rooms on each floor out of service for energy conservation.

Figure 7.2 shows how the room status is updated on a property management system where colour coding is used to denote room status. For example, red is used for dirty rooms, green for inspected rooms etc. This will vary from hotel to hotel depending on which system they use to maintain the records. This aids in quick communication between the front office and housekeeping department reducing delay and the miscommunication.

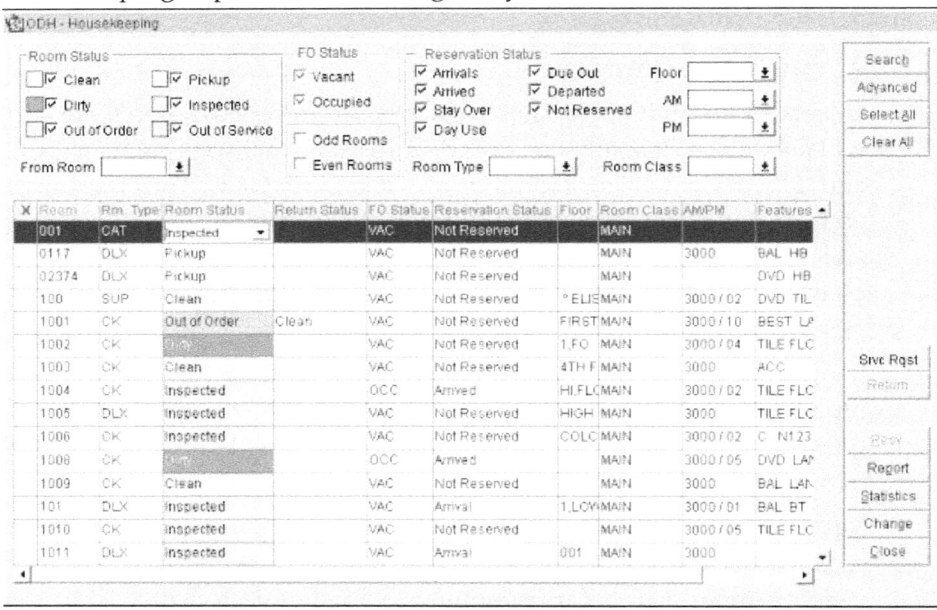

Figure 7.2: Room status display on a hotel's property management system

Cleaning checklists

A cleaning checklist is a tool to carry a consistent service in all the guest room. It acts as a guide and prevents the staff from missing any surface to clean thus avoiding guest complaint and dissatisfaction. A checklist confirms the performance standards expectation from the staff.

Examples are given below. Note that these will vary from hotel to hotel.

Figure 7.3: Sample checklist for a room, to be done as soon as the room becomes avaiable.

Sequence	Check
Check if privacy light and doorbell are working	
Check for any maintenance faults in the room	
Check if TV, A/C, telephones and speaker are working	
Check the ceiling in room and bathroom for any leaks, stains, damages, or dust	
Check for any damages/ stains on furniture, carpets, upholstery and curtains	
Organize any deep cleaning if needed: high dusting, vacuuming under and behind heavy furniture, cleaning bathroom air vents, steaming of bathroom, descaling shower heads, replacing valances	
Check for any guest preferences/ organize set ups/ storage IN/ OUT, flowers	
Check if all the surfaces and furniture clean: start clockwise from the entrance door all around the room and finish by the entrance door	
Check all lights: if clean and working - standing lamps, desk/ bedside lamps, headboard reading lamps, wardrobe/ shelf, night lights and wall LED lights	
Check wardrobe clean and fully stocked: hangers, laundry drawer set up, slippers, yoga mat, hairdryer, shopping bag, suit bag, luggage racks and safe	
Mini bar and arrival amenity - check if no missing items	
Check desk, stationery drawer, magazines, books, and if speaker present	
Check the bed: headboard, linen, and presentation	
Check heavy curtains/ nets/ blinds opening and closing, windows and double glazing clean,	
If applicable, check if balcony and balcony furniture clean, and plants in good shape	
Check if carpet thoroughly vacuumed, wooden floors cleaned	
Check all bathroom surfaces if they are clean: floors, walls, doors, sinks, bathtub, shower cubicle, toilet; check if functions work,	
Check all bathroom lights - if clean and working ceiling lights, wall lights, make up mirror lights, cabinet lights, night lights (lollypop mirrors - charge if needed)	
Check if underfloor heating and radiators working	
Check if all toiletries placed	
Check if all towels and bathrobes placed, in good condition and clean	
Quality check/ presentation - stand at the door of the bathroom/ room and look around to ensure everything is in place and presented well	

Figure 7.4: Sample checklist of a vacant room

Sequence	Check
Ring the doorbell and check if privacy light is working	
Check that connecting doors are locked from both sides	
Switch ON and OFF all the lights to see if they are working	
Switch on TV to check if it is working	
Check if both telephones are working - by calling to your device	
Check A/C is working and that correct temperature set: BST- 21'C, BWT- 23'C	
Check lobby, bedroom/ sitting room for any leaks/ damage on walls or ceiling	
Check that there is a speaker in the room, and it is ON	
Check bathroom walls and ceiling if there are any leaks or leak damage	
Check toilet to ensure is not used and flush the water	
Quality check/ presentation- stand at the door of the bathroom/ room and look around to ensure everything is in place and presented well	
If room on arrival, check and organize any specials, IRD (In room dining) amenity, flowers if needed	
If room had been vacant for more than 2 days, re- dusting of surfaces might be needed. If TOP VIP arrival, more thorough inspection to be carried out	

Figure 7.5: Housekeeping deep cleaning sample checklist

Room #_____ Attendant _____date_____		
Housekeeper Signature		
	Attendant Check	Housekeeper check
Entrance		
Dnd in excellent working order		
Wipe/clean all door frames, tops & sides		
Wipe/clean dust door closer		
Wipe/clean A/C vent		
Wipe/clean all door hinges		
Vacuum carpet including edge		
Closet		
Wipe/clean all door hinges		
Wipe/clean all door frames, tops & sides		
Mirror must be spotlessly clean and in good condition		
Wipe all shelf surfaces		

Luggage racks clean, dust free and in good condition		
Satin hanger – in good condition		
Clip hangers – must all match		
Regular hangers – must all match		
Suit bag – in good condition		
Closet rod must be dust free and in good condition		
Umbrella and collateral must be in good condition		
Vacuum carpet including edge		
Bedroom		
Dust armoire and contents		
Wipe/clean all electrical cords		
Wipe/clean all drawers		
Wipe all bulbs and top of lamps		
Wipe/clean table and chair legs		
Remove glass and clean tabletops		
Clean all phones		
All stationery and supplies in excellent condition		
New or clean mattress pad and duvet		
Wipe/clean headboard		
Vacuum behind bed, sofa and table		
Clocks must have correct time		
Open sofa and clean – must be in good condition		
Sofa fabric in good condition and free of stains or tear		
Wipe/clean bedboard		
Trash can clean with liner in good condition		
Wipe/clean desk & drawer		
Desk lamp and phone cords cleaned and neatly wrapped		
Ensure all stationery and magazines are current and clean		
Remove coffee table glass and clean metal frame		
Drapes and sheers must be clean and free of stains		
Drapes and sheers tracks clean and free of dust		
Wipe/clean glass door and frame on the inside		
Scrub/clean glass door tracks		
Vacuum – special attention to edges		
Clean mattress protector, pillow protectors, cushion covers		
Deodorize and shampoo carpet and upholstery		

Bathroom		
Steam clean the bathroom		
Wipe/clean all light fixtures		
Bathroom vase clean with flowers		
Clean vents		
Wipe/clean all door frames, tops & sides		
Wipe/clean all door hinges		
Clean amenity trays and soap dish		
Scrub/steam clean shower walls and floor		
Scrub/ steam clean bathtub		
Polish tub and basin faucets		
Scrub entire bathroom floor		
Wipe/clean base of toilet		
Toilet seat, handle, base clean		
Toilet paper peaked; spare w/ sticker		
Supplies place correctly throughout room		
Bathtub clean/mildew free		
Robes placed correctly & tied at front		
Sink clean; stoppers clean & open		
Bathroom glasses spotlessly clean with new coasters		
Hair dryer clean and in good working condition		
All mirrors clean & streak-free		
Make-up mirror spotlessly clean and light working		
Trash can clean with liner and in good condition		
Floors clean; hair free – check corners		
Wipe/clean baseboard		
Clean bathroom scale (suites only)		
All linen bright and in excellent condition		
Mop floor		
Other tasks		
Chandelier cleaning		
Marble polish including sink		
Window and mirror cleaning		

Turn down service

This is also known as evening service, and is offered in the luxury hotels by preparing the room for a good night's sleep for the guest. During the turn down service the following procedures are followed and this may vary slightly from hotel to hotel depending on their set standards and procedures.

- Bed cover is removed, folded, and kept in the cupboard.
- Pillows are put flat on the bed near the head of the bed.
- The duvet is folded 90 degrees for the guest to get into bed comfortably. For single occupancy this is done on the side where the telephone is kept and for double occupancy this is done from both the sides.

- The foot mat is placed on the side of the bed and a towelling slipper is kept on top of that.
- Turndown amenities and the breakfast card are placed on the 90-degree fold.
- Bedside light is turned on.
- The drapes and the curtains are closed.
- Trash is emptied and the room and the bathroom are given a quick freshen up service.

Cleaning of public areas

Public areas in a hotel means the common areas for all the guests and are shared amongst them. As the areas remain busy during the morning and the day due to check in and check outs, deep cleaning is done at the night when the traffic is less. The most common public areas that are cleaned by the public area attendants are:

- **Front desk/lobby/entrance**: As the guests enters through the hotel's main entrance it is important to regularly clean the front entrance. If there are glass doors, they need to be cleaned to ensure there are no smudge marks on them. Lobby floors, reception desk, telephones, computers need to be regularly cleaned and disinfected.
- **Restaurants/cafes/dining areas**: Need to be cleaned when they are not operational, and special attention should be given to the furniture, lighting, floor, and any decorative items used in the area.
- **Elevators**: The elevators are used quite frequently during the morning and the day hours so care must be made to regularly clean the call buttons, floor, and the mirrors.
- **Swimming pool**: Cleaning includes catching any leaves or any particles, cleaning and disinfecting the water (chlorination), cleaning the surrounding areas of the pool including the pool beds, changing rooms, shower etc. Swimming pools are cleaned either early in the morning before the opening or in the evening after the pool is closed. The engineering departments in the hotel are generally responsible for the cleaning and chlorination of the swimming pool.

> **The main cleaning procedures of the swimming pool**
>
> 1. A visual inspection and remove any thing that is visible if the pool is in an open area close to trees or any landscaping features. Mostly done early in the morning or late in the evening after the closure of the pool.
> 2. Frequent chemical checks to ensure the pool is hygienic and safe. Testing the choline level is generally non-disruptive to the guests.
> 3. Thorough pool cleaning involves scrubbing and brushing of the entire pool, cleaning the waterlines and the filters. Modern pools have automatic cleaners.
> 4. For regular pool cleaning, nets on telescopic poles are used to clean the hard to reach spots.

- **Garden and the periphery**: The team of gardeners are responsible for trimming, watering and fertilizing the trees, shrubs, lawns, hedges etc. They regularly sweep the main gate, periphery of the hotel and rake all the dry leaves, weeds etc, ensuring an inviting entrance for everyone.
- **Parking area**: Maintenance of the parking area is the responsibility of the public area attendants, and it should be kept well maintained, with appropriate signages in place for the guest's convenience.

Post Covid-19 cleaning and maintenance of leisure facilities

When Covid-19 started most luxury hotels shut their leisure facilities to reduce the transmission of the virus. However, a major reason the guests visit the luxury hotels is to avail themselves of their leisure facilities, such as the spa and gym, as these leisure activities help the guests to unwind and rejuvenate. Most of the hotels started using health declaration/disclaimer forms, and thermal scanners to ensure the safety of the staff and the guests. The frequency of the cleaning in the public areas was increased and they began cleaning touch points every 30 minutes or even less, to ensure added safety and security for the guests. This typically involved the use of alcoholic wipes to clean the door handles, elevators buttons, etc., and detailed checklists and maps were given to the public area attendants. The staff had to tick every touchpoint as when they were cleaned to ensure detailed hygiene and disinfection. Thorough cleaning and disinfection during night, using stronger disinfectant, ensured that the facilities were kept clean and hygienic.

Summary

The standards, frequency and principles of cleaning is critical in providing a comfortable, hygienic and safe environment to the guests. Devising and adhering to the cleaning checklists helps in ensuring thorough and consistent cleaning, thus, offering highest possible standards to the guests. Post Covid-19 more stringent cleaning regulations and guidelines were adopted, and the effectiveness of cleaning was monitored and adjusted to offer safety and wellbeing to the hotel guests and staff. The frequency of cleaning was enhanced, and housekeeping roles were more visible to the guests. New and effective cleaning agents and disinfectants were introduced to offer utmost safety. A new era of cleaning, sanitisation, updating and enhancing standard operating procedures in the housekeeping department was established to retain customer confidence and satisfaction.

Activity:

1. Discuss in groups the principles of cleaning and how will you get the cleaning organised in your hotel. (Cleaning of guest room, public area).

2. Suppose you are a housekeeping manager, within your groups discuss the points to be considered when maximising the efficiency of the housekeeping room attendants.

3. Make a list of product and process adaptations in housekeeping post Covid-19.

4. Discuss within your groups the pros and cons of removing daily cleaning of occupied rooms. (During the pandemic occupied room cleaning was stopped and the rooms were cleaned only after departure)

5. Could housekeeping services be merchandised (added charges for occupied room cleaning and other housekeeping related services) in the near future, as some low fare airlines charges low base fares but with add-ons. Make a list of things that can go on add-ons.

Key terms

- **Room Status Report**: The housekeeping status of each guest room generated after the physical check by the housekeeping department.

- **Room Assignment Sheet**: This is used to allocate the guest room to each guest room attendant (GRA) for cleaning and indicates the room status.

- **Sleep-out**: A guest is registered to a hotel room, yet the bed has not been used.

- **Skipper**: The guest has left the hotel without settling the account (also called a walk-out);

- **Sleeper**: The guest has settled the account and left the hotel, but the front office staff has failed to correctly update the room's status.

- **Double Locked Room (DL)**: A room which cannot be opened by any key other than a grandmaster key.

- **Stayover rooms**: Also called *occupied rooms*, where the guests are continuing to stay.

References and further reading

Neog, R. (2021) New hotel cleaning procedures after COVID-19: A study of new housekeeping practices in hotels, *Atithya: A Journal of Hospitality*, 7(2), 1–7.

Roy,H., R. Faroque,A.R., Gupta, V. & Gani, M.O. (2022) Mitigating the negative effect of COVID-19 from the lens of organizational support in Bangladesh hotels, *Journal of Human Resources in Hospitality & Tourism*, 21(1), 105–129. doi:10.1080/15332845.2022.2015235.

Wood, D.F., Moreo, P.J. & Sammons, G. (2005) Hotel housekeeping operational. audit: a questionnaire approach, *International Journal of Hospitality & Tourism Administration*, 6(3), 1–10. doi:10.1300/J149v06n03_01

8: Budgeting for Housekeeping

This chapter will help you to:

- Understand the concept and purpose of budgeting.
- Learn about the different types of budgets based on different factors.
- Review the ways to ensure quality management in housekeeping, and controlling the standards.
- Learn about the ways to control expenses in housekeeping or budgetary control.

A budget is defined as a tool, guide, or a standard to control expenses. Budgeting is one of the most important planning activities of an Executive/Head Housekeeper. The front office department is mainly responsible for room sales and generating revenue. The housekeeping department forecasts the expenses required to generate the anticipated revenue. It is important that careful and efficient budgeting is done to control the operational expenses as well as to meet the financial goals of the hotel.

Budgeting is done normally for a period of one year and a head housekeeper investigates the past records (occupancy, staff salary, purchase of equipment etc) to prepare the budget. Although the budget is done yearly it can be broken down to into monthly budgets, and it can be adjusted if the need arises due to unforeseen circumstances.

Therefore, the aim of the department is to create a budget that is cost effective as well as robust enough to deal with any emergency in the future.

Purpose

The purpose of a budget is:

- To allow projection of revenue and expenses and thus efficiently plan people, material, and the finances.
- To foresee the financial plans of a hotel in future based on its organisational plan and performance.
- To compare the projected expenses to actual expenses.
- To plan for capital expenses, operational cost planning and short-term expenses etc.

Budget cycle

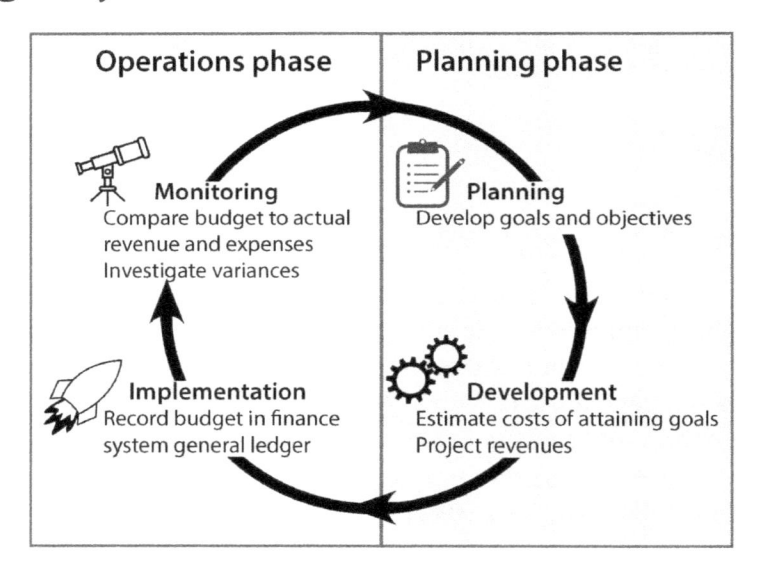

Figure 8.1: The budget cycle

The budget cycle involves two main phases: one is the **planning** phase and the other is the **operations** or controlling phase. It is a cycle because the figures and performance from each year feed into the next.

The **planning** phase has two stages.

- In the *planning* stage the overall goals and objectives of the department are set: What is it we want to achieve? What are the most important goals? What are our key constraints.
- In the *development* stage, costs and revenues are estimated, based on the past performance and on what is currently known about future costs and future business projections.

The **operations** phase likewise has two stages.

- In the *implementation* stage the budget is recorded and verified by the financial department for accuracy.
- In the *monitoring* stage the budget is compared to actual expenses and the variances are calculated. This is typically done monthly, or in response to a significant unexpected expense. In this stage appropriate corrective action is taken in case of deviation from the budget to actual.

Budget classification

Based on the **type of expenses**, budgets are classified as below:

- **Capital budget**: This involves the expenses that are made for procuring the assets like furniture, equipment, linen, and uniform. These assets have a longer life and are not used up in the day-to-day operation.
- **Operating budget**: This involves the expenses that are made during routine operation. The most common operating expenses are salaries, wages, cleaning products and supplies.
- **Pre-opening budget**: The expenses that are made for a new hotel to establish its operation is termed 'pre-opening budget' and this involves expenses on furniture, equipment, linen, cleaning agents, guest supplies, recruiting staff etc.

Budgets can also be classified based on **flexibility** of expenditure:

- **Fixed budget**: As the name suggests this is a type of budget that remains unchanged for the time frame it is planned for. Therefore, planning a fixed budget requires great level of precision in forecasting the sales, expenses, and revenue. It will typically cover specific cost areas, for example, stationery budget, marketing budget.
- **Flexible budget**: This type of budget varies depending on the volume of sales. It is based on the expenditure and the anticipated revenue for that period. For example, the cleaning supplies and guest amenities budget will vary based on the occupancy for the period the budget is prepared for. During unforeseen times a flexible budget allows for the changes to accommodate the needs of the operation.

A third classification of budgets is based on the time frame:

- **Long term budgeting**: This is a type of budget which is prepared for a long term, say 3-5 years. Preparing long term budgeting requires monitoring government policies, market trends and competitors. The biggest challenge of long-term budgeting is accuracy because as the

time frame increases it becomes more difficult to accurately forecast the expenditures and the expected revenue.
- Short term budgeting: For this the planning covers a period of three to twelve months. Due to the nature of the short-term budgeting, it allows for better evaluation of the hotel's performance.

Controlling expenses

Housekeeping is one of the largest expenses in a hotel. By controlling expenses, hotels can save money and increase their profitability. When expenses are controlled, housekeeping operations can become more efficient. This can result in faster turn-around times for rooms, better use of resources, and improved customer satisfaction. Controlling expenses in the housekeeping can be a challenging task, however adopting certain strategies and processes can help in minimising waste and cost control.

- It is important to **train the staff** and provide the right tools and equipment. Educating housekeeping staff on how to reduce waste and use resources efficiently can help to minimize costs.
- Another important factor to consider is **inventory control** (avoiding excess inventory on the shelf). Buying in bulk keeps down prices, and there must always be sufficient products and materials to meet the usage needs, but excess stock ties up capital unproductively. Consumption can be easily calculated once the occupancy is known, thus, better forecasting and planning of housekeeping operation will assist in controlling the cost and ensure successful operation.
- One of the important ways of controlling cost is to **avoid wastage** and misuse, constant inspection and check will help the department to find out ways to reduce the wastage. For example, storing dry amenities in the trolley with the wet items can lead to wastage as the piles of tissue could get wet and have to be thrown in the dustbin. Noticing this, a hotel decided to offer a zipped pouch to all the room attendants to store the dry amenities, ensuring theys are not damagedand thus avoiding wastage.
- Tracking **manpower productivity** has become easier in housekeeping due to technology therefore staffing can be carefully planned to ensure the operation is smooth and there is sufficient work for each employee as per the set standards.
- Equipping the showers and bathrooms with **refillable dispensers** results in cost savings of soap, shampoo and conditioners as it is more

economical to purchase them in bulk rather than pay for the packaging cost for every purchase of single use plastic. It may cut the housekeeping time to replenish these amenities in the occupied room, as topping up dispensers can be quicker than removing and replacing single use items. Dispensers soap are more convenient to use as the customers don't need to fumble to open the tiny bottles and can use the soap with one press – the sensor dispensers do not even require pressing. Thus, adding to the customer's positive experience.

Advantages of budgetary control

- Allows the department and the hotel to have clearer purpose and direction by allowing them to look ahead to the future and set detailed plans to achieve the set targets and the goals.

- As a budget is a controlling tool, this allows for assessing the performance of the department by analysing the actual results compared to the budgeted plan.

- Calculating the variance allows the department to investigate the reasons for deviation from the budget, identifying the reasons for the differences (controllable and non-controllable expenses), thus fostering better control.

- Enables the department to undertake corrective actions to overcome the variance.

- Promotes efficient communication, coordination and allows the managers to evaluate their individual control skills by being responsible for the achievement of their budget targets.

- Improves staff morale by allowing them to participate in the budget process.

Purchasing

Housekeeping purchasing involves procuring and managing the necessary supplies, equipment, and services needed to maintain a clean and comfortable environment for guests. The process typically involves identifying the needs of the housekeeping department, selecting vendors, negotiating contracts, and managing inventory. Effective hotel housekeeping purchasing is essential for ensuring that guests have a clean and comfortable stay, while also managing costs and optimizing the hotel's operations.

To keep the cost under control it is important to stop oversupplying the room attendants. With the advent of just-in-time purchasing software, hotels are avoiding storing excessive supplies on the shelves. Digital solutions that track inventory and alert supervisors when supplies are running short are an excellent example. This programme gives managers important insight into supply consumption and ordering cycles, allowing them to order in bulk and save money on essential products. All the amenities in the hotels are labelled with barcodes and this makes the stock taking quick and efficient.

Covid-19 and purchasing

Covid-19 added to the challenges of purchasing and procurement as the guest supplies and amenities got delayed due to lockdown. Most hotels have tried to find out ways to maintain the sufficient stock to ensure smooth operation. For example, procuring slippers and umbrellas took more than the expected lead time as the deliveries got stuck at the borders of the countries from where they are procured, and the shortage of these essential amenities added extra pressure on the hotels. To cope with this hotel shifted to weekly stock-taking rather than monthly stock-taking to ensure sufficient stock for hassle free operation.

> ### In-sourcing for cost savings
>
> Some of the leading hotel chains, post pandemic, have in-sourced their night cleaning, public area cleaning, fumigation, and other specialised cleaning tasks like carpet cleaning by training their internal permanent staffs that has resulted in a major cost saving as well as developing skills from within the department. In-sourcing the skills allow flexibility of cleaning and instead of monthly cleaning the cleaning can be done weekly. This offers better control and security.

Total Quality Management

Total Quality Management (TQM) is a systematic approach that focuses on continuous improvement of quality in all aspects of an organization's operations. In the context of housekeeping in hotels, TQM can be applied to improve the quality of the cleaning, laundry operations, linen-uniform tasks and other guest services offered to guests. Applying TQM principles to housekeeping in hotels can help ensure that guests have a positive experience and that housekeeping operations are running smoothly and efficiently.

Key principles of TQM that can be applied in housekeeping operations in hotels:

Customer focus

In the hospitality industry, the customer is always the top priority. In housekeeping, this means focusing on meeting the expectations of guests by providing them with clean and well-maintained rooms. TQM emphasizes the importance of understanding customer needs and expectations and using them as a basis for improving service quality.

Continuous improvement

TQM involves an ongoing process of improvement, with the goal of constantly improving quality and efficiency. In the context of housekeeping, this means continuously improving cleaning methods, equipment, and products to ensure that rooms are cleaned thoroughly and efficiently.

Employee involvement

TQM recognizes that employees are a valuable resource in improving quality. In the context of housekeeping, this means involving housekeeping staff in the improvement process, providing them with the training and resources they need to perform their jobs effectively, and empowering them to make suggestions for improvement. *Investors in People* offers accreditation in people management as well as solution to improve employee engagement. Visit their website to find out more about their work: https://www.investorsinpeople.com

Process management

TQM emphasizes the importance of managing processes to ensure that they are efficient and effective. In the context of housekeeping, this means implementing standard operating procedures for cleaning rooms, conducting regular inspections to ensure that cleaning standards are being met, and using data and feedback to identify areas for improvement.

Data-driven decision making

TQM involves using data to make informed decisions about how to improve quality. In the context of housekeeping, this means collecting data on cleaning performance, analysing it to identify areas for improvement, and using the findings to make changes to cleaning methods, equipment, or products.

Quality Management Systems

QMS stands for Quality Management System, which is a framework that helps organizations to ensure their products and services meet customer requirements and regulatory standards. In the context of hotel housekeeping, a QMS can help to maintain high standards of cleanliness, safety, and guest satisfaction. By implementing a QMS in hotel housekeeping, the service quality is improved, guest satisfaction is enhanced, and compliance with regulatory standards is ensured. It helps in the elimination of errors and waste thus reducing the operating costs.

An approved QMS gives assurance to guests that the hotel is committed to quality. Poor quality management results in:

- Wasted work
- Reworking
- Reinspecting
- Lost business
- Lack of repeat business
- Liability
- Complaints
- Staff demotivation

Measuring standards of accommodation

Various methods can be used to assess the standards.

- **Internal measurement**, e.g., guest satisfaction scores, are easy to apply and help to answer the key question of whether the guests' experience is as good as what they expect. Survey results should be read alongside the figures for repeat business. Do guests return at the level you'd expect, given the location and type of hotel?
- **Formal measurement** using organisational criteria, e.g., compliance with brand standards. Hotel chains will have their own inspection regimes to assure compliance.
- **Formal measurement** against classification criteria from an external body such as:
  - ☐ ISO – International Standards Organisation (www.iso.org)
  - ☐ Hospitality assured (https://hospitalityassured.com)
  - ☐ AA hotel star ratings (https://www.theaa.com/hotel-services/quality-assessment/hotels)
  - ☐ LQA – Leading Quality Assurance (www.leadingquality.com)

  Visit their websites to find out more about their schemes.

Summary

When expenses are managed effectively, hotels can budget more accurately for housekeeping expenses. This can help to prevent unexpected expenses and ensure that adequate funds are available for routine maintenance and repairs. Controlling expenses can help hotels to reduce waste, conserve resources, and promote sustainability. This can be achieved through measures such as using eco-friendly cleaning products, reducing energy consumption, and minimizing the use of disposable items.

> **Activities**
>
> 1. What are the customers' quality expectations in relation to housekeeping? (Consider room, public areas, and laundry)
> 2. What does quality mean to you?
>   What words do you think of when you think about Quality?
>   Write down any 3 brands that you feel are not good quality
>   Write down any 3 brands that you feel are good quality
> 3. Draft a purchasing policy for a five-star hotel. What factors will you consider when it comes to purchasing?

Key terms

- **Inventory:** The list of items, supplies, or goods available in a space or facility.
- **Inspection:** A thorough examination of a space using a specific checklist to ensure it meets certain standards.
- **Forecasting:** The process of estimating future financial trends based on past data and current market conditions and data.
- **Expenses:** The costs incurred in running a business.
- **Revenue:** The income generated by a business; in hotels it will be income generated by selling the rooms.
- **Procurement:** The process of obtaining goods and services from suppliers.
- **Purchase order:** A document that authorizes the purchase of goods or services.

References and further reading

Jones, T.A. (2008) Changes in hotel industry budgetary practice, *International Journal of Contemporary Hospitality Management*, 20(4), 428–444. doi:10.1108/09596110810873534.

Kaynak, H. (2013) *Total Quality Management and Just-in-Time Purchasing*. Taylor and Francis.

Pavlatos, O. & Paggios, I. (2009) A survey of factors influencing the cost system design in hotels. *International Journal of Hospitality Management*, 28(2) 263–271. doi.org/10.1016/j.ijhm.2008.09.002.

9: Linen, Uniform and Laundry Operations

This chapter will help you to:

- Understand the importance of crisp clean linen in hotel housekeeping.
- Learn about the right way to store and launder the linen as per the industry standards
- Review the ways to ensure laundry operations is smooth cost effective.
- Learn about the uniform design and the prerequisites of the careful selection of the uniform

Linen and its importance

Clean, immaculate linen adds to the guest satisfaction and therefore it is vital to pay attention to the quality and cleanliness of the linen. Supplying the finest cotton bed linen and luxurious soft towels and robes adds to the guest experience and encourages them to come back to the hotel property time and again. The main concern of the guests while checking in a guest room is about the hygiene and cleanliness of the bed and bath linen.

Figure 9.1: Luxurious towels add to the guest experience. These are from Star Linen, one of the UK's major suppliers. View their ranges at https://star-linen.co.uk

The companies which manufacture the linen are building hygiene into it by managing the moisture content of the linen and ensuring unfavourable conditions for the bacteria and mildew. This built-in hygiene is a boon and will reduce the stress for the guests.

The more recently manufactured linen is designed to be biodegradable and thus the condemned linen will not put a threat to the environment, another important concern which is being addressed by the manufacturers. Hotels are making a choice of sustainable and hygienic linen to offer a safe stay to their customers.

Figure 9.2: High thread count cotton feels soft and silky. These 800 thread count cotton Savoy pillowcases from Richard Haworth, one of the UK's oldest linen suppliers, are sure to give your guests an unforgettable night's sleep. Explore their range at https://www.richardhaworth.co.uk

Points to consider while storing linen:

- It is important to allow the linen to rest for minimum 24 hours before it is used, as this allows the wrinkles to smooth out, especially in poly-cotton fabrics.
- However, care needs to be taken that linen is not held for a long time after wash – prolonged storage is to be avoided.
- The linen storage room should be well-ventilated and free of humidity. It is important to ensure that linen is kept dry, otherwise mildew and moulds will grow as it is made up of natural fibres.
- Good quality shelves, or snag-free storage racks need to be used to store the linen, to avoid tearing of the fabric. Metal storage shelves should be used to store, as wooden storage can lead to the growth of micro-organisms.

- The linen store needs to be free of obstructions, well organised, with clear labelling, and large enough to avoid crushing and crowding the linen.
- Effective stock control measures must be in place to minimise the loss, theft and misuse of the linen.
- Rotation of the linen is important on the shelves and on the trollies.

Laundry operations

This is vital to hospitality operations and has a significant role to play in ensuring health and safety of the customers. Guest expectations is highly impacted by the clean and crisp bed and bathroom. Perfect linen is the basic demand of every guest.

Washing is a science, and a thorough understanding of every type of textile helps you to select the right wash cycle for each type, ensuring consistently high quality results. It is essential to use the right product for each fabric and to follow the washing instructions when setting the temperature, time and the wash cycle. This will bring the expected results, and help to maintain the life of the fabric as well.

Disinfectants are added in the wash cycles and linen is washed in the warmest water setting and dried completely to prevent cross contamination and make the linen safe and secure.

Washing pillows requires the lowest agitation setting and they should not be washed in warm water for more than 5 minutes. They should be surrounded with bedsheets and towels, which acts as buffers. Using pillow protectors helps to an extent to maintain the quality of the pillows and changing the protectors with each departure will ensure the hygiene.

Waterproof mattress covers have polyurethane barriers which trap moisture and stop it from seeping into the mattress. They are great for rooms with kids, and for accessible rooms, but also prevent staining due to spillage of tea, coffee, coke etc.

Incorporating technology in the laundry operations eases the operation and makes it efficient. Some of the common technological features that can be deployed in the laundry are :

- Tracking linen stock using RFID technology,
- Using clever cameras to spot blemishes,
- In-house laundry analysis
- Mobile laundries and antibacterial bedding and linen.

The wash cycle

The laundry flow or wash cycle includes different stages.

1. The soiled linen is **collected** and pre-sorted by textile family, like cotton together, synthetics and delicate separately. This will allow the different textiles to be washed in their appropriate wash formula without causing any damage.
2. Next step is **transportation** of the soiled linen in appropriate packaging and following the set route to avoid cross-contamination, as the dirty linen is the source of potentially harmful bacteria.
3. In the **sorting** stage, the linen is sorted and checked for any sharp objects to prevent the risk of harming the linen. It is also checked to see if the linen requires any stain removal treatment.
4. The dirty linen is then **washed** at the right temperature using the right chemical to preserve their quality.
5. **Drying** and **ironing** is the next step in the cycle and is done immediately to avoid recontamination.
6. The linen is folded immediately after ironing.
7. Washed, ironed and folded linen needs to be sorted and stored.
8. The linen is then put back into use.

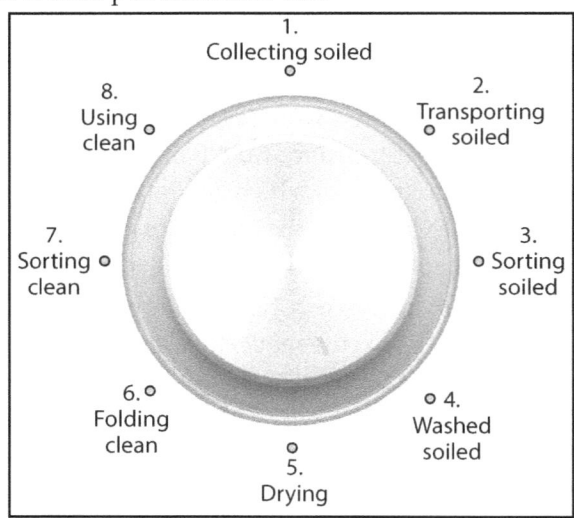

Figure 9.3: The laundry flow, or wash cycle.

> Rust in the water causes discoloration of the sheets and cleaning the linen using such water may result in guests' complaints. If this is a problem, the hotels use water softener products to remove the minerals.

Points to consider when investing in laundry equipment
- The efficiency of the machines in their use of water and electricity.
- Which tasks are automated and which required manual operation, as this will decide the time the employees need to spend in the laundry.
- The number of washes the linen can withstand without losing quality.

Labour-saving laundry machines

Here are some example of labour-saving machines that can be found in hotels' laundries.

Milnor's 30022VRJ washine machine comes with a comprehensive set of programmes which helps to save on labour costs and enhances efficiency. Options include an overnight soak, which eliminates the need of extra washes, and bath soak which saves time during the morning shift and is effective on tough stains. Find out more at https://www.milnor.com/products/30022vrj/

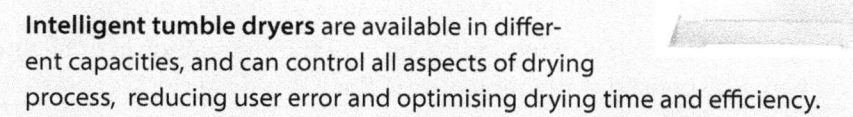

Intelligent tumble dryers are available in different capacities, and can control all aspects of drying process, reducing user error and optimising drying time and efficiency.

The Girbau Compact 5-in-1 Ironing system automatically feeds, irons, dries, folds and stacks large and small bed and table linen. The finishing side is the most labour-intensive area of the laundry, so this system can significantly reduce the labour hours while upping the production, quality, and efficiency. Find out more at https://gnalaundry.com/commercial-compact-ironers.html

LinenTech laundry management software is a cloud-based system to automate and optimise laundry services. It is easy to setup and generates evaluation reports on dashboards which are easy to comprehend. It measures the critical performance indicators, allowing the required improvements to be made quickly thus enhancing the efficiency. Find out more at https://www.linentech.net

Laundry costs

The average cost of a laundry process breaks down like this:

- Energy and water   10%
- Detergent   5%
- Textile replacement   20%
- Labour   50%
- Indirect costs   15%

Clearly the biggest cost saving are to be found in reducing labour.

Laundry dispensing systems

Automatic detergent dispensing systems can be connected to washing machines for greater efficiency in the laundry. Reasons to select laundry dispensing systems:

- Improves safety by minimising the employee's exposure to the chemicals.
- Automatic dosing helps to minimise the potential downtime and enhances the results by ensuring accurate and reliable dosing.
- The life of the linen is extended because of the right amount of chemical being dispensed every time during the washing cycle. Thus, results in saving of linen replacement costs.
- Improves efficiency by eliminating the need of manual labour and rewashing.

Ecolab

Ecolab is a global leader in providing global solutions for optimizing water and energy usage, with world class service to provide a clean and safe environment. It supports hotels in their efforts to improve operational efficiencies, being mindful about the need for sustainability. Their products are used by most of the leading hotel chains.

The wide range of services offered by Ecolab include OPL, an On Premises Laundry comprehensive partnership programme, that covers detergents, equipment etc, and has cost effective solutions for managing water and energy use.

Read about Ecolabs laundry dispensing systems here: www.ecolab.com/solutions/commercial-laundry-dispensing-solutions and here: https://en-uk.ecolab.com/offerings/aquanomic-eu

Figure 9.4: LQA standards for laundry operation

LAUNDRY DATE :		LQA Score	0.0%	
	STANDARD	Performance Classification	Met	Below	N/A
	COLLECTION				
1	Was the telephone answered within 3 rings or 10 seconds with an appropriate greeting?	Efficiency			
2	Was the laundry/pressing collected within 10 minutes of request for urban hotels and 15 minutes for resort hotels?	Efficiency			
3	Did the employee knock on the door/ring the doorbell and if required wait 10 seconds, and then knock or ring again and announce their department before asking to enter the room?	Service			
	DELIVERY AND PRESENTATION				
4	Was all the laundry/pressing delivered within specified time?	Efficiency			
5	If laundry delivery was requested, was it delivered to the room within 15 minutes of the request?	Efficiency			
6	If any delay in the delivery time, was the guest informed immediately?	Service			
7	If a 'privacy' sign/light was present was a calling card/doorknob card left under/on the door, or a silent message left on the telephone?	Service			
8	Were all collected items returned and if so, were they returned as requested (i.e. folded, on a hanger, etc.)?	Efficiency			
9	Were all laundry items appropriately cleaned, pressed and free of odour?	Service			
10	If a stain could not be removed from a garment was the guest informed through a printed card or via a telephone message?	Service			
11	Were any personal items left in clothes (e.g. money, business cards, etc.) returned and was the guest informed verbally or in writing?	Service			
12	Were all hanging garments returned on good quality hangers (i.e. not wire) and if covered was this either reusable (i.e. canvas) or biodegradable (i.e. not plastic)?	Service			
13	Were folded garments delivered in a box/basket/tray?	Service			
14	Were minor repairs automatically carried out where required (e.g. buttons replaced if fallen off or loose, collar stays replaced, etc.) and was the guest informed verbally or in writing?	Service			
15	Were the garments free of any staples, pins or laundry tags?	Service			
16	Were any shoes given for cleaning returned on time, cleaned/polished to a good standard & well presented?	Service			

	THE EMPLOYEE - BEHAVIOURAL STANDARDS				
17	Were employees well-groomed and neatly presented in clean, well fitted uniforms including clean masks (where applicable) and, if applicable, wearing name badges, resulting in a positive first impression?	Emotional Intelligence			
18	Was the employee's speech clear and use of English satisfactory, enabling engagement in two-way conversation with the guest (intelligently fair approach given some limitations due to face masks)?	Emotional Intelligence			
19	Did the employees engage in a well-paced, natural (non-scripted, jargon/slang free), friendly and interested manner (intelligently fair approach given some limitations due to face masks)?	Emotional Intelligence			
20	Did the employee use the guest's name naturally and discreetly without overusing it?	Emotional Intelligence			
21	Did employees collaborate seamlessly to ensure service was organized and professional without being intrusive or repetitive?	Emotional Intelligence			
22	Did the employee actively listen, avoid interrupting and give the caller their undivided attention (i.e., the guest should not have to repeat themselves)?	Emotional Intelligence			
23	Where applicable, did the employee display self-control and empathy in challenging interactions and offer a suitable alternative/resolution?	Emotional Intelligence			
	BRAND CORE				
24	Did employees take ownership of guest requests and effectively communicate them to other departments as needed (i.e. guest does not need to repeat request)?	Service			
25	Did employees show a genuine sense of care during interactions by smiling, making eye contact and using positive body language?	Service			
26	Were all written communications to guests (i.e. notes, email, etc.) on hotel branded stationery, personally addressed where applicable (i.e. use of guest name) and signed by a named individual?	Service			
27	If the guest was staying for a special occasion, did the employee show recognition of this?	Service			
	BRAND SIGNATURE				
28	Was a small amenity in the laundry basket to reflect the hotel's brand personality (e.g. lavender sachet)?	Product			
29	Was all tissue paper and wrappings printed with the hotel's logo or signature design?	Product			
30	Were shirts returned with cardboard inserts and were jackets returned with tissue covering the shoulders and inserted in the arms?	Product			
31	Did the laundry amenities include a 'Going Out' one hour valet service for rapid pressing and shoeshine during early evening hours (i.e. 17h00 - 20h00)?	Efficiency			
	TOTAL NO. OF STANDARDS		Met	Below	N/A
	31				

> Fabric is one of the most porous materials, even when treated with stain resistant or antimicrobial coatings. As much as possible, the hotel should avoid fabric upholstery and look for synthetic alternatives. Nowadays there are non-porous surfaces that are fashionable, but durable, imitating the look and feel of fabrics on tables, storage items and desks. Compared to other synthetics, vinyl has the most durable and cleanable properties and can withstand industrial solvents and constant cleaning.

Aquanomic Laundry Solution

Ecolab is one of the leading suppliers of detergents and other laundry products. Below is their Aquanomic solid product line, which shows the range of treatements for specific type of washes, and their attributes.

THE AQUANOMIC SOLID LAUNDRY PRODUCT LINE			
	AQUANOMIC SOLID DETERGENT	Phosphorus-free concentrated solid detergent is formulated to deliver premium results leaving linens whiter and brighter.	4,08 kg
	AQUANOMIC SOLID UNIVERSAL DETERGENT	Concentrated low alkaline solid one-shot detergent which delivers premium clean & bright linen, boosts whiteness, highly effective against fat, grease, oils, body and food soils. Suitable for hard water and delicate textiles.	3,5 kg
	AQUANOMIC SOLID OXY	Provides colour-safe laundry destaining in a safe and stable solid formula for achieving optimum whiteness whilst maintaining textile strength and integrity.	1,36 kg
	AQUANOMIC SOLID DESTAINER	Solid destainer chlorine formulated to obtain highly effective bleaching power and excellent stain removal.	1,81 kg
	AQUANOMIC SOLID SOFT M	Premium performance solid fabric softener leaving outstanding softness and antistatic touch.	2,72 kg
	AQUANOMIC SOLID NEUTRA-PLUS	Solid neutraliser reliably brings textiles to a neutral pH, eliminates residual chlorine, provides a pleasant smell, helps to improve whiteness and to prevent yellowing of textiles.	2,72 kg

- Aquanomic products are safe and convenient to handle. There is less physical strain and spillage as the product comes in solid capsules instead of liquid canisters.

- Aquanomic products are more sustainable and have a lower environmental impact as they have lower transportation cost (as the washing tablets are smaller and lighter) and require 70% less packaging.

- Aquanomic intelligent service software helps to track the key metrics like number of loads washed, the weight of each load, the wash programmes and number of cycles run, with an easy to read dashboard that indicates the critical actions undertaken.

Ecobrite low temperature laundry programme:

- Improved performance and brightness at low temperature.
- Extended textile life
- Reduced carbon emissions and thus offering highest sustainable impact.
- Optimised water and energy cost
- Compliant disinfection according to BPR (Biocidal Product regulation).
- Controlled dosing

Ecobrite Delicate Clean offers gentle treatment, with colour protection of items made of wool, silk, polyester, cotton, linen, viscose. The textile has a pleasant soft fragrance after the wash.

Ecobrite Delicate Finishing used in combination with Delicate Clean provides textile protection to delicate and wool fabrics. Special ingredients in the finishing agent add strength to the fibres restoring the life and minimise shrinkage, pilling and felting.

Ecobrite Des is a mild oxygen-based laundry disinfectant suitable for all textiles including wool and viscose. The textiles come out brighter and with a high level of antimicrobial protection.

Ecobrite Magic Emulsion Clean, suitable for all washable textiles made of cotton, linen, polyester or viscose, removes heavy dirt and grease and restores the brightness.

StainBlaster ™

Stainblaster Stain Management Programme is a cost-effective part of laundry process as it helps to save time, labour, water, energy and linen investment. The stain removal process helps to achieve spotless and bright linen, enhancing guest experience and satisfaction. Using Stainblaster with the wash process removes the need for rewashing and reduces linen replacement.

Points to consider while laundering the linen

- The linen needs to be categorised/ sorted according to the material or cloth type: linen cotton, silk, polyester etc.
- Sorting of the linen should also consider the severity of staining.
- Shake out all the clothes carefully before loading them in the washer extractor to see if any guest belongings have come through.
- While washing, the coloured fabrics should not be mixed with the whites. It is always advisable to wash the coloured fabrics before wearing so that the colour doesn't run into the skin.
- If washing at 40 degrees, then tumble dryer at warm and if washing at 50 degrees then tumble dry at hot, but note that over-drying can make the garment shrink.
- Once the washing or extracting cycle is complete, the linen needs to be immediately removed from the machines.
- A cool down period should be used if washing any cotton or polyester linen at a temperature above 140 degrees. Allow cold water to run in the machine to reduce the water temperature at least 3-4 minutes before the hot water is drained.
- Good quality detergents and soaps should be used to lengthen the life of the linen and the machine as well as maintaining the quality and standards of the linen.
- Blue torch (UV) checks of the linen will show if the quality is up to standards.

Outsourcing linen laundering

- Removes the need for the hotel to invest money in setting up the laundry space and purchasing expensive equipment.
- Allows the hotel to focus on room and public area cleaning and maintenance, and taking care of guest needs.
- Specialist commercial laundries invest in the latest laundry technology, thus making the job more consistent and efficient.

To find out more about the services offered by commercial laundries who cater to luxury hotels, visit one of these specialists, Royal Jersey Laundry at https://rjlaundry.co.uk

Or explore the linen hire services offered by Empire Laundry at https://empirelaundry.com/hotel-linen/

Garment care advice labels

Garment care advice labels are usually sewn inside garments, and need to be followed to maintain their colour and condition.

Washing

Usually the first item is the washing instruction: what temperature, and whether it should be washed in a machine or hand washed.

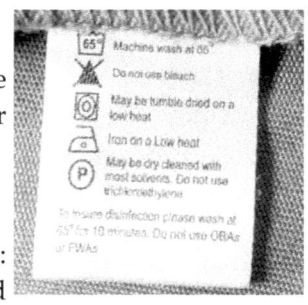

Maximum wash temperature advised.

The temperature advised for industrial wash.

The garment should be delicately washed whether by hand or on hand wash cycle.

Figure 9.5: Washing advice symbols

Special care

Other instructions may be about ironing, the use of bleach, whether it can be dry cleaned and other notes.

Bleach resistant. The garment can be washed in bleach and not lose its colour.

Crease resistant. The garment has been treated to make it easy care and resistant to creases.

Suitable for dry cleaning.

The garment has been treated with a finish to help easy cleaning of the garment.

The garment features technological fabric to help keep you dry and cool.

Iron on cool.

Iron on warm.

Iron on hot.

Tumble dry safe.

Safe to bleach.

Do not bleach.

Figure 9.6: Garment care advice symbols

Laundry and dry-cleaning equipment suppliers

Here are two of the UK's leading laundry and dry-cleaning equipment suppliers. Visit their websites and explore their ranges of equipment and laundry solutions.

- Electrolux Professional: https://www.electroluxprofessional.com
- Dane Realstar: https://www.danerealstar.com

> **Standards and compliance**
>
> Suppliers should be up to date with the industry standards and be members of industry bodies like SLEAT (Society of Laundry Engineers & Allied Trades) or the Guild of Cleaners and Launderers (GCL). The SLEAT code of conduct was drawn up in consultation with DEFRA (Department of Environment, Food, Rural Affairs) and SEPA (Scottish Environment Protection Agency). Machines must be compliant with Solvent Emission Directive regulations.

Hotel uniform

Planning and designing a hotel uniform for all the employees is a huge cost and therefore requires careful planning and execution. The uniforms in the luxury 5-star hotels are designed by famous designers and are typically changed every five years to match the current trends and styles.

Factors to taken into consideration while choosing the uniform designs are as follows:

- Design trends
- Employees comfort, as an employee does a lot of lifting, bending, and stretching tasks so they need to feel comfortable while working in the uniform to be productive and efficient.
- Uniforms should complement the hotel's vision and also impact the customer experience. Witnessing a well-dressed groomed employee always builds a positive impression about a hotel brand.
- The uniform should be made from high-quality fabric for durability and long life.
- Unifroms should be easy to care for, crease resistant and able to withstand frequent machine washing.
- Some hotel brands get their logo embroidered to give their uniforms a unique look.

Steps in planning uniform design

Meeting/briefing phase
The first step to uniform planning is setting up a meeting between the uniform supplier and the hotel, which allows the hotel to communicate to the supplier their aspirations and requirements which include budgets, timelines, aftercare etc.

Design selection
In this phase the hotel chooses from a varied selection offered by the designers, the style of uniform that matches their need. Mostly the attributes a hotel seeks are a uniform that depicts their culture, that the material used in the uniform is breathable, durable, convenient to carry out tasks as required in each department, has an excellent fit for every shape and achieves production efficiencies.

Designing phase
In this phase the uniforms for various departments as specified by the hotels are sketched and mood boards are created, showcasing the fabric, colour, texture etc.

Product trial
Once the uniform design is agreed, sampling is carried out before the final approval by the hotels to ensure the product is of highest quality, is functional, durable and can withstand the harsh working environment.

Bulk production of uniform
Once the samples are approved, all the necessary quality tests are done, and the size breakdown of staff is agreed, the production of the uniform is done matching all the specifications supplied by the hotels. After inspecting the quality, the delivery is made to the specific hotels.

Uniform fitting and alterations
Professional tailors make sure the uniform trial is done for each staff member. This ensures each member of the staff is wearing the correct size and if any final/ minor alteration is required, this is done. Final stock count is run, and any remaining stock is handed over to the hotel.

Some uniform suppliers and designers offer warehousing facility as well, if space is a constraint for the hotels, and they can store the uniform in the ideal storage space. Using their order management system, the hotels can order the uniform stock required and the same can be delivered very next day. The hotel's stock management system will show when the stock is low, and orders can be sent, thus ensuring efficient management.

Logos and name labels

Embroidery and printing services are offered by uniform suppliers. The logo of the brand and employee's name can be embroidered on the uniform for personalisation and uniqueness. Embroidery samples and digital visuals are created by the supplier to enable you to choose before proceeding with the order.

Some of the leading uniform suppliers

- **Fashionizer Couture Uniforms** design bespoke uniforms for luxury hotels and brands. They recently launched a new sustainable range in their housekeeping uniform collection. Explore their styles at: https://fashionizer.com

Figure 9.6: Housekeepers can dress to impress with uniforms such as this design from Fashionizer

- **Dennys brands** is a family of six brands - Dennys London, Le Chef, Comfort Grip, AFD, Joseph Alan and Soho Knives. Between them they supply a full range of hospitality uniform and clothing. Find out more at: www.dennys.co.uk

- **NoUniform** is the UK leader in high end bespoke uniform designs that are functional and iconic. Their website showcases their designs, but is challenging to navigate. Visit them at: www.nouniform.com

Determining par levels and inventory levels

Par level is defined as the number of sets of linen in hand for the operation. Most hotels maintain a par level of three for their room and food & beverage linen. Thus means that there is one set of linen is in use, one set is in the laundry for wash and the third set is in the housekeeping storage. As there is a huge cost associated with purchasing and maintaining linen, some budget hotels decide to go with two par and the key challenges associated with this is short linen life as the linen will not have sufficient resting time in the store if it will be in continuous use. This will impact the life of the linen and the need for the replacement of the linen will arise soon due to excessive washing. As the cotton fabric regains its strength from the humidity in the atmosphere, allowing it to rest on the shelves makes them regain their hydration and strength, thus, elongating the life and the quality of the linen.

Reduced par of linen puts pressure on the laundry and the cost of laundry increases due to increase in the usage of chemicals, water, and energy. Delays in processing the linen in the laundry, due to a machine breakdown or other issues, will result in customer dissatisfaction. The third par acts as the buffer during such circumstances to avoid any discomfort to the guests. Many hotels allow an allowance of 0.25 par to the standard three par which is ideal for the hotels with on premises laundry. Some hotels go for par of four and five, or even six, in case the laundry is outsourced, as the delay in the linen delivery can happen due to heavy traffic, vehicle breakdown or any other unavoidable circumstances. Extra par allows peace of mind and ensures sufficient linen supply for smooth operation.

Use cycle stage	in circulation
On the beds (clean and dirty)	1 par
On the trolleys to be used that day	1 par
In your linen store	1 par
Used linen and towelling being processed by the laundry	1 par
Clean linen and towelling being delivered to the hotel	1 par
Total	5 par

Figure 9.7: Laundry use cycle for a typical hotel

Establishing a par stock level for a hotel that uses an external laundry operation, and supplies three sheets for each of its 300 king-size beds

300 king-size beds × 3 sheets per bed = 900 sheets per par number

One par in the guest room	1 × 900 =	900
One par in floor linen closets	1 × 900 =	900
One par soiled in the laundry	1 × 900 =	900
One par replacement stock	1 × 900 =	900
One par for emergencies	1 × 900 =	900
One par for linen in transit	1 × 900 =	900
	Total no. of sheets	5400

Thus 5400 sheets ÷ 900 sheets per par = 6 par

Note that if such a hotel uses an on-premises laundry operation, 5 par will be sufficient.

Figure 9.8: Calculating the linen par stock level (Chibili et al., 2019)

Factors influencing par stock calculations
- Occupancy of the hotel
- Frequency of delivery of clean linen by the outsourced laundry service
- Average length of stay
- Level of service (For a luxury hotel an extra par of linen will be required during the turn down service)

Linen inventory management

This is the process of physically counting of all the linen items in use, store, and laundry. Linen is the most expensive recyclable item in the inventory and the hotel need to ensure appropriate control procedure for storing, using and replacement. Monthly inventory check-up results in better control as this helps to diagnose the shortages in the linen quickly and to curb the problem as soon as possible. Shortages in linen can bring in negative impressions from the guests as well as the staff. Though inventory taking is a time-consuming process it is essential to monitor linen usage, and a stock check needs to be planned monthly or quarterly, depending on the hotel operation and need.

RFID (radio frequency ID) chips can be attached to items of linen, and with scanners and suitable software, the location of each item can be known at all times. This eliminates the need for manual inventory checks, reducing labour costs. If an external laundry is used, automated scanning as the linen is sent out and returns makes it much simpler to identify items lost by the external operation.

Summary

Offering a clean and crisp linen to the guests is part of creating comfortable and hygienic experience. Hotels need to use innovative laundry equipment and supplies to preserve linen for long-time and reduce costs. The digitization of the laundry operation has reduced the decision-making of the laundry staff and brought consistency in the chemical usage, avoiding too much chemical usage as it can ruin the linen. Uniforms are essential part of hotel operation as they provide a professional appearance to the hotel employees, offer comfort and convenience to the employees while working, and improve the brand image with consistency and enhanced appeal. Efficient management of linen, uniform and laundry operation is imperative for the hotel's overall profitability.

Actvities

1: Case Study Analysis: The Hilton Prague

Read this case study, adapted from Ecolab's website, and answer the questions.

Ecolab's OxyGuard™40 detergent is gentle yet effective on linen and results in reducing the water usage up to 20%. In 2013, the Hilton Prague hotel laundry, which washes linen for the Hilton Prague and the Hilton Prague Old Town as well as several other hotels, faced poor dosing equipment and a lack of data management, which made it difficult to monitor system efficiency and look for opportunities to make improvements. Ecolab worked together with Hilton and completely changed its approach to the washing process. By installing dosing systems and implementing digital monitoring platforms, Hilton was able to get full control of the washing process, follow all the required steps and adjust the parameters any time during the process to optimise and maximise the results. By making the switch from a 90°C process to one at 60°C while keeping washing efficacy, Ecolab was able to lower operational costs by 10% during the first few months of operations. Then in 2017, Ecolab successfully deployed a new technology for low-temperature washing: OxyGuard40. This is a programme based on a wash temperature of 40°C, which generates water and energy savings.

From a sustainability standpoint, Hilton also appreciated OxyGuard 40's EU Ecolabel, as a mark of its commitment to reducing the environmental impact of its laundry operations. With support of the Ecolab Textile Care team, the focus was put on total cost optimization and quality improvement through a holistic approach combining service and technology.

1. What objectives and goals were set to be achieved by this programme?
2. What benefits were achieved by following this new programme and can you think of any challenges to adapt to this?

2: Case Study Analysis: The soft toy

Read the real case study from a leading luxury hotel and answer the questions.

At a luxury hotel, while stripping the bed a room attendant by mistake collected a child's soft toy (which the child use to cuddle while sleeping and was greatly attached to). We all know how precious these toys are to each child, as they comfort and give a feeling of safety to the children. Realising that the soft toy is missing in the room, the child and the parents panicked, and rang the front desk to enquire about it. After checking with the housekeeping department and intense searching the soft toy was finally found.

The hotel made some genuine effort to offer service recovery and create an unforgettable experience for their little guest. They took the little soft toy to several departments and clicked photographs of it performing hotel operational tasks and even took it to a shopping arcade and clicked photographs showcasing the toy had so much fun outside. Then the hotel took the effort of putting all these pictures in a little diary and captioned the diary as "Let me tell you how I spent my day today". Reading all about this and witnessing the pictures of the little soft toy the child and the parents were really thrilled and forgot about the panic and thanked the housekeeping staff for creating this unforgettable memory. They posted about this incidence on several social media praising the hotel.

1. Why did the hotel staff put so much effort while returning the lost soft toy to the child?
2. How could this situation of losing the little soft toy have been avoided?
3. Can you think of an incidence when the HK department had created a WOW moment for their guests and created a lasting memory for them?

3: Uniform design

Research the uniform design of a luxury hotel and discuss how the designers have incorporated the cultural heritage into their uniform design

Key terms

- **Linen par**: The sufficient level of linen inventory, defined as the amount of linen needed to outfit the hotel property at 100% occupancy.
- **Upholstery**: The linen that is used for decorating the furniture, for example the sofa set, chair etc.
- **Linen chute**: A passage from each floor pantry which is used for sending the soiled linen to the laundry for cleaning.
- **Stock taking**: The physical verification and counting of linen periodically.
- **TSA (Textile Services Association)** is a trade association for the textile care service industry. It provides information and guidance on commercial laundry and textile rental business. Find them at: https://tsa-uk.org

References and further reading

Brunet, R. (2018) Clean sweep: Forward-thinking equipment manufacturers help make housekeeping easier, *Eastern Hotelier*, 10(3), 35–39.

Chibili, M. , de Bruyn, S., Benhadda, L., Lashley, C., Penninga, S. and Rowson, B. (2019) *Modern Hotel Operations Management*. Taylor and Francis.

Mest, C.E. (2012) Electronic integration with housekeeping, *Hotel Management*, 227(13), 22.

Wai Chun Choy, M. & Ching Ching Shih, C. (2022) The effect of employee uniform on job satisfaction: A case of the housekeeping department in a luxury five-star hotel in Hong Kong, China, *Tourism & Hospitality Management*, 28(3), 559–574.

10: Safety and Security

This chapter will help you to:

- Understand the safety and security features in the hotel.
- Review the legislation to ensure the safety of the housekeeping staff and the guests.
- Learn about the comprehensive health and safety programmes and their considerations.
- Know how to deal with emergencies.

The safety and security of the hotel and its guests are always paramount and any guest arriving at a hotel expects that they and their belongings will be safe and secure throughout their stay. The hotel must implement measures to protect and secure their assets. Staff are valued and should also be protected. There must be safety and security of systems, equipment, food poisoning and against any criminal activity, such as theft, abduction, murder, etc. The safety and security of guests are vital for maintaining positive reviews, as weak safety and security measures at a hotel may pose a threat to the life of the guests and staff and can tarnish the reputation of the hotel.

The hotel needs to formulate strict safety and security policies and guidelines which needs to be communicated thoroughly to the staff, as well as briefly to guests on arrival to showcase the hotel's duty for care. Regular checks and inspection will ensure any items or any processes causing threats to safety are identified in a timely manner and removed to prevent any mishap.

It is essential to keep the guests and staff informed by planning regular drills and training, and placing signages where they are clearly visible to guests. Actions that may result in a threat must be banned and regular monitoring by the security department and housekeeping team needs to be carried out.

Security and safety features include:

- Access control is essential. Only authorised guests and staff should be able to access anywhere other than public areas.
- CCTV cameras should be present to monitor all vulnerable areas and detect ptoential threats.
- Room safety measures include a safe (for valuables), a peephole in the entrance door and a safety door lock (unlock when handle is turned manually).
- In some hotels, guests can access CCTV surveillance of their room from a smartphone or tablet.
- Slip-strips or other slip-proof surfaces are required on bathroom floors.
- Hand rails must be fitted in baths.
- The temperature of the hot water outputs should be regulated at not more than 55 degrees to prevent burns and scalds.
- A hairdryer in the room is the common reason for short circuits and therefore measures need to be exercised to ensure safe wiring and placement.
- Any balcony should be structurally solid and should not have any climb points.
- Windows may be kept closed, or have restricted opening to prevent any accidents. It is up to the hotel whether visitors can open their room windows, and if so, to what degree.
- All in-room safety features should be checked regularly by the housekeeping staff.
- Signs indicating the emergency evacuation route (fire escape) must be put behind the bedroom door, as well as at meeting spots.
- Fire alarms, smoke detectors, carbon monoxide detectors, sprinklers, and fire extinguishers must be installed and in excellent working condition. They must be checked on a regular basis and replaced as needed.
- Swimming pools should not be accessible by unaccompanied children, and should have lifebelts or safety flotation devices, and lifeguards and/or signages notifying guests that they swam at their own risk.
- To safeguard against the spread of viruses like Covid, chemicals such as sodium hypochlorite (NaClO) and products based on ethanol should be used while cleaning the floor.

Legislation

To reduce risks, it is important to carry out risk assessment on all housekeeping operations and activities, and to implement organisational and technical measures when necessary. Recognising that the safety of the employees is one of the most important things, hotels invest time and resources to ensure the staff safety. For example, recently the housekeeping department of a pre-opening hotel in London had written close to 230 procedures and 78 risk assessments, which detailed the right procedure for doing each task and for avoiding any related risks. In housekeeping, most of the jobs involve repetitive tasks, prolonged muscular load, and awkward and constrained postures. Such factors can lead to work-related musculoskeletal disorders (WMSDs) in the neck and shoulder regions. Correct use of the right equipment can reduce the development of such disorders.

The emphasis on health and safety training is paramount and the training is refreshed each year, followed by an audit and inspection by an external company, wherein all the training records are checked and verified to ensure each member of the staff has undergone mandatory training.

Unsafe work environments cause:

- Medical costs
- Legal issues like fines and lawsuits tarnishing the hotel's reputation
- Decreased productivity
- Low employee morale and management concerns (resulting in reduced productivity)

Health and Safety legislation

Some of the Health and Safety legislation relevant to the hospitality industry and particularly to the housekeeping department are discussed below.

Health and Safety at Work Act 1974 (HASAWA)

HASAWA sets out the general duties which:

- employers have towards employees and members of the public
- employees have to themselves and to each other

It requires employers and employees to take the necessary measures to control and reduce all risks to an acceptable level, to safeguard the health and safety of anyone who may be affected by the activities at work.

Details can be found here: https://www.hse.gov.uk/legislation/hswa.htm

Below are some examples of HASAWA procedures in the prevention of slips and trips, which are of fundamental importance to housekeeping:
- Clean all spills immediately and clearly marking wet area.
- Sweep all debris and removal of all obstacles.
- Secure (tacking, taping etc.) mats, rugs etc..

Control of Substances Hazardous to Health Regulations 2002 (COSHH)

COSHH was introduced to control the use of any materials, mixtures or compounds used at the workplace, which have the potential to cause harm to people's health. They can include bleaching agents, which can be toxic, corrosive or irritant, and are commonly used in housekeeping for cleaning purposes. The employer is responsible for ensuring that all employees are trained and aware of hazards, that all items should be correctly labelled and that employees to wear the necessary protective equipment (provided by employer).

The COSHH website tells us that you can prevent or reduce workers' exposure to hazardous substances by:
- Finding out what the health hazards are.
- Deciding how to prevent harm to health (risk assessment).
- Providing control measures to reduce harm to health.
- Making sure they are used.
- Keeping all control measures in good working order.
- Providing information, instruction and training for workers and others.
- Providing monitoring and health surveillance in appropriate cases.
- Planning for emergencies.

Find out more about COSHH here: https://www.hse.gov.uk/coshh/

Health and Safety Regulations 1981 (First Aid)

The First Aid regulations 1981 require employers to provide some employees with adequate training and appropriate equipment to ensure that anyone ill or injured will receive immediate attention. First Aid procedures should include at least one trained First Aider on site, a first aid box or even first aid room.

Find out more about the First Aid legislation here https://www.hse.gov.uk/firstaid/legislation.htm

Manual Handling Operations Regulations 1992

Manual handling operations regulations covers areas such as lifting or lowering heavy objects or loads. This also includes moving, pulling, and pushing by hand or using bodily force. Housekeeping job functions require a lot of manual handling and employees must be trained to avoid injury. Some procedures used for reducing manual handling risks can include:

- Relevant information on load weights etc.
- Diagrams showing correct heavy lifting methods
- Regular risk assessments and updates.

Find more details at: www.hse.gov.uk/msd/manual-handling/the-law.htm

Regulatory Reform (Fire Safety) Order 2005

This is the main law covering employes' responsibilities in relation to fire safety. It states that all employers must carry out, or find a 'competent person' to carry out, a suitable and sufficient Fire risk assessment. Risk assessment procedures should do the following:

- Identify all fire risks
- Identify locations of people most at risk in case of fire
- Keep assessment under review and updated

Any risks identified in the assessment must bemitigated.

For good advice about on fire safety go to https://www.hse.gov.uk/fireand-explosion/fire-safety.htm

---

Government departments

While every country has laws and guidance to promote health and safety in the workplace, the regulations and advice vary.

In the UK, the relevant department is the Health and Safety Executive (https://www.hse.gov.uk/index.htm). A full range of guidance is available on its website, or as free downloads, or in book form.

In the US, the relevant department is the Occupational Safety and Health Administration (https://www.osha.gov), part of United States Department of Labour. The mission of OSHA is to ensure safe and healthy working conditions, by setting and enforcing standards, conducting compliance inspections, training, assistance and taking legal action when there is nonfulfillment.

Make sure that you know where to find health and safety legislation and guidance for your country.

Risk and risk assessment stages

Risk is defined as a possibility of occurrence of an unfortunate event. The purpose of **risk assessment** is to understand the factors that influence the risks, to identify the range of outcomes and to estimate the likelihood of the outcome.

1 The first step in in risk assessment is the identification of the potential risk (injury, diseases) or the probable cause of its occurrence.
2 Then the severity or the impact of the risk needs to be assessed.
3 Next the probability of the occurence must be assessed.
4 A risk assessment matrix can help now. Which square does the risk fit into in terms of impact and probability?

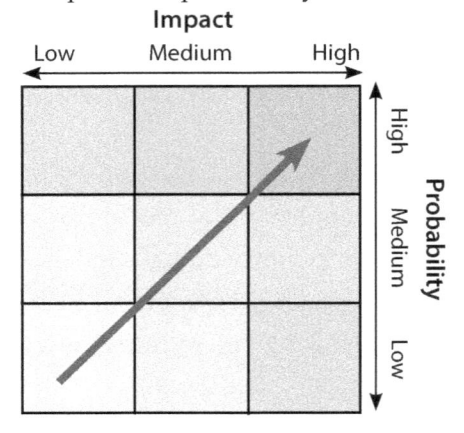

Figure 10.1: A simple risk assessment matrix.

5 If the risk is of low impact and low probability, it can probably be ignored. The higher the impact or the higher the probability, the more important it is to either eliminate or reduce the likelihood of its occurrence by applying some practical control measures and evaluating its effectiveness, and also to have a plan to deal with the consequences should it occur.

Risk management is defined as a courses of action which to seek risk reduction as well as cost reduction. Common strategies used to manage risks are:

- **Risk-informed decision making**, which involves reduction and avoidance of risks using risk assessment.
- **Cautionary or precautionary measures** which involves the abilities of reading signals and precursors of major events.
- The **discursive strategy** involves measures to develop confidence by clarification of facts, deliberations, reduction of uncertainties.

10: Safety and Security   145

WE CARE PROGRAMME
at Mandarin Oriental, Hong Kong

In response to the current COVID-19 pandemic, Mandarin Oriental, Hong Kong has implemented an additional *'We Care' programme* of stringent protocols to further safeguard the comfort, health and safety of guests and employees. Our existing high standards of health and hygiene have been enhanced, and we remain alert to local advice from health experts and government authorities, adapting best practices accordingly. Lloyds Register, an internationally recognised independent assessor, audits our rigorous Fire, Life, Health, Safety & Security standards on an annual basis and have verified the new additional methods in place. Examples of some of the new initiatives that have been introduced at Mandarin Oriental, Hong Kong include the following:

Connect with our colleagues through instant messaging to avoid unnecessary contact

Temperature checks for all guests and employees at all points of entry

Paperless check-in and express check-out service

"We Care" kit (face mask and hand sanitiser wipes) will be provided upon request

High traffic areas are treated with Nano Titanium Dioxide

Sanitise all guest touch points with neutral disinfection cleaner every hour

Suitcase disinfection service is available upon request

Clean and sanitise all air conditioner filters on a bi-monthly basis

COVID sensitive rooms with enhanced cleaning protocols and contactless service

All colleagues are equipped with face masks and gloves when cleaning the room

All gym equipment, spa treatment rooms and limousines are sanitised after each use

All restaurant dining tables are disinfected after each use and menus are offered through a QR code

Hotel Stay Safe - This certificate has been issued following verification of cleaning and hygiene standards in the hotel that meet the Lloyds Register guidelines.
For more information, please contact us on +852 6015 7211 or via email at mohkg-amo@mohg.com.

VERIFIED LR
Hotel Stay Safe

Figure 10.2: Hotels responded to the Covid-19 pandemic with a wide range of risk-reduction measures, and most sought external certification of their hygiene standards to reassure their guests. Notice the Hotel Stay Safe logog.

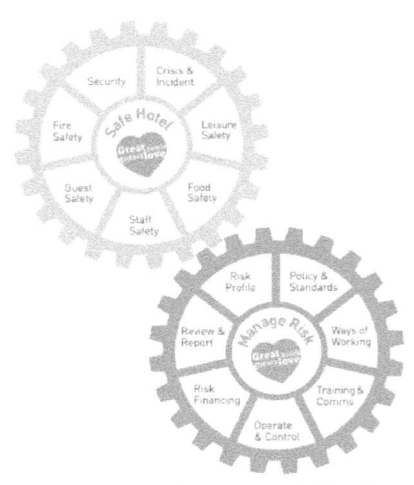

Figure 10.3: Like all hotel groups, InterContinental Hotels group (IHG) takes their risk management very seriously. Read their annual risk report here: https://www.ihgplc.com/en/-/media/ihg/annualreports/2022/our-risk-management-2022.pdf

Common accidents

The work that the housekeeping staff are involved in could easily become an accident-risk if they are careless with equipment and chemical procedures. One of the leading luxury hotel in London identified that the most common cause of accidents while cleaning the guest rooms was for the room attendants to get cut while do polishing the glasses in the room. In response, they stopped this procedure and instead purchased more stock of wine glasses so the room attendants can just replace the used with freshly polished glasses to avoid these accidents.

Another common accident in the guest room occurs while emptying the rubbish bins, as guests sometimes dispose of used needles there, which poses risks to the room attendants. In they do get scratched or pricked by a used needle, the room attendants should be sent straight away to the hospital to for infection and ensure their safety.

Reporting of Injuries Diseases & Dangerous Occurrences regulations 2013

As per the law and RIDDOR regulations, the employer needs to report any occurrences of workplace accidents that causes death, serious injuries or diagnoses of any work-related diseases. A serious, reportable, injury is one that causes the employee to be off work for at least 7 days. If the injury causes incapacitation for between 3 and 7 days it must be recorded by the company. Less serious injuries, or when employees are taken to hospital as a precaution, do not need to be reported.

Dealing with emergencies

Correct training and continual monitoring are necessary to keep both employees and guests safe. The executive housekeeper must write and enforce a health and safety programme that complies with local and federal regulations. Effective health and safety programmes should be designed to prevent accidents, by this means reducing injuries and insurance costs.

Key points to be covered in a comprehensive health and safety programme:

- Setting up a safety committee. Some hotels have an ERT (Emergency Response Team) which comprises of the duty manager, shift engineer, and security manager to ensure safety and security of the staff and guests.
- Safety should be of key concern to the hotel's management as well as its staff and any repeated failure should be handled as a disciplinary problem.
- Each department must encourage a safety-conscious attitude. People in charge can set an example by following safety procedures themselves when operating equipment etc.
- Developing safety training programs
- Enforcing the existing safety rules
- Making sure everyone knows what to do in case of an accident

Fire safety

The fire safety training programme should include safety training and refresher training to be given to all the employees. Safety audits and checks need to be performed by external companies as well as by the internal team. All staff should be trained and given regular fire drills. Everyone needs to be aware of the procedure in case of fire, lthe ocation of all the fire exits and the location of fire points (safe meeting points, where people should assemble after an evacuation). Staff should know the correct type of fire extinguisher to be used in relation to the fire type.

When a massive fire broke out in one of the luxurious 5-star hotels in Knightsbridge in 2018, close to 120 firefighters were sent to the scene. The entire hotel was evacuated in four minutes and there were no casualties. This was impressive and showcased the hotel's exemplary fire safety training.

> **Personal safety**
>
> Some hotels offer panic buttons to their staff to ensure a piece of mind while working.

Lost and Found

Any item that is left unattended by a hotel guest should be stored by the housekeeping department safely until it is claimed and returned to the guest. This procedure showcases the concern and care of the hotel towards the guests' belonging. All the lost items, whether valuable, non-valuable or perishable, need to be recorded in a lost and found register. Care needs to be taken in case of an expensive item like a phone, jewellery, watch, Ipad and similar.

The hotel's property management system should have the facility to add a note on the guest profile about a lost and found item. This ensures quick communication with the front desk. If the guest enquires with the front desk the front desk team can quickly view this note and coordinate the return of the item, ensuring guest satisfaction

Palms

Lost and found form

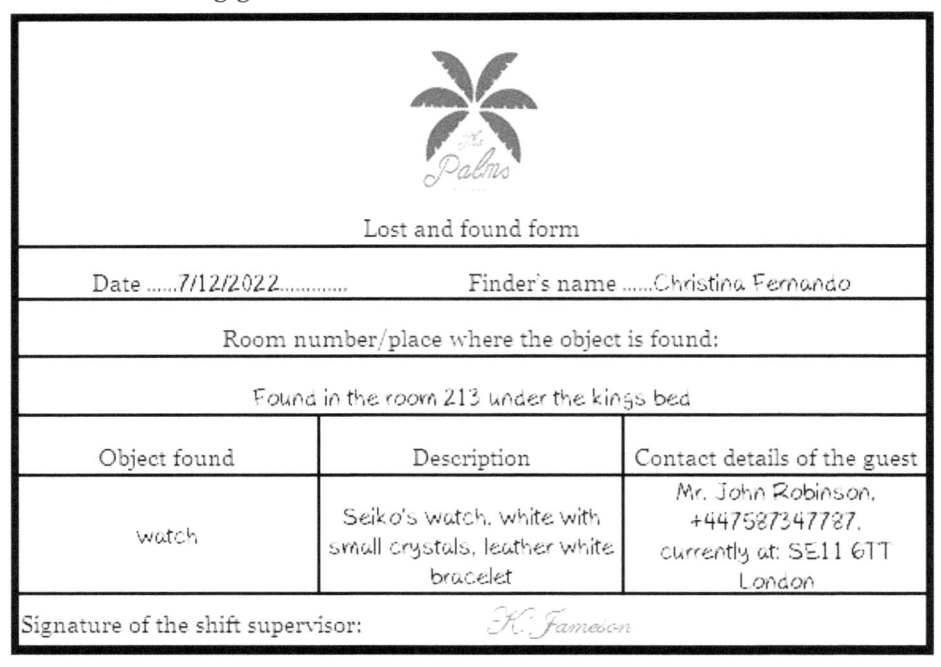

Date ……7/12/2022……………		Finder's name ……Christina Fernando
Room number/place where the object is found:		
Found in the room 213 under the kings bed		
Object found	Description	Contact details of the guest
watch	Seiko's watch, white with small crystals, leather white bracelet	Mr. John Robinson, +447587347787, currently at: SE11 6TT London
Signature of the shift supervisor:	K. Jameson	

Figure 10.4: A typical lost and found form.

Pest control

According to the food safety laws and health and safety laws, hotels have the duty of care to provide a safe environment, free from pests, to the employees and the guests. The housekeeping department is responsible for coordinating the pest control measures between the pest controlling agencies and the various department. It maintains the Pest Control logbook and ensures the necessary pest preventive procedures are followed as per the schedule (monthly/weekly/periodically depending on the area).

Before contracting a pest control agency, the hotel must ensure that the agency's staff are all trained and certified and compliant with all the important legislations like Health & Safety at Work Act 1974, the Control of Substances Hazardous to Health Regulations 2002, Food Safety Act 1990, Control of Pesticides Regulations 1986-97, and Poisons Act 1972.

The pests that need to be controlled include:

- **Insects** that eat textiles, paper, wood and other materials, and that are unsightly and carry disease, like ants, bedbugs, cockroaches, carpet beetle, sliver fishes, wasps, moth etc.
- **Rodents** that eat foodstuffs, but can also damage the wiring and fabric of the building, like rats, mice and squirrels. They are typically removed by poisoning or trapping.
- Birds, especially **pigeons**, whose droppings can cause some serious mess. The control measures for these are normally designed to to stop them nesting in the hotel surroundings. Pigeon proofing can be done with netting deterrents, spiking, trapping, wiring, gel-based deterrents and blocking pigeon nesting areas.

A major consideration in selecting a pest control agency is to ensure that they are conscious about the health, environment and safety while using any of the pest control methods.

> **Find out more about pest control**
>
> You can find out more about the pests that can infest hotels, and some of the techniques of pest control by visiting one of London's leading agencies, Protech. Details at https://www.protechpestsolutions.co.uk

Innovative pest control technology

Modern technological advances and imaginative design have produced some innovative methods of pest control. Here are three examples:

Figure 10.5: Ecolab's thermal enclosure is an inflatable structure that gently raises the temperature throughout the bed and kills any bedbugs.

Figure 10.6: The STEALTH™ Fly Station is an innovative dark, reflective device that uses multiple stimulating characteristics to attract and kill flies. It is best used outside in a strategic position where big flies gather in mass, such as near garbage bins. By eliminating them there, it reduces the number entering the building.

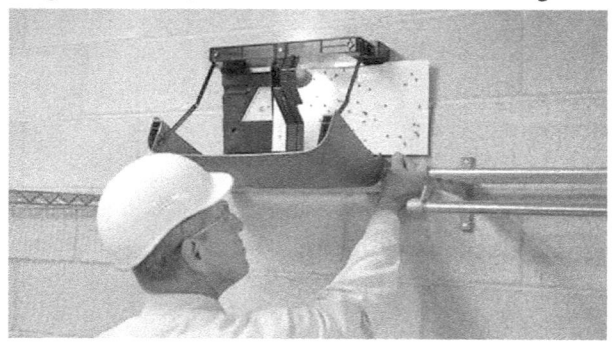

Figure 10.7: The STEALTH™ Fly Light is another non-pesticide innovative design for the interior of the building and uses the LED lamp that attracts the flies, which get glued to the fly trap board. This is a low energy and discrete fly removal technique. It ensures the environment is clean healthy and safe for the employees and guests.

Summary

Safety and security are paramount for the well-being of the hotel staff, guests and the property. The hotel must be have comprehensive safety and security policies and procedures and all necessary safety features, including CCTV monitoring. Training staff and preparing them to respond effectively during emergency situations is critical. Conducting regular safety audits, installing and maintaining safety equipments is essential to mitigate any potential threat or emergency situations. Pest infestations must be prevented if possible or dealt with promptly if they occur.

Activities

1. Select any area in the hotel that the housekeeping department is responsible for (room, or any public area). Identify the risks that might affect it, and what you could do to remove or prevent the threat.

2. Read this case study, adapted from HSE website, and answer the following questions.

The health and safety managers in a hotel decided that they needed to replace an old floor in a kitchen area following several slipping accidents. They decided on a new bespoke epoxy-based floor with an anti-slip surface. The floor was duly laid and sometime afterwards the flooring supplier was asked to visit the site because they were having problems keeping the floor clean. The supplier was surprised to find the floor was stained in various areas and generally didn't look very clean. He discussed the problem with the cleaners who said that the new floor was extremely difficult to clean, was becoming slippery in parts and in fact was damaging their mops. The supplier discovered that the cleaning instructions appropriate to the new floor were not being followed, but they were filed on a shelf in the health and safety manager's office. He asked for a stiff brush and a bucket of warm water with the appropriate amount of cleaning detergent, and then set to work on the floor. He merely swilled the cleaning solution across the floor, leaned on his brush for a few moments and then brushed away the dirty liquid. The supplier explained that if the floor was not cleaned properly, it would lose its slip-resistant properties. The cleaners were amazed to see that, almost immediately, the stains were lifted from the surface and the original floor colour had returned.

1.How this situation could have been avoided. Imagine you were the housekeeping manager at the hotel.

2. What factors do you consider while choosing a floor covering?

3. How do you plan the cleaning regime for the new surface?

3. Why is it important for management to include employees when developing safety programmes? Discuss within your groups.

Key terms

- **Safety**: Is defined as creating an environment and minimising risks where staff and guests can feel protected and secured.
- **Security**: Secuity involves the measures and the precautions taken to mitigate risks, ensure safety and protection of people and property.
- **Crisis management**: Preparation, communication, and decision-making to minimize the negative impact of the crisis and promote recovery.
- **Hazard**: Unsafe condition or a source of danger.
- **OSH Standards**: Occupational Safety and Health standards
- **Job safety analysis**: a procedure which ensures the staff undertaking any task are safe.

References and further reading

Ambardar, A. & Raheja, K. (2017) Occupational safety and health of hotel housekeeping employees: A comparative study', *International Journal of Hospitality & Tourism Systems*, 10(2), 22–31.

Global Secure (n.d.) Accrediation for hotel security. https://www.gsaccreditation.com/services-for-hotels-and-serviced-accommodation/

Global Secure (n.d.) Royal Lancaster Hotel case study. https://www.gsaccreditation.com/royal-lancaster-london/

Wang, M.-H., Chen, Y.-L. & Chiou, W.-K. (2019) Using the OVAKO working posture analysis system in cleaning occupations, *Work*, 64(3), 613–621.

Yap, M.H.T. (2011) Hotel housekeeping occupational stressors in Norway, *Tourism & Hospitality Management*, 17(2), 291–294.

11: Hotel Guest Rooms

> **This chapter will help you to:**
>
> - Understand the various types of hotel guest rooms and designs.
> - Evaluate the layout and design of different categories of rooms and their features.
> - Review the selection and trends in guest room amenities and their role in customer satisfaction.
> - Learn about the impact of Covid-19 on the changing dimensions of customer behaviour.

A good night's sleep is central to guest satisfaction. When customers leave the comfort of their homes and travel, they look for a clean, safe, and comfortable stay, and therefore planning and designing guest room is vital to meet the guest expectation. With globalisation, and people travelling to distant places and different countries for work and for travel, the importance of safety and comfort has grown proportionately.

Types

Hotels have different types of rooms to cater to the different needs and preference of guests. Booking an appropriate room while travelling is the biggest prerequisite for a guest ,and therefore researching a room type that matches the need and budget for a customer is important.

Hotel guest rooms are classified on the following bases:

- Size of the room
- Type of the beds (single, double, queen, twin, king etc)
- Interior of the room
- Number of occupants
- Accessories and amenities in the room

Types of hotel guest rooms

- **Single room**: A small room with a single bed for one person/single occupancy
- **Double room/ Standard room**: Will have a queen or king size bed meant for two people.
- **Twin room**: Will have two single beds separated by a bedside table. Suitable for business travellers sharing a room.
- **Hollywood twin**: Has two single beds joined by a common headboard. Suitable for families with small children.
- **Queen size room**: With a queen size bed suitable for single or double occupancy.
- **King size room**: With king size bed and comfortable for double occupancy.
- **Double-double room**: Usually contain two double beds, can also have queen beds and are suitable for guests travelling with young kids.
- **Quad room**: Designed for four individuals and mostly used by families. Such rooms have two queen size beds.
- **Accessible room**: Designed for guests with special needs. Such rooms have enough space for wheelchairs, furniture is at a lower height. Bathroom design is such that it allows the guests to use them efficiently.
- **Suite room**: Has a spacious living area and a luxurious bedroom. The room is expensive, décor is beautiful and offers a range of excellent amenities. Depending on the size, they can be further classified into *junior* and *presidential* suite rooms in many hotels.
- **Connecting rooms**: Have a connecting door between them, and separate doors from outside. It allows the guests to move freely between the rooms. Suitable for families with young children as well as friends travelling together.
- **Adjoining rooms**: Share the same wall, but do not have a connecting door. Suitable for families with older children who do not require too much supervision.
- **Cabana**: are spectacular rooms overlooking a swimming pool.
- **Lanai**: have a balcony overlooking a beautiful garden.
- **Studio room**: Will have a sofa-bed, with a living area, kitchen and bedroom combined in a one ample space. Suitable for one person.
- **Aparthotels**: Also called *apartment style hotels*, suitable for long stay guests, with a kitchenette for guests to cook their own meals if they wish.

- **Villas**: Found in some luxury hotels/ resorts which are in a natural environment like near mountains, forests. They include a range of luxurious and spacious amenities for the guest's convenience.
- **Executive/club rooms**: These expensive rooms are mostly available in a 4–5-star hotels. The rooms are designed on a particular floor of the hotels and come with additional perks like access to the lounge, meeting space and overlooking scenic view of the city. The facilities and availability of these rooms varies from hotel to hotel.

Design

Hotel guest room design are paramount to the hotel's success as the major revenue is generated from the room sales. It is important to design a guest room to meet the expectations of the customer and provide a home away from home. While selecting a hotel, customers search for the safety, familiarity, and security of their homes. Guest room design has a direct impact on the hotel's ADR (Average Daily Rate), Rev PAR (Revenue Per Available Room) and occupancy rate.

Guest room design acts a factor for establishing price discrimination. The investment in the guest room design is a crucial decision, no matter if the hotel is a budget/economy, upscale/ luxury, resort, or mid-priced. The decision has long term impact, and mistakes can be expensive. Therefore, it requires a longer lead time of planning, developing, and realising. For the successful design planning of a guest room, it is important to identify the user target groups and their needs. The age and gender of the customers is important to consider while planning the colour scheme of the guest rooms, as male guests prefer the rooms decorated in masculine colours like blue, green, and brown, while woman like both masculine/feminine colours like orange, purple, pink, etc. Younger customers prefer contemporary styling while older customers prefer more traditional design.

Market segmentation is the process of splitting the target group based on their similar needs and characteristics. The segmentation can be geographic, demographic, psychographic etc. Researching and understanding what is important for the target groups will enable an optimisation of the guest experience by meeting and exceeding their needs. Therefore, it is pivotal to determine the target market for the hotels. To meet the needs of the evolving breed of customers some international companies have different brands in their portfolio targeting several segments of customers.

Layouts of various types of room

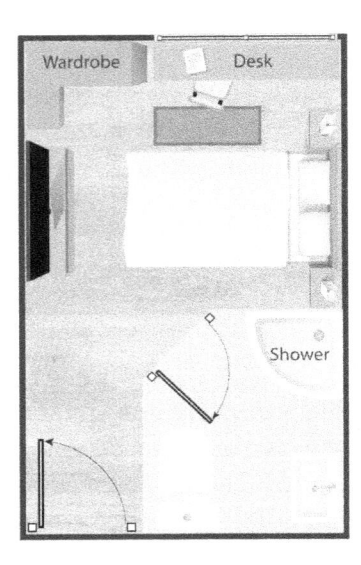

Figure 11.1: Layout of a standard double room (Ibis One Central Dubai)

Figure 11.2: Spacious twin room design (Treehouse Hotels)

Figure 11.3: Standard room with double bed (Park Plaza County Hall London)

11: Hotel Guest Rooms   **157**

Figure 11.4: Hollywood twin room

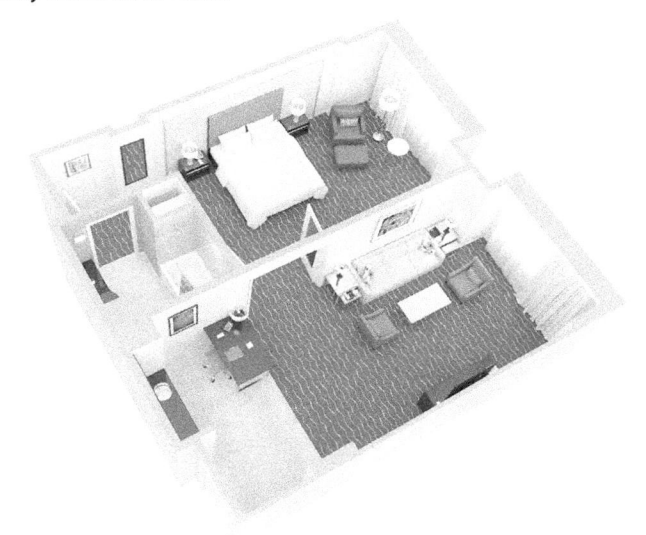

Figure 11.5: Suite Room layout

Figure 11.6: Suite Room layout (Rosewood Hotels, London)

Figure 11.7: Private pool cabana (Ritz Carlton, Florida)

Figure 11.8: Executive floor Lounge- The Langham Hotel, London

Figure 11.9: Villa rooms overlooking scenic beauty (Cntraveller.com)

Trends

Cleanliness

The recent pandemic has reminded us of how critical the housekeeping department is, and has resulted in a new breed of customers – *Generation-Clean*. These customers worry too much about cleanliness, and the moment they check in the hotel, they start to worry about who was the last guest in the room, has the bed and the linen been sanitised, has the room being cleaned and disinfected as per the set standards and the guidance. The psychological impact of Covid-19 is seen in the booking decisions of the hotel guest rooms. The cleanliness of the hotel and the guest room are always the top priority when these customers make booking decisions. The guest expectations concerning the cleanliness and sanitation have elevated and it is quite evident the hotels who will invest in the meticulous cleaning, sanitation and disinfection processes will be ahead of the game.

Cleanliness visibility is another trend, while earlier housekeeping was more a back of the house operation, today the brands are communicating to their guests about their heightened cleanliness and disinfection standards by ensuring the increased visibility of their housekeeping staff. A customer who is constantly watching the safety standards clearly adhered to will have more confidence as "seeing is believing". According to the guest perspective, when they see the elevator call buttons, door handles, surfaces and floors being regularly sanitised and cleaned, it instils a sense of safety and confidence, thus differentiating the brand from their competition.

Technology

Technological adaptation is important for enhancing the customer experience. Irrespective of the hotel size and type of customers, in-room technology for controlling the lighting, music and temperature are greatly valued. Higher end hotels will provide in-room tablets which allows guests to order in-room dining or request housekeeping services at the tap of their finger.

Environmentally friendly

Another popular trend is the use of environmentally friendly design elements such as recycled materials, and locally sourced products with reduced or zero carbon footprints. Hotels have designed sustainable lighting solutions using solar cells to power several LED lights in a lamp with the remaining energy is stored in a battery and used to charge a phone via a USB port. Sensor technology is a lighting strategy to save energy, as this does not rely on the customers to switch off the light when not in use, either in the guest rooms and the communal areas.

Sleep tourism

Another rising trend is sleep tourism, where the primary goal of travel is seeing new places, having adventures, or exploring, but staying at hotels which promise to provide the best eye shut possible for the guests.

Guest room amenities

An amenity is defined as an item given to the guest at no extra cost, but as part of the room charges. Room amenities will include stationary, tea/coffee making facility, slippers, iron and ironing board, and electronic safe; bathroom amenities include shampoo, conditioner, body lotion, soaps, shower cap, pumice stone.

Luxury amenities

Those items that add comfort and ease but are not necessary. They are typically provided by luxury brands and the motive of the providing luxury amenity is connect emotionally with the guest. Examples will include personal care items (like shaving kit, dental kit) toiletries, electronic devices like headphones, hair dryer, coffee machine, massage chair, minibar, massage shower, pillow options (offering down, foam, cotton, hypoallergenic pillows) printers/scanners for business hotels, in-room cocktail station etc. A personalised amenity showcases care and concern for the guests.

Some luxury hotels have customer experience teams who research their incoming guests try to find out the reason for their stay, which enable theme to customise the in-room amenities, thus showing they take pride in knowing their guests. For example, if the hotel knows guests are staying to watch *Frozen* at the theatre, they will ensure they keep some Frozen designed cupcakes in the room. Similarly, if the guest is staying to watch a football match, then an amenity designed to match the colours or the logo of the team the guests are supporting will add the personalised touch. Curating the amenity to match their needs is one way to go above and beyond and create a 'WOW' experience for their guests.

Women value luxury in the feminine room amenities. Careful selection of the amenity will lead to guest satisfaction and helps in achieving the hotel's profitability. Therefore, it is imperative for the hotels to research and understand the target market's perception and willingness to pay while planning the in-room amenities. The range of amenities provided will act a price discriminator (setting up pricing for the room) by hotel brands.

Keeping up with trends

Study of the changing needs of customers is necessary, and some of the amenities are now seen as essential for every customer, despite their age, gender, ethnicity, etc, such as Wi-Fi internet access. Similarly, today the presence of multiple charging point in the rooms is another important amenity as the guests travel with different gadgets and devices. The unavailability of an amenity can lead to guest dissatisfaction.

Some hotels let their guests select their preferred amenity to avoid dissatisfaction. Conrad Hotels offered their guests to choose their personal care bath amenities. They offered three different options for the bath range to choose on arrival and thus the guests had the flexibility to customise their own experience. Changing trends also adds to the preferred amenity in the guest room. The trend of wellness travel and healthy hotels has led to the inclusion of the in-room workout, spa, yoga programs, jogging routes and option of gluten-free and vegan in room menus, etc.

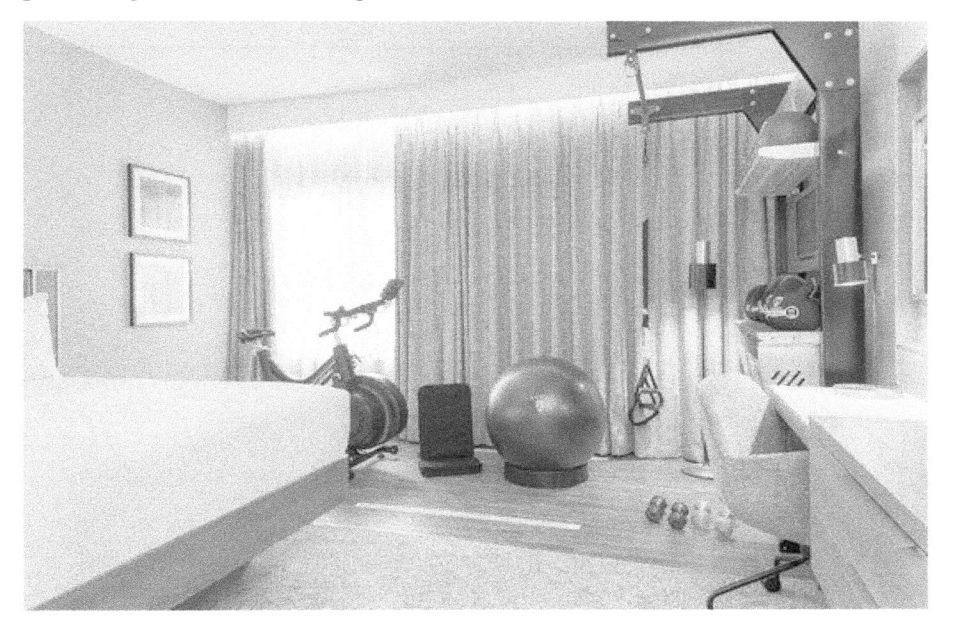

Figure 11.11: Room in Double Tree by Hilton, five feet to fitness: Lifestyle-focused amenities, meant to deliver a full set of flexible services

> **Initial** are suppliers of hygiene and sanitary products and have a signature range of washroom products that have got great functionality and sleek design matching the needs of the hotel. Explore their range and note the uses of their products. Initial can be found at https://www.initial.co.uk

Summary

Careful guest room design and careful amenity selection helps in achieving and enhancing customer satisfaction. Unique amenities can enhance the guest experience, making their stay convenient and comfortable as well as differentiating hotels from their competitions. In the age of social media, a guest who stays in an aesthetically pleasing hotel guest room, surrounded by amenities that add to their convenience and comfort is most likely to leave a positive review, posting pictures of the room and recommending the hotel to their friends and family. Therefore, providing a well-designed hotel room can influence a guests' decision of booking a particular hotel, generate loyal customers, positive word of mouth referrals, enhance customer experience and satisfaction. Welcoming guest feedback, monitoring and adapting trends in hotel guest room design and amenities can play a critical role in generating repeat and loyal customer base and thus making the hotels more profitable.

Individual activity

Research a global international brand and find out:

- The categories of room in their brand portfolio.
- The guest room designs are based on certain themes if yes what are those.
- What considerations about the target market is shown in their guest room design?

Group activity

This group activity will help you to summarise and apply your understanding of design concepts and cleaning principles.

Design a mood board and display a hotel guest room keeping in mind the hotel type (business, leisure) and the customer segmentation (family/tourist /business).

> A mood board is a type of visual presentation or a collage consisting of images, text, and samples of objects in a composition. It can be used to convey a general idea or feeling about a particular topic.

Design considerations

- Type of Hotel – budget, boutique, international hotel chain etc.
- Geographical location of the hotel.

- Target market – business traveller, family/leisure/ elderly /single lady
- Dimension of the room and bathroom depending on the category of room chosen – standard room/suite room
- Layout planning of the room/bathroom – to include all the amenities and in-room facilities provided.
- Furniture/ fixture/furnishings/lighting/colour scheme/flooring/wall covering
- Safety considerations in the guest room – Room features and amenities to enhance the safety and security of the guest.

Cleaning & Maintenance (Cost and ease)

- Briefly explain the daily /periodical annual cleaning schedule planning of the guest room and the bathroom.

Customer experience

- Which innovative housekeeping service or amenities can help to enhance the customer experience. (These needs to be in sync with the hotel type and target market, and should be something unique and creative.

Key terms

- **Down pillows**: Also called duck and goose pillows, made of soft fluffy feathers of duck or swan used for stuffing pillows and cushions.
- **Dust ruffle**: Decorative, pleated floor length skirting around the foot and the sides of the bed. This gives an elegant and luxurious look to the bed.
- **Fixtures**: The hardware items which are fixed in the rooms and cannot be moved easily for example bath fixtures, Water closet (WC) or bathtub etc.
- **Amenities**: These are the items which are given by the hotels at no extra cost to the guests for comfort. For example, bath amenities, turndown amenities (a small gift/chocolates)
- **Guest loan items**: The guest supplies which are not available in the room however they are given on guest request, for example adaptors, sewing kits, iron/ironing boards, cribs/cots etc.

References

Ogle, A. (2009) Making sense of the hotel guestroom, *Journal of Retail & Leisure Property*, 8(3), 159–172. doi:10.1057/rlp.2009.7.

Thomas, C. (2012) Keeping up with guestroom trends, *Hotel Management*, 227(6), 30–33.

Jadallah, R. (2018) *An exploration into how design can better align the attributes of luxury and sustainability for 'high-end' hotel guest rooms*, PhD thesis, De Montfort University. Available at https://ethos.bl.uk/OrderDetails.do?uin=uk.bl.ethos.768228

12: Design and Interior Decoration

This chapter will help you to:

- Understand the basic concepts of design and interior decoration of a guest room and public spaces.
- Review the important considerations in design concepts and planning aesthetics.
- Learn about designing spaces for differently abled guests

Designing spaces in an aesthetically pleasing manner to attract customers requires a great deal of planning and research. Interior *design* looks at the functionality of the room and therefore consideration needs to be given to the end user, that is the targeted customer for whom this is designed. Interior *decoration* looks at the enhancing the appeal and look of the room design, without initiating any changes to the structure, by careful selection of the furnishings, paints, floor covering, wall covering, lighting, furniture and fixtures. etc.

Design considerations

Design follows the story

The most important consideration while designing a hotel is to keep in mind that the design relates to a story, or a theme, can be historical or based on location. Merging the theme in the design helps the customer to have an enhanced experience and offers uniqueness to the hotel. The theme and the story that the hotel or the brand is going to tell the customer should be depicted in thearchitecture, the service offerings like the restaurant food, the wellness options, spa, etc. The theme of the design is narrated in a beautiful story by the marketing and communications team to the guests, helping the customers to connect.

Geographical location

The location of the hotel greatly impacts the exterior and interior planning and design. External elements, like the weather, govern the choice of materials, furnishingsand colour scheme. The position of the sun in relation to the building will decide the positioning of the rooms to make most of the natural lighting.

Functionality and aesthetics of the public area

Focus needs to be given in designing the entrance and positioning it in a way that the guests do not struggle to locate it, otherwise the very first impression of the hotel will be frustrating to the guests. The entrance must relate to the story the brand is depicting. Another important space is the lobby, as many guests love to take a picture in the lobby and share it on their social media platforms. Therefore, the designer should consider creating Instagram moments and refer to some of the architectural guidance on how to create the best hotel space design. The hotel lobby, being the focal point, needs to be tastefully designed, as the pictures posted on social media by the guests help the hotel gain some free marketing and publicity.

Focus and flow of story in guest room design

A guest spend most of their time in the guest room and expects value for money, especially in a luxury or boutique hotels. Therefore, the hotel guest room should focus on the smallest details, while the design ensures that the story is depicted in each element of the guest room: in the comfortable bed for the guest to relax, in the functional and recreational zone where the guest can work and entertain, in the bathroom and even in the storage space.

Environmental impact

Hotels are increasingly showing environmental consciousness in choosing products that are ethically and locally sourced to reduce the carbon footprints. Increasing the energy efficiencies of the operations through design considerations is a must in today's time.

Market segmentation and target market

To get most of the experience from the communal areas of the hotel like lounge, restaurants, bar it is important to bear in mind the segment of the market that the hotel serves, but noting the cultural diversity and different experiences and expectations of customers within that segmeny.

The focus on the branding, aesthetics and functionality of the space helps the customers to gain a top-notch experience.

Unique Selling Point (USP)

A business's unique selling point is an advantage they have that makes them stand out from other businesses within the marketplace. It's what they offer that no one else does, which can vary from more affordable prices to something that's entirely innovative that no other company offers. For example, here are four brands in different segments of the market. Look at what makes them stand out.

Hotel Name	Hotel Type	Unique Selling Point
BANYAN TREE HOTELS & RESORTS	Luxury	Banyan Tree has many exclusive offers and experiences for their guests to enjoy, giving their holiday that extra special touch. Some offers are for special occasions like weddings, anniversaries and honeymoons – perfect for a romantic getaway – whilst others are simply great deals. These experiences included are destination dining (private dinner for 2 in breath-taking locations), private cruises, spa treatments, villa romantic set ups and plenty more.
mantis HOTELS AND ECO ESCAPES	Premium	Mantis focuses on providing an unforgettable experience for their guests with their hotels, eco-lodges and waterways situated in beautiful remote locations where nature is at the heart of the experience. Depending on the location they have different activities, from safaris to all sorts of adventure travel. This is all done sustainably, respecting the environment, as well as the local communities.
Mercure HOTELS	Midscale	Through the hotels' *Discover Local* programme, guests during their stay have an opportunity to learn about the area of their destination through workshops, masterclasses and tastings given by local artisans and entrepreneurs to ensure a richer experience.
JO& JOE	Economy	Jo & Joe youth hostels are spread across the globe in amazing locations. Each hostel has an individual style inspired by the local area, whilst still giving the guests that "home away from home" experience. Affordable, amazing value for money as they have outdoor spaces, bars, restaurants and lounges for guests to enjoy.

Budget

Budget and the finances are the most crucial factors that need to be considered in design consideration. Costs and value for money are key components in the decisions when selecting materials and items. The careful planning of the funding is important to achieve the desired results.

Durability

The selection of material needs to be carefully done to balance the aesthetics, with the expected lifespan and long-term maintenance costs to ensure the selected material is cost-effective.

Health and safety

The materials selected should be fire safe and safe for the guests and staff to operate and use. The surfaces, especially in potentially wet areas should be slip resistant. The acoustics of rooms should be matched to their uses: voices should carry clearly in conference rooms, but not in snug bars, and there must be adequate sound proofing between guest rooms. Clearly visible signages are needed for guest room safety features, hot water, etc.

Cleaning ease and frequency

A new aesthetically designed hotel looks attractive and exuberant to everyone, however the challenge is to ensure that the same look and appearance is maintained for long, as the investment will have been huge. So, materials which are easy to maintain or replace without compromising on the overall aesthetic should be selected. Investing time and research in choosing the right material will show advantages in the long run as they will be less stressful for the staff to clean and will be more hygienic and safer.

Colour schemes

The colour scheme has a great importance in enhancing the overall appeal of the guest room, as customers look at the photo gallery, in addition to the reviews, before booking the room. Selecting the right colour to match the style of the hotel and guest room is vital for the hotel's success. Choice of the right colour tone adds to the entire guest experience. Creating an effective colour scheme is crucial in developing a stress-free environment. Colour can invoke a variety of emotion and provide each room with a sense of identity. Therefore, while choosing colours for a specific area, it is important to understand the market segment, the customers' demography and the experience that is going to be offered.

The bedroom is a space where the guest is going to relax and sleep, therefore the choice of colours should be such that the provide calm, relaxed and peaceful ambience. The bedroom colour is generally more of a neutral shade like white, cream, beige etc. As well as being restful, neutral colours offer the additional benefit that they make the space look larger and they blend well with other colours. Colours like blue and green make the rooms look more peaceful and offer a relaxing experience to the guests. In the room design inspired by love of the environment, the use of green is made to offer a serene and tranquil experience to the guest, connecting with the nature.

Other spaces in the hotel like a bar can be seen use shades of vibrant colours like red, which depicts energy and excitement, and stimulates appetite. The choice of colour for the lobby and reception should be warm and welcoming, but with at least a hint of grandeur, and therefore we see the use of metallic colours in those areas.

Colour is present in the paintings, accessories, furniture and furnishings, and therefore the careful planning of the colour scheme is crucial to the hotel's success.

Lighting

Hotel lighting is important to create the perfect environment for the guest and creating ultimate guest experience. The implications of different lighting techniques can influence the atmosphere, mood, and the illusion of space. A hotel interior, whether it is a lobby, restaurant or a guest room, need to have lighting that adds to the interior of the space, is efficient and enhances the guest experience. Lighting makes the colour of a space more evident and is the best way to highlight the furnishings of the interior. LED lights take little power and generate less radiant heat than the others, but have a high brightness and intensity, as well as an excellent color spectrum.

Table 12.1 illustrates the types of lighting that we will use within a standard room design. The appropriate selection of the lighting can make a space pleasant and welcoming whereas the wrong selection will lead to making the space dark and gloomy. Poor lighting can bring in customer complaints if the reading light or vanity mirror light is not sufficient. Being able to operate the lighting from a single switch panel can add to the convenience of the guests.

Guests often prefer to keep a light in the bathroom on during the night, to avoid any accident which could interfere with their and accompanying guests' sleep. The installation of sensor-based low level floor lighting is a relatively trend, offering improved safety to customers in a new space during the night.

Lighting designs are used in hotels to create special effects. For example, warm lights have relaxing features, therefore they are used in the guest room and the lounges. Hotels can be decorated using different types of LED lighting that comes in varied design and functionalities like floor lights, pendant lights, decorative chandeliers, reading and picture lights, crevice lights etc.

The guest experience starts to be built at the front desk and therefore a guest who checks in at night will feel welcomed by the use of warm lights, whereas the guest arriving in the morning will be impressed if there is sufficient natural bright light.

Location	Type of light	Colour of light
Bedside	Lamp	Yellow
Bedroom	Ceiling light	Yellow
Living room	Pendant light	Yellow
Bathroom	Vanity and ceiling lights	White
Hallway	Ceiling light	Yellow
Walk-in closet	Recessed light	White
Bar	Under cabinet light	White

Table 12.1: Lighting for different spaces

Figure 12.1: Lamp for ambient lighting. Brand: John Lewis & Partners, Colour: Beige,

Figure 12.2: Ceiling Light for ambient lighting. Brand: Plastra, Colour: White

Flooring

Flooring plays an important role in making or breaking the guest experience and therefore suitable care must be exercised while selecting the flooring. Flooring adds to the aesthetic appeal but must be tough enough to withstand the pressure of long working hours, and offer ease of maintenance. For example, acoustic vinyl flooring is a great choice for busy areas like restaurants or bars as this reduces the footfall noise remarkably and has high wear-resistance.

While selecting the flooring care must be taken to see the location in the hotel where it will be used. For example, the flooring for the lobby entrance will be completely different from the flooring for the back of the house or receiving area of the hotel.

Carpet tiles

Carpet tiles in varied colours, design and textures and add beauty to the spaces where used. The tiles are warm, have high acoustic properties and are comfortable on feet.

Luxury vinyl tiles (LVT)

These are more durable and low maintenance floor solutions, with the additional benefit of stain and scratch resistance. LVT usually have a high level of recycled content and therefore offer a more sustainable solution.

Laminate floors

Laminate floors offers a wooden finish look and are great for the bar, restaurant and other guest facing spaces. They are durable and low maintenance floor solutions.

Natural wooden flooring

Well, maintained wooden flooring can last for extended periods. It is hygienic as it does not harbour parasites and has an easy to clean surface. Beige and browns are natural colours that do not cause strain to the eyes.

Marble flooring

Marble flooring is durable and can last for extended periods. It is easy to clean and resists stains, and aids in illuminating the surface and the space where used. In the bathroom, the floor is an integral and crucial part of the design. It should have a visual impact and reflect the hotel's style, but should be non-slip and feel warm and comfortable to the soles of the feet.

Porcelain tiles

Porcelain tile is arguably the best choice for bathroom flooring. It is durable, stylish, and cost effective as it tends to last much longer than other tile varieties. They are as comfortable and convenient as ceramic tiles. Porcelain tiles are water resistant as their water absorption rate is exceptionally low.

Wall covering

The wall covering designs in the hotel guest room can create warmth and set a grandeur vibe in the space where used. But in selecting the wall covering, the design is only one aspect – the choice of materials is also important. The professionals involved in guest room design include architects, contractors, and interior designers, and while selecting the wall covering, they will look at that key operational aspect, the maintenance of the chosen covering.

For example, if the hotel decides to use a hand painted wallpaper, before approving it, the housekeeping department will be given a sample. They will put wine, lipstick, ketchup, crayon, pen, tea, coffee, and other possible stains on the sample and see if it is easy to clean, maintain and replace. Based on the feedback from the housekeeping staff the wallpaper will be adapted and checked again to see if every possible stain can be removed.

While wallpaper is more expensive than paint, a premium quality wipe-clean wallpaper has a far longer lifespan and is much easier to maintain. In the past, the two main reasons for not selecting wallpaper were the patterns and colours become too dated and it does not allow the walls to breathe. However, the new trends in the design are allowing more classic patterns and colours and thus the dating issue can be avoided. Additionally, recent developments in wallcovering design are helping to prevent moisture build up and mould formation.

In bathrooms and wetrooms, wall panels are both practical and aesthetically pleasing.

Points to consider while choosing wallcoverings

- **Durability:** Sculptural finishes and wall-panelling systems can greatly extend the expected life span, resulting in reduction of cost, as well as they create options for branding and featured walls.

- **Antibacterial properties:** Since the design will be in the spaces where the guests can touch them, using materials that have antibacterial properties will be add to hygiene and cleanliness.

- **Low fire ratings:** To tick the box of safety, the material must have low fire ratings compared to classic materials.

- **Non-polluting:** Hoteliers should look for products that are free from PVC (polyvinylchloride), mercury and cadmium, made from recycled content, and emit either low or no VOCs (volatile organic compounds).

- **Nature inspired designs:** Simple, clean, calming, accent colours assisted by lighting offer great natural flowing design options.

Bathroom

In a luxury hotel, the bathroom to a suite should be more than just functional, but should create a feeling of tranquility, space and elegance. Some of the elements that can help to create such an ambience include:

- Italian marble tiles
- A jacuzzi bath with mood lighting
- Shower lighting with water features
- Floor to ceiling window
- Ocea TV (a waterproof, touch-controlled, smart TV that works as a mirror when turned off).

Figure 12.3: Examples of luxury bathroom design. (Top) This is from the Dorchester collection at Heritage Bathrooms. (Below) The Heritage Orford Freestanding Acrylic Bath. Explore their different styles and ranges at https://www.heritagebathrooms.com/collections/dorchester

Figure 12.4: Jacuzzi baths can give a relaxing massage that will be greatly appreciated by the guests at the end of a long journey. Soak up the luxury at https://www.jacuzzi.com/en-gb/bathroom

Planning for differently abled guests

According to the Accessible Hotel Rooms best practice guidelines, it is clear that all hotel operators should meet a target of 10% accessible rooms welcoming differently abled customers. New hotel developments, in addition, should consider guidance provided by Building Regulations (mandatory) and British Standards (advisory).

All accessible rooms in a hotel should have following features as per the Building Regulations.

- **Wheelchair accessibility**: the doors of the main room and bathroom must be wide enough to accommodate a wheelchair.
- **Rational bathroom layout**, which includes level shower, low heigh of the toilet and washbasin etc. Allowing access of the wheelchair.
- Availability of the **handrails** for support in the room and bathroom.
- **Easy to operate** switches, taps and control, multi-sensory alarms and emergency pulls, double height spy hole with wide angle viewer, and card activated locks.
- **Bed height** to allow use of mobile hoists

- **Wardrobe** with adjustable height cloth rails.
- **Allowing choice of essential equipment** like bath board, shower or bath seats and desirable equipment like vibrating alarm clock

> Read about the commitment of Walt Disney World in providing access and accommodation:https://www.disneyholidays.co.uk/walt-disney-world/help/guests-with-disabilities/

Flower arrangements

Flowers enhance the look and appeal of wherever they are used in a hotel be that the hotel lobby, reception desk, banquet tables, spa, or guest rooms. Each hotel is designed in a unique style and to match that the flower arrangers will use their creativity. Some hotels have their own in-house floral experts, while others will rely on specialist firms; in the UK, Moyses Stevens, McQueens Flowers, and Igloo Flowers are three of the major suppliers of flowers to the luxury hotel brands. They offer consultation and design ideas as well as supplying flowers and arrangements for special events, weddings, and conferences. The pictures in Figure 12.5 show some of the excellent flower arrangements at luxury hotels.

The important elements of flower care:

1. When flowers are first delivered, you should cut at least 2 cm off each stem at 45° angle, using a clean sharp knives, scissors or secateurs. Preferably, knives should be used as scissors can close the stem inside when cutting. Once the stem is cut the flowers should be placed in water withiin two minutes otherwise the stem will start drying.
2. The stem needs to be handled carefully, as if it gets crushed the structure will be disturbed, which will prevent water from being absorbed.
3. The vase needs to be filled with fresh water daily, after a good rinse and the flower food needs to mixed gently, one litre of water to one sachet of food.
4. Do not use metal containers as the nutrients in the flower food will be destroyed, and the metal containers will get affected by the oxidants.
5. Do not place flower in direct sunlight, or near ripe fruit as they give off ethylene gas which causes flowers to deteriorate.
6. Flower arrangements that are placed in oasis should be kept moist but not waterlogged and should not be allowed to dry out.

12: Design and Interior Decoration   **177**

Figure 12.5: Floral arrangements by McQueens Flowers, at Claridges (top) and Mandarin Oriental Hyde Park (below)

7 Some flowers, like lilies and berries, leave colour, care must be taken so the stain doesn't come on the fabric.

8 The stem of the flower breathes just like our skin, so it is advisable to clean the 2/3 of the stem.

9 For plants in pots, tepid water should be used as cold water will shock the roots.

Ethereal Blooms

The flower scientists at Ethereal Blooms are using biotechnology to create sustainable long life, natural flowers that have been treated to look and feel fresh for 12 months. They have a unique process whereby the water content is removed and replaced with natural oils. The flowers treated this way are 100% natural and require minimal maintenance.

Details at https://www.etherealblooms.com

Photo: Ruth bouquet from Ethereal Blooms

> **Plants create better places**
>
> Creating a green environment helps to offer a positive and safe place. Indoor plants bring along a lot of benefits, like balancing the humidity levels, controlling dust pollution, absorbing noise and odours, and cooling the surroundings. Plants can also absorb some of the the toxins (like VOCs) emitted by modern buildings and furnishings, thus purifying the indoor air and reducing the minor ailments linked to sick building syndrome, such as coughs, headaches, and fatigue. Biophilic (plant-loving) design in working environments helps to reduce stress, enhance creativity and productivity, and supports overall well-being.

Summary

Hotel design today is greatly influenced by the environmental awareness and sustainability concerns, as well as technological developments and the local geography, climate, culture and heritage. The focus of sustainable design is to ensure the energy is conserved and the functioning is efficient. Adopting design strategies to match the changing trends and consumer demand, is crucial to maintaining the brand image and enhancing revenue growth in today's competitive world. Careful planning and considerations in hotel design needs to be executed to ensure the satisfaction of the end users as well as to meet the financial constraints.

> **Activities**
>
> 1. Carry out in-depth research about carpet and stone flooring and make notes about:
>   a) The types of carpet flooring, their advantages and disadvantages.
>   b) The types of stone flooring, their advantages and disadvantages. Where will you see the stone flooring in the hotel?
> 2. Discuss the latest trends in hotel floor covering and lighting.
> 3. Make a list of different areas of the hotel and suggest the type of flooring that you will use. Provide a brief justification for your choice.

Key terms

- **Inclusive or accessible hotels:** Those which welcome all their guests and have provision to accommodate the needs of the differently abled guests.
- **Biophilia:** A love of the natural world. Biophilic design establishes a link between humans and the natural world which contributes to wellbeing, productivity and health. The designers mainly use organic building materials and maximize the use of daylight and natural ventilation.
- **Boutique hotel:** Also termed *design* or *lifestyle* hotels depicting exquisite and interesting design in their architectural innovation as well as unique interiors. For example, The Ritz in Paris, Savoy in London.
- **Atmosphere/ Ambiance**: The mood of a place, created partly by the design, but includes its sounds, scents, emotions and interaction.

References and further reading

Magnini, V.P. & Zehrer, A. (2021) Subconscious influences on perceived cleanliness in hospitality settings, *International Journal of Hospitality Management*, 94, 102761. https://doi.org/10.1016/j.ijhm.2020.102761.

Penner, R., Adams, L. & Rutes, W. (2013) *Hotel Design, Planning and Development*. 2nd edn. Taylor and Francis.

Plunkett, D. & Reid, O. (2013) *Detail in Contemporary Hotel Design*. Laurence King.

Tieng, S. (2019) *Hotel Design, Planning and Development.* Society Publishing.

Useful links

Access to and Use of Buildings, 2004 ODPM https://www.gov.uk/government/publications/access-to-and-use-of-buildings-approved-document-m

Accessible hotels in London, https://www.london.gov.uk/sites/default/files/gla_migrate_files_destination/archives/accessible-hotels-draft-BPG.pdf

British Standard 8300:2009 Design of buildings and their approaches to meet the needs of disabled people - Code of Practice http://www.acornironmongery.com/dda/Guide%20to%20standards%20BS%2083000.pdf

13: Ecotels

This chapter will help you to:

- Understand the concept of sustainable hospitality and the nature of environmental management systems.
- Review the important certifications and environmental considerations.
- Learn about the environmental initiatives of some of the international hotel brands.

Environmental considerations

The primary goal of luxury hotels is to give their visitors the best possible service in the most comfortable environment. Reaching the necessary high standards in, for example, heating, cooling, lighting, ventilation, cleaning, and laundry means that they have very high levels of energy and water use. The hospitality sector has historically had a dramatic environmental impact through energy and water consumption, use of consumable and durable goods, and solid and hazardous waste creation.

That is changing as hotels try to become more eco-friendly and make their operations more sustainable.

- **Eco-friendly** can be defined as actions taken to reduce detrimental environmental effects.
- **Sustainability** can be defined as adopting holistic policies and measures to reduce adverse effects on the physical, social, and natural environments. The World Commission on Environment and Development (1987) defines it as *"fulfilling current demands without jeopardising future generations' ability to meet their own needs"*.

Because the public's perception of global warming is changing rapidly, the tourism sector must quickly change to green practices using new technologies and intense employee training. Environmentally responsible hotel management includes solid waste management (e.g. waste reduction and recycling) and natural resource (e.g. water and energy) conservation.

Sustainability refers to an ecosystem's ability to retain its core functions and processes, and to retain the balance between activities and the supportive environment in which they interact without negatively influencing one another. Standard practices associated with sustainability in the hospitality industry include:

- reducing water and energy consumption by implementing energy-saving technological systems and renewable energy,
- reducing plastics, especially in packaging and disposable items,
- food wastage management,
- using products made from recycled material and which are recyclable,
- a responsible purchasing policy,
- carbon emission control, and
- responsible consumption.

When it comes to being sustainable in the tourism and hospitality businesses, a well-known term is "green hotels". Green innovation has emerged since the late 1990s, looking to safeguard the environment and the local communities – protecting nature and honouring cultural diversities. Nowadays, being green is crucial to tackling the environmental emergency to preserving the planet's resources. In addition, adherence to green practices within hotels is becoming increasingly popular and a fundamental requirement to remain competitive within the market.

There are two main approaches to environmental management: **reactive** and **proactive**. A reactive approach covers the strategies used to respond to external pressures, whereas the proactive approach covers strategies that are voluntary responses for reducing the environmental impact. Guests' attention has considerably moved towards sustainability and environmental issues, and there is a trend for people to orientate towards environmentally friendly products and services. Sustainability has been adopted by the big chain hotels because they want to show their respect and support towards the environment in different methods throughout the hotel departments.

Most housekeeping departments have adopted green cleaning methods, and hotels have chosen to go with environmentally friendly chemicals such as products made from plant fibres, products that are hypoallergenic, dye-free, and fragrance-free. Some luxury hotels have achieved the commitment of no longer having single-use plastic items, and for this the guest room amenities like toothpaste in a tube has been replaced by toothpaste tablets; shaving foam comes in a soap form which can be rubbed to make foam, plastic water bottles have been replaced by glass bottles and are refilled from the water station.

> Read about toothpaste tablets here: https://parlatoothpastetabs.com

Some hotels have adapted each product to such an extent that even a little plastic ring in the bag of the vacuum cleaner had to be changed by the respective supplier to support this goal of the hotels. The products are strictly rejected by the more committed hotels if the suppliers fail to replace plastic components either in the packaging or in the manufacture. Going plastic-free is a long-term project and it takes close to 5-7 years to adapt every single product and process to make them plastic-free. Luxury hotel chains are showing the proactive approach which shows positive impact on the environmental competitiveness.

Reusing and recycling

Earlier environmental strategies involved the **3 Rs** – Reduce, Reuse/Repair and Recycle). Today strategies include **Upcycling** – transforming waste into material – to further minimise the waste of resources.

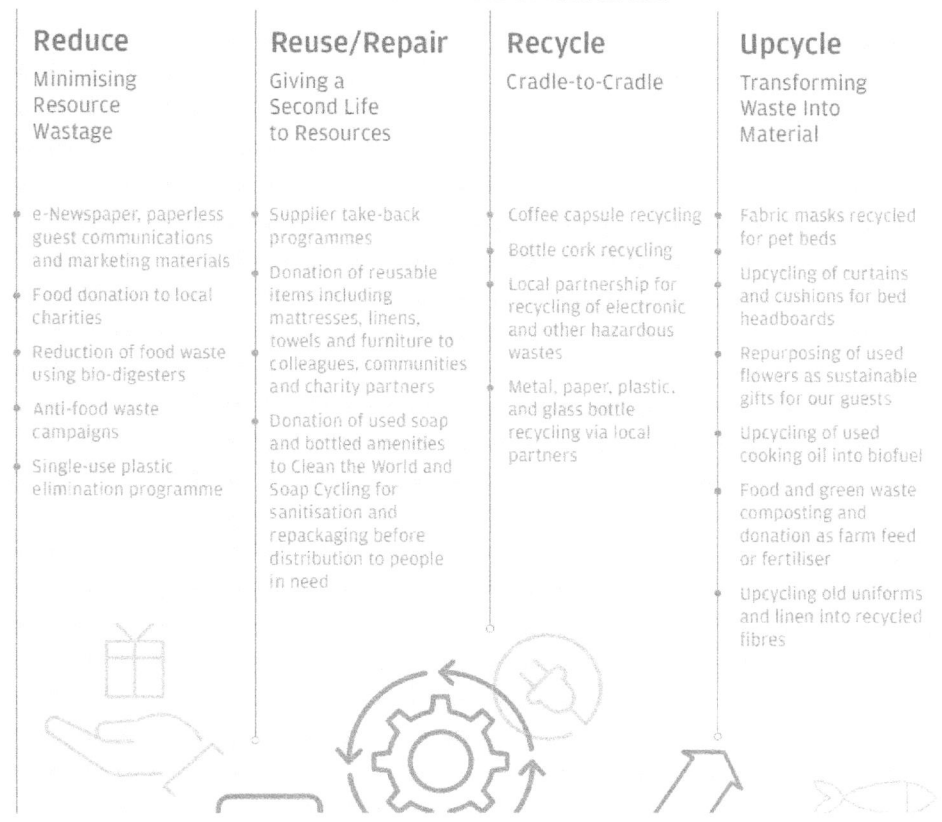

Reduce	Reuse/Repair	Recycle	Upcycle
Minimising Resource Wastage	Giving a Second Life to Resources	Cradle-to-Cradle	Transforming Waste Into Material
• e-Newspaper, paperless guest communications and marketing materials
• Food donation to local charities
• Reduction of food waste using bio-digesters
• Anti-food waste campaigns
• Single-use plastic elimination programme	• Supplier take-back programmes
• Donation of reusable items including mattresses, linens, towels and furniture to colleagues, communities and charity partners
• Donation of used soap and bottled amenities to Clean the World and Soap Cycling for sanitisation and repackaging before distribution to people in need	• Coffee capsule recycling
• Bottle cork recycling
• Local partnership for recycling of electronic and other hazardous wastes
• Metal, paper, plastic, and glass bottle recycling via local partners	• Fabric masks recycled for pet beds
• Upcycling of curtains and cushions for bed headboards
• Repurposing of used flowers as sustainable gifts for our guests
• Upcycling of used cooking oil into biofuel
• Food and green waste composting and donation as farm feed or fertiliser
• Upcycling old uniforms and linen into recycled fibres

Figure 13.1: Environmental strategies

Reusing differs from **recycling** in that recycling breaks down an item into its basic parts and makes new products out of them, but reusing an item keeps the material in its original form and uses the item repeatedly for the same or different purposes. For example, sustainable wall coverings: newspapers, coconut fibres as well as glass fibres can be recycled to produce green wall covering options. Using material such as pre-used Italian marbles helps the hotels to receive LEED certification.

Ecolabel certification schemes

- **Green Globe** is the global leader in sustainable tourism certification. Find out more at: www.greenglobe.com

- **LEED** (Leadership in Energy and Environmental Design) is the most widely used and best recognized green building rating system in the world. It is run by the US Green Building Council. Find out more at: www.usgbc.org/leed

- **Green Key** is a leading standard of excellence in the field of environmental responsibility and sustainable operation within the tourism industry. It is based in Copenhagen. Find out more at: https://www.greenkey.global

- **ISO** (International Standards Organization) was established in 1947 and sets quality standards for many things, including ISO 14063 on *Environmental management*. Find out more at: https://www.iso.org/news/ref2500.html

- **EU Ecolabel** is the official European Union voluntary label for environmental excellence and certifies products with an independently-verified low environmental impact.

- **Earth Check** is an Australian based worldwide certification scheme benchmarking sustainability schemes in hospitality and other industries.

- **Green Leaders** is the TripAdvisor's badge that showcases green initiatives in hotels. This is not an accreditation scheme, but does give a measure of hotels' environmental commitment.

Waste management

In the United Kingdom, the Environmental Protection Act 1990 regulates the management of waste and control of emissions into the environment. Section 34 of the statute imposes a Duty of Care on importers, producers, carriers, keepers, treaters or disposers of controlled waste to prevent unauthorised or harmful activities. All commercial and industrial organisations must hire licenced waste carriers to store and dispose of rubbish appropriately and safely. The act five key actions:

- decide to waste less;
- buy with eco-intelligence;
- use well to generate much less trash;
- repurpose waste ingredients; and
- segregate and recycle waste.

Practical steps for housekeeping

Different actions can be incorporated into daily operations to minimise harmful environmental effects. These include using recyclable materials such as paper and cloth; fitting refillable dispensers and recycling containers for both employees and customers in common areas and rooms alike; removing all disposables, such as paper napkins and plastic cups.

The hotel should follow an eco-procurement/purchasing policy, choosing products and services that have minimum negative impact, and undertaking a thorough environmental impact analysis of those products and services, from cradle to grave. This will involve tracing the origin of the raw materials, assessing the manufacturing process for any toxins and pollutants produced, assessing the packaging, transportation method and impact on the environment while using a product, and finally considering the disposal of the item and its packaging after use. Few hotels will have the staff capability to do this kind of environmental impact analysis in-house, but buying from certified suppliers means that the impact analysis will have been done upstream for you.

Sustainable Hospitality Alliance

The vision of the Sustainable Hospitality Alliance is responsible hospitality for a better world. It brings together engaged hospitality companies and uses the collective power of the industry – 270 brands and 50,000 hotels – to deliver impact locally and on a global scale. Find out more at: https://sustainablehospitalityalliance.org

Benefits of recycling in the hospitality industry

1. Environmental impact
Recycling prevents materials ending up in landfill. Some materials, such as plastic can take up to 450 years to decompose, others, such as glass, paper, steel and aluminium can be valuable raw materials for industries.

2. Cost effective
Reducing waste through recycling will have a positive impact on your business's waste disposal costs. It is often cheaper to organise the collection of recyclable material than it is of general waste.

3. Positive company image
As well as saving your business money and reducing your carbon footprint, recycling and sustainability will promote a positive company image.

According to a survey done by Booking.com, 70% of the travellers mentioned they check if the hotel is environment friendly or not before proceeding to book. The eco-friendly practices entail:

- Reduction in the amount of water and plastics being used.
- The products that are purchased are sustainably manufactured and packaged.
- Using cleaning products that are more environmentally friendly
- Careful monitoring of energy usage
- Introducing more opportunities to reduce, recycle and reuse.

> **Bottle alternatives**
>
> The individual amenity bottles in the guest bathroom for shampoo, conditioners and body wash add up to a humungous plastic waste. By installing reusable dispensers in the bathroom, hotels can eliminate this plastic waste. The use of glass water bottles in the guest room will also aid in reducing the pollution generated using single plastic. Most of the luxury hotel brands have switched to these sustainable and environmentally friendly options.

Energy conservation

Energy conservation is an important element of an EMS (Environmental Management system). Some of the energy saving initiatives include better training of hotel staff, making them aware of the actions that waste energy; installing energy efficient equipment; utilisation of renewable energy sources; and efficient building design to maximise the use of the natural lighting.

To reduce energy use, some strategies include motion sensor-controlled lighting throughout the hotel; intelligent HVAC (Heating Ventilation Air Conditioning) systems; efficient glazing designed to maximize solar gain where warmth is needed, or to reduce heat build-up where this is a problem. Simply cleaning bulbs and reflecting surfaces regularly will maximise the lightning efficiency. Passive building techniques involve efficient insulation with a ventilation system that allows heat exchange and recovery, using the thermal mass of the materials in the building, and setting the building's orientation to get the most natural lighting and heat.

Carrying out regular energy audits and purchasing green energy, by referring to the local/regional companies' information on sourcing renewable energy, will enhance the energy management of the hotels.

Water saving systems

Investment in water saving technologies and developing water efficiency and water management programmes are essential to quantify the use of water. Water recycling system (using recycled grey water from laundry) and rainwater harvesting, highly efficient showerheads, premixed hot water, faucet aerators, and toilet dual flushing systems are all great ways to reduce the potential consumption of water. A low flow water-saving systems could be integrated into bathrooms, toilets, sinks, and showers. In addition, bio-toilets, low-energy consumable products, reusing greywater and practising proper sanitation habits are ways to reduce water use. This approach brings significant environmental and economic benefits.

Case study

A leading hotel brand avoided nearly 8 million plastic bottles a year. They noted that plastic water bottles are one of the most heavily used single-use plastic items in a hotel. They replaced plastic bottles with either glass or aluminium bottles across all operational areas from restaurants and bars, meeting venues, guestrooms, spa and fitness areas, to airport-hotel transfer vehicles and back-of-house areas. Over one third of their hotels implemented in-house water bottling, using premium water from quality water filtration systems such as Nordaq and Natura. Bottling their water in-house helps to cut the plastic waste and transportation footprint associated with transporting water bottles.

Ethical sourcing of the uniform

To comply to sustainable business practices, hotels should ensure they procure uniforms from suppliers who are compliant with sustainability guidelines and follow these principles throughout their supply chain. Identity and traceability certification, such as that by Oeko-Tex, ensures awareness of the origins and the footprints of the materials, and endorses environmentally friendly and socially responsible production of textiles and the uniforms. If the garments are produced locally, this will reduce the overall carbon footprint.

The ethical and ecological initiatives followed by hotel brands are supported by the leading uniform suppliers, who constantly refine their initiatives, processes, and materials to achieve a first-class sustainable approach.

MADE IN GREEN by OEKO-TEX®

This is a traceable product label for products that have been "manufactured using environmentally friendly processes and under socially responsible working conditions". Find out more at: www.oeko-tex.com/en/our-standards/oeko-tex-made-in-green

Points for achieving sustainability goals while designing uniform:
- A design that allows a greater range of staff to fit fewer garment sizes will reduce the quantity of unused stock.
- The uniform suppliers should have the technical expertise to calculate accurately the usage of the fabric, based on the staffing numbers, leaving zero surplus fabric and thus eliminating the wastage.
- Using high quality fabrics to make the robust uniforms will allow the uniforms to be used for longer duration, as they will withstand the rigorous working environment.
- Responsible sourcing ensures that the raw materials used for the uniforms can be recycled and consume less water to manufacture.
- Reduce the carbon footprint by minimising the transportation by ensuring the proximity of the factory and the fabrics, and consolidating shipments to keep air freight to a minimum.
- Regular audits of the factories where the uniforms are manufactured to ensure good working conditions, fair salaries for the staff, in-house recycling, wastewater treatment plant and use of renewable power if possible.

- Check if the factories are Bluesign approved. The bluesign® system checks for eco-friendly and resposible production practices across the entire textile value chain to reduce impact on people and the planet.
- Look for responsible packaging that uses recycled polybags or FSC (Forest Stewardship Council Certified) approved paper bags.

Pro-environmental behaviours (PEB)

These refer to behaviours that create little or no harm to the environment or even benefit it. PEB in the workplace refers to all voluntary actions that individuals take to be more environmentally friendly, such as double side printing, utilising recyclable materials, turning off lights when not in use, using reusable dining utensils, recycling, and conserving. PEB from employees are how they execute their work obligations in an ecologically sustainable manner.

PEB are determined by the individual's own decision, even if support mechanisms exist from the organisation or society. There are three types of workplaces PEB. Information-seeking, program-starting, and environmental activism are examples of these behaviours.

- The first type of behaviour is employees' attempts to learn about an organisation's sustainable policies and procedures.
- The second type of behaviour concerns how employees behave at work, such as reducing waste, power, and water use and improving paper usage and ecological norms.
- The third kind includes people's efforts to promote environmental information within their organisations.

These sustainable behaviours benefit businesses. First, the environmental challenges attract the interest of many stakeholders and have financial ramifications; second, they are essential for both nature and humanity's long-term existence; and last, waste minimisation and resource conservation are crucial because of the Earth's limited resources.

Employees' pro-environmental conduct at work may be influenced indirectly (via organisational identity) by the company's CSR (Corporate Social Responsibility) policy. Employees' CSR perceptions influence the appeal of their organisation's internal and external reputation since it adds to workers' self-identification and meets their self-enhancement demands. Improved job performance is aided by successful environmental efficiency.

Environmental management systems (EMS)

An EMS provides firms with practical direction on how to concurrently establish, develop, and analyse their business processes to achieve corporate and environmental goals. Organisations engage in routine procedures to mitigate environmental damage as part of sustainability strategies. Sustainable practices entail taking management activities to keep resources safe and secure and implementing operational strategies that benefit the environment. As part of an EMS, it can also assist hotels in lowering their operating expenses.

International hotel brand initiatives

Encouraging Sustainable thinking that is allowing the guests to opt for the Eco-friendly programmes and encouraging guests to request pitcher of water during turndown service, placement of recycling bins in the rooms and the option to skip daily changing of linen and towel in the room. Most of the hotel brands communicate this on the website saying, "Bed linens and towels are laundered every three days which deviates from the standard daily change. "The challenge the luxury hotels face is to make these programmes visible to the guests while not burdening the guests who pay premium prices for their stay at the five-star hotels. Hotels are encouraging their employees and customer to use the environment conscious transportation and provides on-site bike storage facilities.

Accor

Accor is dedicated to long-term sustainable value creation and actively particiapates in giving back to the environment and community. They are doing this through their Planet 21 Acting Here programme. Their aim is to steer a change towards 'Positive Hospitality'. Their mission is to:

- Be an inclusive company and ensure the welfare of our people
- Encourage our guests to act as multipliers of the positive effects of our actions
- Establish a lasting relationship with our partners, who share our commitments and are working with us to produce innovative solutions that have a positive impact
- Work hand-in-hand with local communities, because our commitment does not end at the hotel door
- Provide healthy and sustainable food, with a ban on food waste
- Move towards carbon-neutral buildings

(Accor, 2023)

Fairmont Hotels and Resorts

The Green Partnership Programme of this international hotel chain sets out its practices and policies to reduce the environmental impact and to increase their engagement with local communities. As most of their properties are in the unique environments like national parks and bioreserves, they have many opportunities to initiate their environmental programme.

Hilton Hotels

Hilton call their ESG (Environmental, Social and Governance) strategy *Travel with Purpose* and its aim is to redefine and advance sustainable travel globally. They have committed to increasing their positive social impact and significantly reducing their environmental footprint by 2030.

Find out more at: https://esg.hilton.com/our-approach/

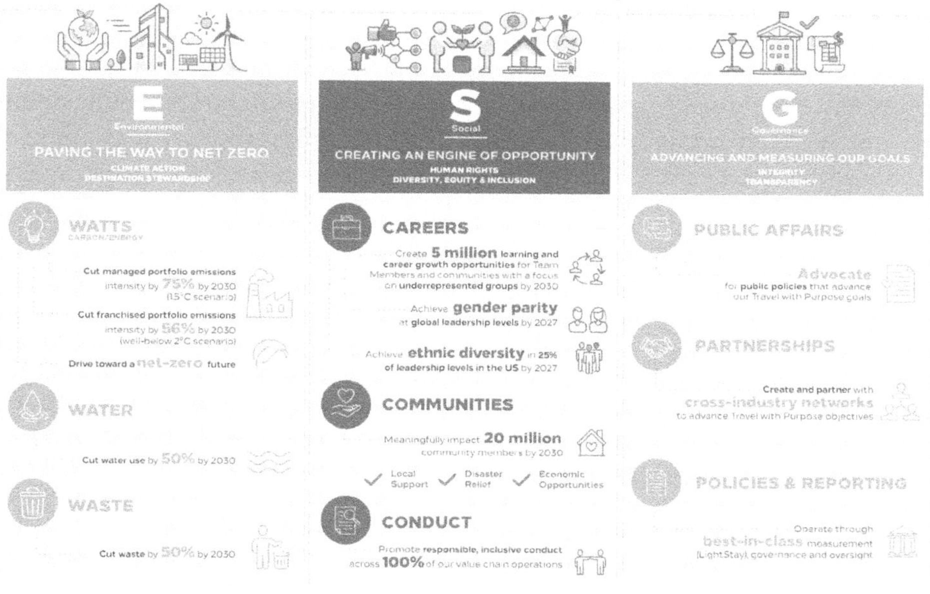

Figure 13.2: Hilton's ESG strategy summed up on a placement

Sustainability post Covid-19

In wake of Covid-19, most hotels are aiming to act more sustainably and help create a meaningful change around the world. Some are focussing on encouraging consumers to make small changes in the ways they behave, for together they can make a big difference, and this can be done in ways to improve the guest's experience. The larger hotel chains have recognised the need to combat climate change and have accepted their corporate responsibility to reduce their carbon footprint.

Since Covid-19, Hilton have committed to doubling their investment to combat their social impact and to cut their environmental footprint by half throughout their hospitality chain, by 2030. (Details can be read at https://esg.hilton.com/toward2030/)

> Several hotel groups ran a "Make a Green Choice" scheme, with incentives for guests who choose not to have daily housekeeping during their stay. Some people thought the scheme was more about reducing housekeeping staffing and costs than helping the environment. During the pandemic, most hotels only provided daily service on request, with a deep clean between stays. The scheme has now largely disappeared.

Summary

Hotels today are trying to become more eco-friendly and make their operations more sustainable. A reactive approach to environmental management covers the strategies used to respond to external pressures, whereas a proactive approach has strategies that are voluntary responses for reducing the environmental impact. There are essentially four key environmental strategies Reduce, Reuse/Repair, Recycle and Upcycle.

Employees who are more aware of sustainability in the workplace are more likely to use sustainable practices and concepts in their job. Internal restrictions, such as a lack of skills, experience, and lack of training, explain employees' unawareness and non-engagement with sustainable practices. Therefore, keeping employees involved and updated regularly will enhance their interest in the topic and consequently positively influence the hotel's environmental footprint.

> **Activities**
>
> 1. Discuss in groups the advantages and disadvantages of environmental policies for the hotel, guests, and other stakeholders (suppliers, government, owners).
> 2. Think of some ways that making a green choice is environmentally and economically beneficial for the hotel brand. Why have such programmes lost their significance post-pandemic? Are there any limitations of sustainable initiatives adopted by hotel brands.
> 3. Read the CSR report of the Oetker Collection and summarise their ethical and sustainable practices. Find the report at www.oetkercollection.com/media/41875/ungc-oetker-collection-csr-report.pdf

Key terms

- **Biodegradable plastic**: Plastic that breaks down in a defined period through a composting process.

- **Green hotel**: Environmentally friendly hotel working on programmes to save water, energy, reduce waste and protect the environment.

- **LEED**: Leadership in Energy and Environmental Design. The world's most widely used green building certification.

- **UNEP**: United Nations Environmental Program is a global authority in the environment focusing on climate, nature, pollution and sustainable development. There are 12 sustainable goals set by UNEP.

- **Green wash**: the act of misleading customers regarding the environmental practices of a firm or environmental benefits of a product.

- **Green organisational culture**: The intersection of environmental consciousness and shared values, norms, attitudes, experiences, beliefs, artefacts, and standards among employees in an organisation, as represented in the obligation or determination to be environmentally friendly.

- **Corporate Social Responsibility (CSR)**: A management concept in which business incorporate social and environmental issues into their operations and interactions with stakeholders.

- **Environmentally sustainable policies and practices**: are defined as fundamental ideas, rules, and practises developed to assist an organisation in achieving its environmental management objectives.

References and further reading

Accor (2023) Positive Hospitality: Acting Here. https://group.accor.com/en/commitment/positive-hospitality/acting-here

Ha, M.-T. (2022) Greenwash and green brand equity: The mediating role of green brand image, green satisfaction, and green trust, and the moderating role of green concern, *PLoS ONE*, 17(11), 1–24. doi:10.1371/journal.pone.0277421.

Jaykumar, P. (2020) The triumphs & challenges in the path of green hotel housekeeping, *Journal of Services Research*, 20(1), 21–37.

TUI (n.d.) *Plastic Reduction Guidelines for Hotels*, https://www.tuigroup.com/damfiles/default/downloads/plastic_reduction_guide.pdf-2f4f4f0e2278382f-cd50d9a530985b84.pdf

Untaru, E., Ispas, A. and Han, H. (2020) Exploring the synergy between customer home-based and hotel-based water consumption and conservation behaviors: An empirical approach, *Journal of Consumer Behaviour*, 19(6), 542–555. doi:10.1002/cb.1826.

World Commission on Environment and Development (1987) Our Common Future. http://www.un-documents.net/our-common-future.pdf

Yusof, N.A.M. & Soelar, S.A. (2021) A quantitative case study on customers' expectations of hotel green marketing, *Asia-Pacific Journal of Innovation in Hospitality & Tourism*, 10(3), 447–462.

14: Changing Trends in Hotel Housekeeping

This chapter will help you to:

- Understand the changing trends in hotel guest room and bathroom design.
- Learn about the impact of Covid-19 on the hotel housekeeping operation and international hotel brands' initiatives.
- Review the changing dimensions of customer behaviour and the role of the housekeeping department.

The hotel industry is constantly evolving and adopting new trends to meet the expectation of the customer. The housekeeping department's role is critical in creating customer satisfaction, and therefore to keep up with the changing world and customer behaviour, traditional housekeeping has evolved in a new era of housekeeping. If hotels are to stay ahead in the business, they need to keep up with the trends that lead to more efficient processes, and follow the best practice guidelines.

This chapter will highlight some of the trends and innovation in guest room design, and the amenities offered to the guest for convenience and to meet changing needs. Among the key changes are the enhanced use of technology and equipment to counter the impact of virus and offer a safe environment to guests and employees. The operational implications of the changing cleaning protocols, and the adaptation of processes in various international hotel brands are discussed.

Design

Good design attracts customers and enriches their guest experience by adding value to the facility's aesthetics and enhancing the visual appearance. But design should be geared to match the tastes and needs of the type of customers that the hotel sees as its key market segments.

Wellness

A significant segment of customers travelling today are looking for an overall wellness experience and therefore the hotel brands are constantly innovating their in-room design, amenities, and products to meet their needs and provide them with a holistic wellness experience. Some of the common healthy design considerations are biophilia, energising lighting, air purification system, exercising facilities, yoga space, vitamin infused shower water, healthy minibar amenities and fresh menu options. Several hotel brands some or all of the above features, either in the room or elsewhere in the hotel, to offer a peaceful and resting experience, impacting the psychological wellbeing of the guests.

Circadian lighting

Circadian lighting is designed to people's internal 24-hour clock. This is controlled by the brain's response to the quality of light, releasing more melatonin – which makes us sleepy – when it gets dark. Circadian lighting is possible because the brightness and colour of LED lighting can be adjusted in different ways.

- With **intensity tuning**, the colour remains the same, but the fixtures have a dimming system, set to low intensity in the early morning and evening, and reaching a high intensity in the middle of the day.
- With **colour tuning**, the intensity and colour are changed through the day to mimic the natural light and colour cycle. .

Biophilic design

This includes natural elements like the use of natural light, and having plants in the room interior, to help establish a connection with the nature, as this results in enhancing the mood and rejuvenating the mind, body, and soul.

Eco-conscious design

Incorporating energy efficient products in the room design is another important trend, for example triple glazed windows offer efficient insulation and greatly reduce the energy requirements, as well as reducing external noise. Blackout window shades offer better sleep. A new design trend is called the 'dual-purpose building', which combining a hotel and a business space into one. This offers a premium working environment for the guests as well as saves the energy of the hotel from being wasted during the day due to the building being only partially occupied.

> When luxury hotel brands are planning new hotels or renovating existing ones, they get the specialists in to work on the design. **Humble Arnold Associates** is one of the leading kitchen, foodservice and back of house design consultancies. They incorporate the latest trends in the design considering the health and the wellness of the customers, and assist with sizing, storage and operational service strategies for housekeeping, laundry, and food services in line with the global and regional practices. Find out more at https://www.humblearnold.com

Design considerations post-Covid

Post Covid-19, guestrooms are typically being made larger, to allow space for sleeping, working, dining, and even exercising. Some hotel brands are even exploring the options of in-room gym facilities for the customers. Corridors are also tending to be built wider to make movement easier while avoiding contamination. In post-Covid design, room collateral will become outdated in favour of digital apps. Handles of door, elevator buttons, bathroom flushes, and electrical switches will all be replaced by sensor or gesture-controlled technology.

Maintaining social distance is projected to become a fundamental component in the design and layout of conference and event rooms soon. Due to normal meeting density, demand is expected to take longer to recover. As a result, the adaptability and multi-purpose usage of such venues, as well as the development of enhanced AV technologies that allow virtual conferences to work alongside and complement actual events, will become increasingly important. Open kitchens, non-intrusive, decorative screens, and more quiet booths in lobbies, cafes, and eating areas come to mind.

Re-designing hotels post-Covid-19 will demand a significant increase of outside, natural space, whether on ground floor open patios or rooftop lounges and bars. There is no doubting that visitors want more outside spaces and activities that will make them feel psychologically secure. The future design of hotels will focus on more circulation space in the public areas and the guest rooms, and will incorporate more environmentally conscious features like the use of sunlight and fresh air.

It is paramount to pay attention while designing, redesigning, or renovating hotel that the materials and the products that are purchased are cleanable and can withstand the disinfection. Less porous surface are easier to clean and repel germs. While selecting the materials for the soft furnishings care needs to be taken and the materials that are difficult to clean and attracts microbes should not be purchased.

In many hotels, the guest rooms are now clutter-free, meaning the beds have no extra cushions or runners, which ensures the guest hygiene while taking the pressure to maintain them from the hotels. The concept of luxury is evolving and now less is seen as more hygienic and safes.

Guestrooms and public areas will be cleaned, sterilized, and disinfected using hospital-grade chemicals and electrostatic cleaning routines. As a visible reminder of the new cleaning schedule, seals will be put on guestroom doors. As we have already seen earlier in this book, some brands are already doing these things in their revised protocols. While pools and spas are among the first areas in hotels where guests express concern due to the pandemic, they are likely to be the safest spaces if properly maintained with correct hygiene practices, as chlorinated pools and disinfected spa waters will inactivate the virus, posing a lower danger than direct client contact.

The way in which we now use space has already been adapted to reflect the impact of the pandemic, but architects and interior architects must continue too keep it in mind as they work on new hotel designs. We will also have to consider how many guests can safely use a space, while maintaining social distancing, and the type of materials that we select for indoor and outdoor furniture, and the surfaces for hotel bathrooms, bedrooms and public areas. It would be highly advisable to replace carpets in reception and guest common areas with hard flooring as it can be more hygienically cleaned.

Amenities

Going digital for greater safety and convenience

Digital apps are taking over from room collaterals – printed menus, notices, brochures and information sheets – which in some places can build up to a big pile of paper. But the in-room tablets don't just give information, they also allow better and safer communication with the hotel staff, reducing contact and avoiding the spread of virus. In-room dining menus are replaced by QR codes in most hotels, to access the in room dining menus from the guest rooms. These thoughtful in-room digital amenities are focused on safety and wellbeing, giving spatial flexibility, invisible service, cleanliness in style and protection. For example, at Hilton hotels, guests will be able to scan a barcode and see all the high touch areas and the way their room was cleaned by housekeeping.

Using a dedicated app on a smartphone, at many hotels now, guests can avoid queuing at the front desk to check-in and get a physical key, but go straight to the room and unlock it with a digital key.

Sustainability and wellbeing

In-room amenities that are eco-friendly and designed to de-stress are gaining more popularity as the customers are aligning more towards health and wellbeing. Keeping this trend in mind, more hotels are procuring soaps, lotions, shampoos etc that are 100% natural and are sourced from sustainable producers only.

Sustainability in room amenities is another big trend like straws made from rice flour or from avocado pits, and canvas laundry bags. Wooden keys and cardboard pens are next level of innovative environmental amenities adopted by fully sustainable hotel brands.

Style and luxury does not have to be sacrificed for sustainability, as these examples show.

Figure 14.1: Do Not Disturb signage for the hotel made of wood, by Bulgari

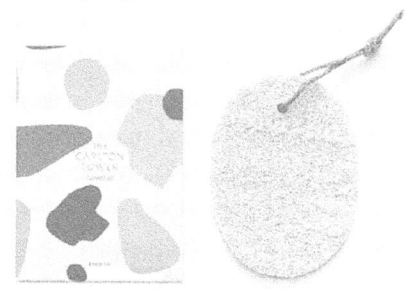

Figure 14.2: An eco-friendly loofah packed in a paper bag for the bathroom amenity, for the Carlton Tower at Jumelrah

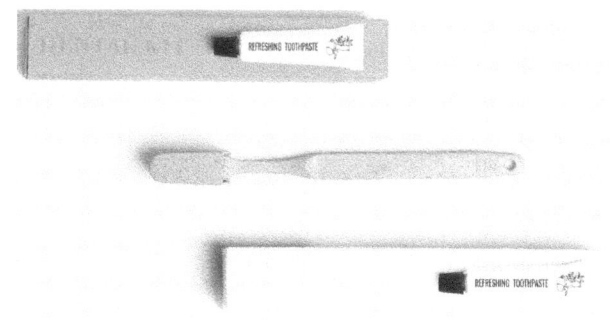

Figure 14.3: La Bottega specialises in eco-friendly products for the bathroom, including dry amenities in cardboard and stone paper, soaps and shampoos in solid form. Find out more at (https://www.labottega.com

> Palatino designs amenities for the luxury hospitality sector, tailored to match the aesthetics of the hotel, using the materials preferred by the clients. Their eco-friendly options, identified by the Terra Stamp, are made from the sustainable and ethically produced materials like organic cotton, bamboo, cork, FSC paper, FSC wood, vegan leather etc. Find out more at http://www.palatinogroup.com/terra.

Creating unique experiences

Many firms cater to the hotel industry, supplying products and services to enable you to create unique experiences for your guests. Here are some to consider – but remember that in this fast-moving business, new ideas are constantly arising, so it is important to keep up with the trends.

- Smart Room designs comes with a "mood creator" since everything is customisable, the guest can choose two mood settings:
    - *Classic*: piano music starts playing on the TV and a scent of lavender is sprayed in the room and ambient lights change every minute.
    - *London feeling*: a selection of teas and biscuits are automatically ordered from the housekeeping; a sophisticated aroma from Penhaligon's is sprayed into the room and on the TV will be playing a collage with the main attractions which are reachable by foot.
- Many hotels now offer a **pillow menu**. For example, at the Montcalm in London, guests can choose from:
    - *Hypo allergenic* pillows filled with 100% cotton fibre balls;
    - *Anti-aging* pillows is fitted with a special cover treated with zitamin E that helps prevent skin aging.
    - *Manly magic* pillows are firmer, with 55% goose feather inside and 45% goose down outside.
    - *Ladies' dainty delight* pillows are filled with goose down, designed for those who sleep lightly.
    - *Shape your sleep* memory pillows mould to your shape, offering perfect neck support.
    - The *ecological pillow* offers aromatherapy in an eco-friendly pillow.
- **Customised room fragrance**: An important element of the experience when the guests enter the hotel lobby and their room is the aroma. Before arrival, guests can pre-order the scent they want for their room from the fragrance wheel selection.

- **I-Music pillows**, with a built-in speaker that can be connected to a smartphone or iPad. The sound is transmitted through the ear when resting on the pillow.
- Smart beds and smart mattresses can revolutionize the way we sleep. They can manage the temperature to keep it comfortable, adjust the firmness, and angle to optimize sleep and even communicate with the blinds to open or close them and lights to switch them on and off, in response to the guest's movement.

Figure 14.4: The Hastens adjustable bed is probably the most luxurious of its kind, with its 1400 spring pockets mattress. Their *Restore* app has a range of carefully selected audios to improve sleep quality.

Guest room amenities post Covid-19

There have been considerable changes in the guest supplies and amenities, in response to the Covid-19 pandemic. The main ones are summarised here:
- Wherever possible hotels are changing the in-room collateral and amenities like pen and pad and directories to digital options using in-room tablet or QR codes.
- Unused disposable amenities, if any, should be disposed off on departure to avoid cross contamination. Amenities like trays, stationary, decorative pillows and remotes should be removed to eliminate the contact from the surfaces through which virus can spread.
- Paper-wrapped amenities like dental kits or shaving kits, which were common in all rooms, are now provided on request as the guests may not be comfortable using the one already lying in the room.
- A care kit of disinfectant wipes, face masks and hand sanitisers to be available for guests as a part of the amenities.
- Minibars should be cleared as a guest leaves, and restocked with fresh items in the room to avoid cross contamination.

- For the environmental and economic benefits instead of single use plastics dispensed amenities are prioritised.
- It is also a good idea to include pamphlets in the guest room detailing the steps taken to maintain the room's hygiene and guest's health.

Processes

The post-Covid-19 era has required the housekeeping department to upgrade its cleaning techniques and practices. In this regard, innovative housekeeping products can make the tasks of the staff less cumbersome and lessen the time consumed for cleaning the rooms and other areas.

Cleanliness theatre

In the wake of the recent pandemic most hotel brands revamped their cleaning protocols to ensure the utmost safety of the guests and the staff. However, these needed to be broadcast to restore the guest confidence and meet the guest expectation. Therefore, the hotel brands came up with the strategy to communicate about their cleaning and safety protocols through newsletters and the short videos which showcase the initiatives taken by the hotel to offer a safe and secure stay to their guests. *'Cleanliness theatre'* – being seen to clean – is also very important, so they scheduled more staff in the public area during the daytime to ensure the high touchpoints are constantly addressed, and installed sanitisation stations in the public areas and the corridors and set staff to refill and check these regularly while being visible to the guests. Thus, addressing the safety as well as the psychological needs of the guests.

Optimising cleaning workflows

Workflow automation is significant in improving the productivity of the housekeeping staff, and can reduce the time spent on repetitive tasks by 50%. In the wake of a renewed influx of guests, workflow automation could be crucial in optimising the operations and communications and meeting targets, with an effective update of tasks in terms of cleaning and sanitising the rooms, andproviding room service to meet the customers' expectation.

Some hotels are adopting digital solutions which embed the real-time workflow for each of the housekeeping staff to keep them in line with the existing and new targets. In this regard, the hospitality technology solutions will help to upgrade housekeeping practices with new protocols of cleaning. The software may be part of a broader package covering many aspects of hotel operations, such as that from Nuvola, or specific to housekeeping, such as CLEANTracker.

> **Nuvola's** hotel service optimization and guest engagement software includes a housekeeping module which facilitates any SOP (Standard Operating Procedure) that is required to be fulfilled by the housekeeping departments ranging from simple tasks of security walkthroughs and daily line-ups to complex tasks such as room inspections, deep cleanings etc. Details at https://www.sabrehospitality.com/solutions/nuvola/
>
> Creating Revolutions has launched **CLEANtracker** technology, which monitors housekeeping staff in real-time to ensure that cleaning protocols and processes have been followed. This has an accomplished through fitting NFC (near field communication) chips on or near all high touchpoints. These communicate with a wrist-strap device worn by the staff. An AI system notes how much time is spent near each chip and compares this with past performance and set protocols, to assess whether the cleaning job has been done properly. It provides proof for the guests that the rooms have been cleaned and sanitised. Details at https://www.creatingrevolutions.com/cleantracker-technology/

Steam cleaning

This new innovative method of cleaning is being adopted by some hotels as it is more sustainable and greener than standard methods of sanitising. It has a higher initial cost however there are no ongoing chemical costs and is safer for the environment as well the wellbeing of the staff. It can clean floors, carpets, furniture, walls etc using cold steam and high pressure.

Steam cleaners vary. Some, like the Delphin, are easily portable; others, like the Vapodil, are much heavier; some offer 'dry steam' – more heat and less water so that surfaces dry very quickly; some have wet/dry vacuuming capability. All can:

- Sanitise the guest room, bathroom and all its fixtures
- Kill bed bugs and their eggs in the mattresses
- Shift stubborn stains from carpets and fabrics
- Clean mould off the grout between tiles
- Clean AC vents and other hard to reach places
- Refresh pillows, cushions, curtains, duvets by removing dirt and odours

And do these without using chemicals, leaving a room dry and ready for re-use very quickly.

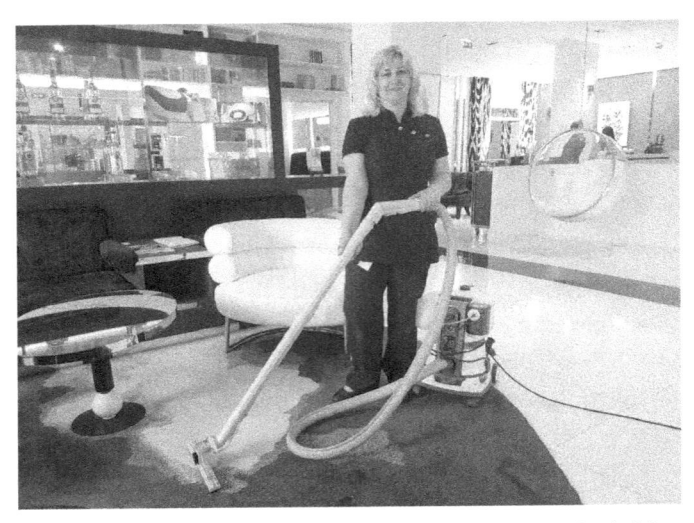

Figure 14.5: The Delphin steam cleaner is designed for use in the lobby and other public spaces.

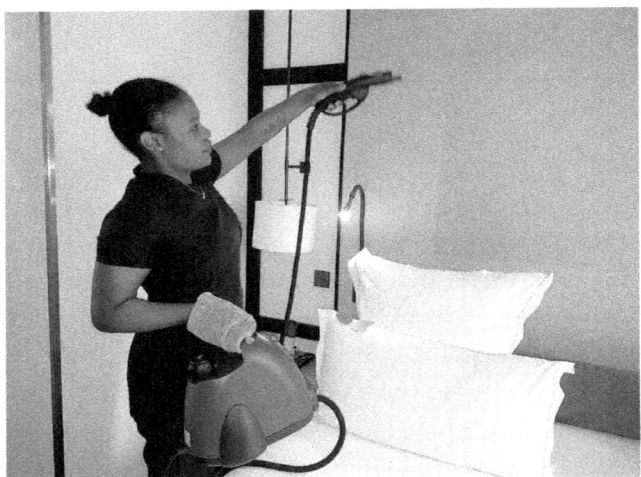

Figure 14.6: The Vapodil is used in conjunction with micro-fibre cloths to lift away the dirt after steaming furniture, fittings, walls and windows. A pipe and head can be added for floor cleaning. Details at www.vapodil.com.

> Hotels can now acquire second-generation electrostatic sprayers that disinfect with immediate effectiveness. The spray is given an electrostatic charge that helps the disinfectant to stick on surfaces providing thorough coverage. Various health organizations recommended its use to sanitise high-touch surfaces quickly and efficiently.

How hotel brands have responded

Marriott

The Marriott Cleanliness Council programme is aimed to enhance disinfection across the hotel and to deliver a holistic approach designed to keep guests and associates safe. The company uses electrostatic sprayers and is implementing ultraviolet light technology used to sanitize keys for guests and equipment shared by co-workers.

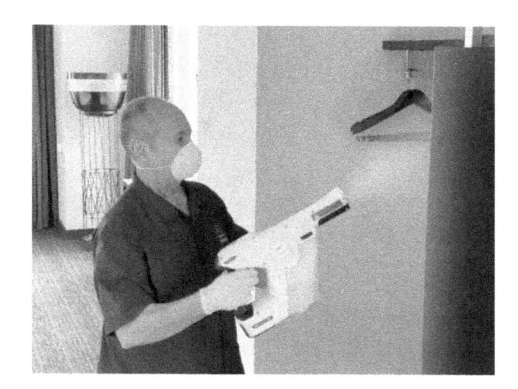

Figure 14.7: Disinfecting surfaces with an electrostatic sprayer.

During the pandemic, Marriott offered guests 500 points on their company loyalty for every day that guests would agree to not have their linen changed, which would be good for the environment but also relieve the pressure on scarce staff time. The initiative was shut down last year. Details of their programme at https://clean.marriott.com/

Hilton

Hilton introduced a cleaning programme called Clean Stay, in collaboration with Reckitt Benckiser. As part of this, it prevents the possibility of contamination in the rooms by disinfecting the most frequently touched areas and applying a seal in the door once the room has been cleaned. Hilton increased the number and visibility of public area employees to guarantee a high-level hygiene in communal areas, such as elevators, lobbies and gyms. Details can be found at https://www.hiltongrandvacations.com/en/cleanstay, but note that the website does not respond properly on all browsers.

Hyatt Hotels

Hyatt Hotel and Resorts announced their Global Care and Cleanliness Programme aiming at "Safety First, Wellbeing Always". This includes:

- Cleanliness accreditation process through Global Bio Risk Advisory Council https://gbac.issa.com/gbac-star-facility-accreditation/
- Trained Hygiene and Wellbeing Leaders at all Hyatt Hotels who are responsible for ensuring enhanced protocols at operational levels.
- Working with trusted medical experts from the Cleveland Clinic.

Details at: www.hyatt.com/info/global-care-and-cleanliness-commitment

Hyatt have recently adopted new cleaning devices that ensure enhanced air quality and less hassle for the housekeeping. Ozone air purifiers were already available on the market, but it could take up to 45 minutes for them to effectively purify the viruses and bacteria from the air in a room. The latest machines take only about 15 minutes to do the job.

Four Seasons Hotels and Resorts

Four Seasons Hotels and Resorts worked with Johns Hopkins Medicine International to devise their health, safety, and security program. In addition to enhanced ventilation and cleaning, improved and focussed employee training, Four Seasons also offers an app for contactless service, and offers masks, sanitisers and – a special touch – portable HEPA air purifiers for guest rooms. Details of their Four Seasons Lead with Care programme can be found at https://www.fourseasons.com/leadwithcare/

ACCOR

ACCOR developed its new hygiene and cleanliness programme under the title AllSafe. It then partnered with a leading French certification company, Bureau Veritas, who audited the group's protocols and practices against its strict requirements before awarding its the Safeguard label.

Details of the Safeguard label can be found at https://certification.bureauveritas.com/certification/safeguard-label

For more on Allsafe, visit: https://all.accor.com/event/allsafe.en.shtml

Intercontinental Hotel Group

IHG redefined its cleanliness to enhance the customer experience and meet the changing consumer needs by their 'IHG Clean Promise' programme. This was developed in partnership with the world leaders in hygiene and cleaning – Cleveland Clinic, Ecolab & Diversey. The program has protocols which is adopted globally to deliver utmost hygiene and safety to the guests.

Details at: https://www.ihg.com/content/gb/en/customer-care/clean-promise

Or for an illustrated guide, read their Stay with Confidence brochure. Download from https://www.ihgplc.com/en/-/media/ihg-way-of-clean_guest-journey.pdf

Ergonomics

Ergonomics is the study of workplace design, equipment, machines and tools, considering the employees' physical and psychological capacities to ensure their safety and security. Improved ergonomic conditions enhance productivity, reduce uncomfortable awkward body postures – bending, twisting, crouching, or kneeling. The risk of musculoskeletal disorder is highest in the hotel housekeeping employee as the job involves repetitive physical labour. There are risks associated with the tasks which can go unnoticed. The luxurious mattresses in the hotel guest rooms that offer comfort and an enhanced experience to the guests are resulting in an increased injury rates to the housekeeping room attendants due to increased strain when lifting while making beds. Other housekeeping tasks performed by the room attendants with higher ergonomic-related injury risks are dusting, polishing, vacuuming carpets, washing windows and walls, bathroom and fixtures cleaning, moving furniture etc.

It is important to assess the physical risks associated with commonly performed housekeeping tasks, and to look for ways to reduce them. By undertaking ergonomic analysis and offering recommendations in terms of lighter tools, different lengths/adjustable handles, and ergonomically focussed training, the physical strain of cleaning tasks on the staff can be greatly reduced. Sometimes simple tools can make a great deal of difference.

Mattress lift tool

This tool reduces the lifting requirement while making the hotel beds. It raises the edge of the mattress allowing the room attendants to tuck in the sheets and the comforter. The use of mattress lifts tool results in reduced strain on the muscle and the spine as well the time required to make beds, thus the productivity is increased.

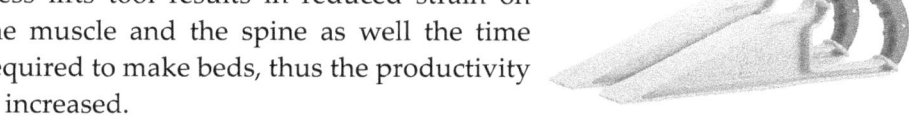

Innovative mobile cart

The traditional maid's cart is heavy and can result in workplace injurys. It also takes a lot of space in the guest corridor. In the latest stylishly designed hotels, placing a maid's cart in the corridor blocks the hallway and detracts from its appearance. A hotel with large inventory requires many trolleys to have enough for each section on the guest floors. During high occupancy when the hotel turnaround is higher, the number of trolleys will result in damage to the walls in the corridors, as the room attendants need to maintain their speed and productivity.

A compact easy to move cart will help to ensure workplace health and safety for the housekeepers. Rubbermaid's suitcase-style Quick carts are compact for easy transport and can be wheeled easily inside the rooms. The supplies and the equipment are stored in an arm's reach in the cart which can be manoeuvred quickly and discreetly. Thus, the hotel hallways look tidy, and the guests do not witness any dirty linen pile or trash while moving in the corridor. The intelligent design also saves back-and-forth movement of the housekeeping staff thus enhancing the productivity as everything it within reach. All the amenities can be saved in the different compartments efficiently and a caddy can be detached and carried into the bathroom for cleaning.

Figure 14.8: Quick carts are a neat and efficient alternative to traditional maid's carts. https://rubbermaidproducts.co.uk/rubbermaid-quick-cart-large/

Occupational health and safety of laundry staff

Poor work organisation and ergonomic problems at workplaces contribute to the rising risks in the occupational health and safety (OHS) problems. Laundry employees are exposed to several critical factors like injuries, accidents, work postures, chemicals, heat, noise, fire etc. and the increase in air temperature and high humidity elevate workplace heat stress and create poor climatic conditions for the workers. Therefore the understanding and application of ergonomic practices is extremely important for the health, safety and performance of the employees during the laundry operations. Hotels must exercise mandatory employee training regarding OHS and procure laundry equipment with those features that help to reduce the work stress by taking care of the right postures and safety. Regular audits to check the effectiveness of OHS practices will ensure the health and safety of laundry employees.

> **Consumer needs post Covid-19**
>
> While COVID 19 has drastically changed every aspect of society, it has also set new standards and norms in the housekeeping department. Specifically raising the sanitary concerns of the people who regularly check-in and check-out of hotels. Following the change in the needs of the consumers, most hospitality businesses have adopted newer technological and management solutions, causing a paradigm shift in the role of housekeeping, both for consumers and for businesses. This paradigm shift is visible in the form of focus of consumers shifting from luxurious food and utilities, to safe and virus free hotels, where they can rest their mind, body, and soul.

Summary

Recent trends in hotel housekeeping have been impacted by the Covid-19 pandemic. This has led to changes in the design of hotels, to greater emphasis on well-being, to increased use of technology and to enhanced cleaning regimes.

Covid-19 has changed the hotel industry significantly and hotels have had to adapt through changes in their operational plan, including new training and improved sanitization methods. These new plans include an increasing shift towards technology to keep the hospitality industry safe for guests and gain customer trust. The role of the housekeeping department has gained extra importance and investing in high quality sanitization equipment has become a priority. These changes and extra protocols are a result of a changing customer expectation that prioritize cleanliness when choosing where to stay. Despite the pandemic causing many challenges in the hotel's previous operational plans, hotels have come up with many innovative technological and systematic ideas to overcome them.

> **Activities**
>
> 1. Research some of the design considerations adopted by major hotels brands to provide an enhanced wellbeing and fitness experience for their guests.
>
> 2. Think about the unique products and amenities you will offer in your guest room for wellbeing travellers and name your concept room. For example, Vitality room by Swissotel Hotels & Resorts. What will be your future room be called?

3. Read this HSE guide on *Ergonomics and human factor at work* and briefly explain what factors need to be considered to ensure health and safety in housekeeping departments. https://www.hse.gov.uk/pubns/indg90.pdf

4. Pick up a housekeeping task and mention the ergonomic intervention that needs to be made to the task to avoid the injury risks. You can suggest any innovative design, equipment, technology that is useful.

Key terms

- **Ergonomics**: The psychological and physiological relationship of human beings to machines and equipment. Ergonomics make sure the tasks, equipment and environment fit with each staff member.

- **Ergonomics intervention**: Reorganising the work process to reduce and eliminate the dangers and promote a healthy work environment.

- **Musculoskeletal disorders**: Include injuries affecting back, legs and joints mostly caused and made worse due to poor work conditions. Read details at https://www.hse.gov.uk/msd/msds.htm

- **Occupational accidents/diseases**: Injuries or illnesses that occurs to an employee while performing their duties at work. Details at https://www.hse.gov.uk/riddor/occupational-diseases.htm

- **Occupational Safety and Health Administration**: OSHA ensures safe and healthly work conditions for employees by setting standards, training, and education. Details at https://www.osha.gov/

References and further reading

Ambardar, A. (2015) Occupational safety and health of laundry employees in hotel industry, *International Journal of Hospitality & Tourism Systems*, 8(1), 32–39. doi:10.21863/ijhts/2015.8.1.005.

Chan, J., Gao, Y. and McGinley, S. (2021) Updates in service standards in hotels: how COVID-19 changed operations, *International Journal of Contemporary Hospitality Management*, 33(5), 1668–1687. doi:10.1108/IJCHM-09-2020-1013.

Jayanti, J. (2020) *Hotel Industry Welcome Back Strategy Review*, Institute of Hospitality. Available at: https://www.instituteofhospitality.org/hotel-industry-welcome-back-strategy-review/

Jiménez-Barreto, J., Loureiro, S., Braun, E., Sthapit, E. & Zenker, S. (2021), Use numbers not words! Communicating hotels' cleaning programs for COVID-19 from the brand perspective, *International Journal of Hospitality Management*, 94, 102-872.

Kim, J.J. & Han, H. (2022) Saving the hotel industry: Strategic response to the COVID-19 pandemic, hotel selection analysis, and customer retention, *International Journal of Hospitality Management*, 102. doi:10.1016/j.ijhm.2022.103163.

Pillai, S.G., Haldorai, K., Seo, W.S. & Kim, W.G., (2021). Covid-19 and hospitality 5.0: Redefining hospitality operations. *International Journal of Hospitality Management*, 94, 102869.

Magnini, V.P. & Zehrer, A. (2021) Subconscious influences on perceived cleanliness in hospitality settings, *International Journal of Hospitality Management*, 94. doi:10.1016/j.ijhm.2020.102761.

15: Technology in the Housekeeping Department

This chapter will help you to:

- Understand the importance of deploying intelligent rooms division technology.
- Evaluate the latest technology used in the housekeeping department.
- Review the role of technology in the post Covid-19 world.

The leading housekeeping departments have adopted world class technology in recent times to offer seamless service to the guests. Housekeeping is the largest payroll, labour-intensive and task-driven department and is critically responsible for a positive guest experience. In the competitive world, hotels are seeking digital transformation to offer their guests innovative services. The housekeeping operation is complex and often changes with the changing needs and expectations of the guests. Technology can greatly support housekeepers and ensure the operation is simplified and streamlined to give effective service delivery. E-housekeeping has brought all the housekeeping operations and other related tasks to a touch of a button at our fingertips.

The impact of COVID-19 has developed strong technological advancement in the hospitality industry. Hotels are spending in systems and technology that help automate procedures, save costs, and improve the guest experience.

Software and apps

The adoption of housekeeping management software impacts the overall revenue by speeding up the process, thus lowering the cost and resulting in improved guest experience. The key to success in today's competitive environment is observation, innovation, and adaptation. Software adds value to the service from the room assignment to the room check, and real time room status notifications, and it allows access from employees at all the levels.

Communication between the departments has become quicker, smoother and quieter, as staff do not need to speak to co-ordinate. The additional benefit this software has brought is accounting for the productivity of the room attendant and other housekeeping staff, as it records the time spent in cleaning or inspecting a guest room.

Integration of PMS with other software

A property management system (PMS) is used by most of the hotels to manage their day-to-day operations and activities. While the core of the PMS is concerned with front-office operations, such as reservations, check-in/checkout, room assignment, managing room rates, and billing, the potential of a PMS can be magnified once it is integrated with the other systems and software. The PMS most commonly used by luxury hotels is Opera developed by Oracle Hospitality. (https://www.oracle.com/uk/hospitality/)

Some of the common integrations are:

1 **Integration with channel managers**: Two-way integration between the PMS and channel managers like online travel agents, Global distribution system and metasearch channels, allows automatic updates of the inventory, thus saving time and improving accuracy.

2 **Integration with payment gateways**: Today most transactions are done through credit cards. A payment gateway integration with the PMS allows the automatic posting of the transactions which saves time, and ensures enhanced security in the online booking system.

3 **Integration with the room locks**: A room access solution is integrated with the PMS which makes the check-in seamless and contactless as the key is encoded while registering the guest.

4 **Integration with the point of sale** (POS) allows for the task to be completed in a real-time, reducing administrative tasks (compared to a manual system), reducing discrepancies, avoiding customer dissatisfaction, and preventing loss of revenue.

5 **Integration with the Revenue Management System** (RMS) results in better inventory and pricing control, and forecasting. Thus, the integration of the two allows enhanced efficiency and revenue.

6 **Integration with the messaging system** allows hotel and guests to communicate instantly and the guest experience throughout their journey is made more efficient.

Housekeeping management software

Technological advances have provided automated solutions to hotel housekeeping operations. As a hotel operation is 24/7, a digital transformation allows faster room turnaround, helps in speedy addressing of the guest requests, and can combine the IoT and operations, for example motion sensors in the public areas can send notifications when an extra round of cleaning is required during busy times. Thus, enhancing the efficiency and effectiveness of the housekeeping operation.

Housekeeping software helps in streamlining housekeeping tasks to enhance the guest satisfaction and empower the staff. Features include:

- Daily cleaning tasks are automated with a real-time overview of room statuses, reducing the paperwork.
- Tasks are prioritised ensuring utmost guest satisfaction (arrivals, guest requests).

> FCS Solutions claim that implementation of their housekeeping software can significantly reduce the time needed: 30% reduction for housekeeping staff, 25% for non-housekeeping staff, and a huge 75% of the time spent on administration. Other software solutions show similar time-savings.

- Staff receive alerts regarding the rooms on privacy as well as rooms requesting service.
- Quick and efficient communication between the room attendant and the floor supervisor – once the attendant completes cleaning of the room and updates it in the app, notification reaches to the supervisor that the room is ready for inspection.
- Live updates of rooms ready for check-in thus ensuring the guests are not made to wait.
- Efficient guest complaints handling by identifying the trends in the complaints, such as recurring issues, areas of improvement for the staff and flawed procedures. If a guest complains, a new incident case is created where the details are recorded. The duty manager receives the notification about it, takes quick action and service recovery is executed, ensuring that the guest experience is not compromised.
- Better forecasting of required levels of manpower, linen, amenity, and other inventories.
- Performance tracking by digital audits helps to maintain a high standard of service, using room cleaning metrics like time taken to clean a room, quality score of the cleanliness and room inspection.

- Creating digital hotel SOPS (standard operating procedures) and checklists can give staff easy access to the internal standards of the practice and the training materials when needed.
- Live recording and tracking of the lost and found items.
- Recording of the minibar consumption.
- Reporting of maintenance requests to the engineering department.

Benefits of using housekeeping management software

- Effective work scheduling allows management to plan the manpower cost more effectively. The data helps to predict the real-time staffing decisions more accurately.
- It allows consolidated communication between the departments and the staff, thus resulting in enhanced guest satisfaction.
- Increased productivity and efficiency enables housekeeping staff to deliver personalised experience to their guests.

Software solutions

Three of the key companies offering software solutions for hotels are:
- **FCS (Fast Connected & Simple) Housekeeping** https://fcscs.com
- **Amadeus Hospitality** at www.amadeus-hospitality.com/hotels/
- **Knowcross** at https://knowcross.com/lang/know-housekeeping/

> **Maintenance matters!**
>
> An efficient maintenance system supports the housekeeping department to offer a zero-defect rooms and public areas to the guests. Engineering job assignments can be automated to enhance efficiency and reduce the paperwork. Engineering jobs can be viewed in real time on the web and mobile applications, so the job can be tracked from start to finish. Preventive maintenance of the equipment can be scheduled using the software and this can increase the life span of the equipment.

Analytics and intelligence

Due to the additional processes and protocols post Covid-19, housekeeping costs have risen and now is the time to take advantage of technological advancements to prioritise hotel housekeeping analytics.

The use of digital housekeeping checklists saves time, avoids miscommunication and lets the housekeeping staff view the comments about their task, focusing on the area as highlighted in the comment and the photo. Data on actual housekeeping task performance duration can be integrated with the hotel's property management system, to enable data driven scheduling decisions. Hotel housekeeping analytics enable managers to analyse the collected data and identify quality patterns. Finding patterns in the quality will assist the housekeeping managers and supervisors to address the issue s arising from a specific staff member, or complimenting a staff member if the quality is meeting the benchmark. Predicted room cleaning times will enable the hotels to minimise the waste of the resources and in turn enhancing productivity and profitability.

The Hilton hotel chain was one of the first to implement technology in their housekeeping department. The *'Perfect Room'* app helps ensure the overall cleanliness of the rooms. The room attendants must press 'start clean' once they have entered the room; then tick a check list which includes key jobs such as disinfecting the light switches, door handles, and remote controls, among others. When they have finished they press 'stop clean' and the rooms go into 'clean' mode, and this is communicated to the Front Desk. The advantage of the app it that it provides real-time information to the Housekeeping Office.

The IoT and the evolution in housekeeping

The IoT (Internet of Things) uses a variety of technologies to connect the digital and physical worlds. Objects are fitted with *sensors*, which can monitor temperature or motion, or other changes around them, or with *actuators*, which pick up signals from sensors and respond to them. The sensors and actuators communicate via wired networks or WiFi with computing systems that can monitor the state of those connected objects and machines.

The IoT has rapidly moved into the hospitality industry and specially into the housekeeping department. It has facilitated intelligent automation, thereby improving the standards of convenience and comfort for guests.

One of the most significant trends is the use of *Near Field Communication (NFC)* technology. We noted in Chapter 14 the CLEANtracker technology, which monitors housekeeping staff in real-time through fitting NFC chips on or near all high touchpoints, and giving staff a wrist-strap device which communicates with them. Similarly, RFI (radio frequency identification) tags can be attached to linen, and items tracked with the use of scanners, greatly simplifying stock control and reducing losses.

TraknProtect

TraknProtect Internet of Things (IoT) platform offers real-time tracking of the location of assets and people. It works through the use of beacons (sensors) on objects, or carried by people, and gateways throughout the hotel which identify the location of the sensors. There are four strands:

- **Inventory** tracking helps the staff with the real time location of guest request items rollaway beds/cribs, ensuring the requests are met quickly and efficiently resulting in exceeding guest expectation.

A TraknProtect beacon

- **Room tray** tracking identifies when room-service trays have been put out in the hallways, so that they can be collected swiftly. This keeps hallways clear, without the need for staff to patrol them.

- **Vendor** tracking ensures the safety of the vendors, as well as guests, on the site by keeping a list of vendors with their real-time location. In the post covid-19 environment this solution makes it easier for hotels to know who was in the building and for how long. The app restricts the access of the vendors to the restricted areas thus ensuring the safety of the guests and the other hotel staff.

- **Safety buttons** assures staff and guests that they can summon help in case they need it. Thus, enabling enhanced peace of mind and providing a safer environment by tracking the exact room number and floor location. This has an added feature of recording the incident and the images.

TraknKleen is a new IoT housekeeping compliance solution designed by TraknProtect. Lke CLEANtracker it uses location data to create an audit trail of date/time and duration of cleaning. Noticeably though non-guest areas, such as staff break-rooms, are excluded from the audit trail; and the data aggregation is conducted intermittently to avoid real-time tracking concerns of housekeeping staff.

Details at: https://www.traknprotect.com/traknkleen

Technological solutions

Air purifiers

Housekeeping is responsible for providing a fresh and safe atmosphere for their guests and therefore need to control the temperature and humidity, and keep the air free from pollutants such as VOC (Volatile Organic Compounds) biological contaminants, ammonia, viruses etc. An efficient HVAC (Heating, Ventilation, Air Conditioning) system is, of course, essential, but an air purification system is also needed.

Some hotels use UV air purifiers. These draw in air and pass it through a filter. The air then goes through a small internal chamber where it is exposed to UV-C light which kills viruses and bacteria in the air. These devices do not effectively remove VOCs from the air, and some emit ozone, which can be harmful, particularly for asthma sufferers.

Filtration using innovative technology now offers more effective air purification, ensuring a fresh and safer environment for the guests and the staff. HEPA (high-efficiency particulate air) filters can capturing 99.97% of the tiny particles in the air, including dust mites, mold, pollen, dirt, bacteria and even viruse. To be classified as HEPA, the filters must be able to capture particles as small as 0.3 micros – a micron is one millionth of a metre.

A typical HEPA air purification unit will have three of four filters. When the air is first drawn in it passes through a micro pre-filter, to trap the larger particles. There may then be a layer of fabric to catch the next level of particle, before it passes through the HEPA filter, and then through a carbon filter to remove odours.

Covid-19 has forced hotels to minimise the risk of the virus by using new technological tools. For example, the UV light card sanitation machine used at Sofitel St James, London and other hotels will kill 99.9% of bacteria and viruses. When different guests or staff members will handle the same card, it will avoid the risk of getting contaminated.

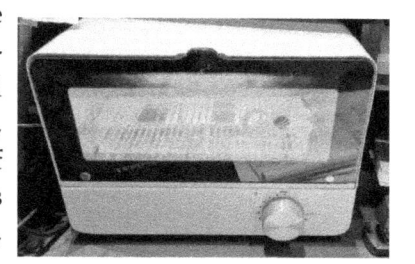

Applications and voice control communication

The purpose of investing in housekeeping technology is to enhance the customer experience. Therefore, addition of smart devices in the room which are controlled by an app makes communication between the guest and the housekeeping staff quick and efficient. This results in addressing guest requests and needs effectively. For instance, if guests want their room to be serviced or need extra water bottles, an app can communicate this seamlessly to the relevant housekeeping staff resulting in a great collaboration between the guest and the staff. Smart speakers and similar devices can allow guests to control some of the aspects of their room as well.

Marriott has implemented technology into servicing and guest requests through their app called *Marriott Bonvoy*. The guest makes a request on the app which is sent automatically to the on-duty public area attendants. The attendant gets a notification on the phone, delivers the product which is left outside the room door and marks this task as 'done'. The guest receives a notification which shows their product is at the door and they can collect. This has produced quicker, smoother service, and was particularly valuable during the pandemic as it reduces the contact between people.

> Check out this article which discusses *How technology has brought revolution in Hospitality Industry* www.forbes.com/sites/forbestechcouncil/2018/06/28/new-technologies-will-revolutionize-the-hospitality-industry

Hilton properties use the Kipsu communicaitons and social engagement system to elevate the guests' experiences around the globe by allowing them to connect with the hotel staff instantly over messages. It allows the guests to share how their experience can be made better by offering feedback and preferences. Kipsu is integrated with the property management system and Hilton Honors app which helps in engaging and building relationship with their guests throughout the guest journey.

Find out more at: https://www.kipsu.com

Robotic housekeeping

Robotic housekeeping technology results in alleviating the pressure on the housekeeping staff, for example a robotic vacuum cleaner can clean the floors without human intervention which is a great news and preferred guest need in the pandemic era.

Further, the robotic vacuum cleaners are efficient battery-operated cleaning devices that can be controlled through the smartphone of the housekeeping staff. The vacuum cleaners are equipped with anti-collision, soft cushion bumpers and anti-drop sensors that would promote a contactless cleaning drive within the hotel rooms by the housekeeping staff.

Rosie is a robotic vacuum cleaner with best-in-class commercial cleaning performance. It uses AI technology to autonomously operate in complex indoor environments, like guest rooms.

Find out more at https://tailos.com

Henna-Na Hotels, based in Japan, take the use of robots further than anyone else. They have:
- Air-cleaning robots
- Floor-cleaning robots
- Window-wiping robots
- Humanoid receptionists

Find out more at https://group.hennnahotel.com

Artificial intelligence in housekeeping

To reduce the burden on the housekeeping staff many of the housekeeping technological solutions rely on artificial intelligence. Deriving insights from the data impactful experiences are offered to the guest by personalising the amenities. For example, remembering their choice of pillow, water/fruit preferences. The smart Television launched by LG offers compatibility with Amazon Alexa and Google Assistant. The voice compatibility allows guests to control the lighting, temperature, blinds (drapes), door locks etc. Digital communication with guests, frees up the hotel staffs and allows them to focus on the core task and the delivery. Read more about the technology and innovation at https://hospitalitytech.com/hotel-future-0

Training using technology

Regular staff training in the housekeeping department is extremely important to deliver quality service to the guests. Technological innovations have resulted in making training more cost effective as well as more engaging. Use of artificial intelligence and machine learning with speech and motion sensors has made the training more effective.

During the Covid-19 pandemic, when the housekeeping staff were required to be trained with some of the additional safety measures and protocols, the cloud-based technology came as a boon to hotels, as it mean that the staff could be provided with digital learning materials which they could assess from their home on their own devices.

Summary

Technology should serve the purpose and enable the employees to perform their operation effectively. By adopting technology, hotel brands can meet and exceed the guest experience and it helps them in wowing their guests. Technology enables hotel managers to manage the complex housekeeping operation smoothly and seamlessly. Choosing the right fit-for-purpose technology can bring meaningful improvements for guests as well as for employees. Using technology to automate the tasks that used to be carried out manually frees up the employees' time, manages their workload and allows them to focus on more creative tasks..

Activities

1. Discuss in groups the impacts of technology in hotel housekeeping operation.
2. How does the Internet of Things influence the experience of the customer in the hotel?
3. Analyse the role of the technology in optimising the housekeeping department's expenditure.
4. Discuss some of the features of the smart guest rooms.

Key terms

- **Hi Jiffy**: A chatbot that connects guests with the hotel staff for instant communication to deliver guest requests and deal with any complaints. Find out more at https://www.hijiffy.com/
- **Smart hotels**: Hotels using a range of information and communication technologies including IoT, cloud computing, mobile internet, smart devices and big data.
- **Technology amenities**: Supplies or facilities provided to the guest in their guest room or outside for no extra charge, example Wi-Fi, face or voice recognition, smart TV, service robots, smart room keys, touch screen panels (to control light, temperature, music, drapes etc)
- **Connected room**: Hilton is delivering its mobile centric Connected Room in which the guest can personalise and control every aspect of their stay.

References

Asafa, T.B., Afonja, T.M., Olaniyan,E.A. & Alade, H.O. . (2018) Development of a vacuum cleaner robot, *Alexandria Engineering Journal*, 57(4), 2911–2920. doi:10.1016/j.aej.2018.07.005.

Shin, H. & Kang, J. (2020) Reducing perceived health risk to attract hotel customers in the COVID-19 pandemic era: Focused on technology innovation for social distancing and cleanliness, *International Journal of Hospitality Management*, 91. doi:10.1016/j.ijhm.2020.102664.

Tieng, S. (2019) *Hospitality Information Technology*. Society Publishing. .

Verma, P., Singh, M. & Aggarwal, N. (2020) 'the effect of next –level housekeeping via technology on the perceptions of the hospitality aspirants', 8th International Conference on Reliability, Infocom Technologies and Optimization, pp. 1150–1156. doi:10.1109/ICRITO48877.2020.9197965.

Vivion, N., (2018).11 Thoughts on the Future of Technology in Travel and Hospitality from CES 2018. Phocuswire.com. Available at: https://www.phocuswire.com/11-thoughts-on-the-future-of-technology-in-travel-and-hospitality-from-CES-2018 (Accessed on 18th January 2023)

Yang, H., Song, H., Cheung, C. & Guan, J. (2021) How to enhance hotel guests' acceptance and experience of smart hotel technology: An examination of visiting intentions, *International Journal of Hospitality Management*, 97. doi:10.1016/j.ijhm.2021.103000.

Index

abrasives 84
accessible rooms 154, 175
Accor's peopleology 62
adjoining room 154
amenities 160, 163
analytics and intelligence 215
aparthotels 154
aquanomic 127
area inventory list 55
artificial intelligence 221
assistant executive HK 32
atmosphere/ambiance 180
attributes 36

back of the house 47
bacterioloical cleaning 93
beekeeper app 61
BICS 86
biodegradable plastic 193
biophilia 180
boutique hotel 180
budget 38, 109
    classification 111
    cycle 110
budgetary control 113
budgeting 30

cabana 154
capital budget 111
carpet tiles 171
chamois leather 75
chandeliers 46
chemical cleaning 93
circadian lighing 196

cleaning 89
    agents 79
    equipment 73
    frequency 90
    specification 78
    supplies 84
cleanliness theatre 202
colour schemes 168
commercial cleaners 46
complete outsourcing 40
connected room 222
connecting rooms 154
continuous improvement 115
controlling expenses 112
COPC 86
COSHH 82, 142
cost control 30
crisis management 152
CSR 193
CSSA 86

degreasers 84
departure 17
design 155
detergents 84
dilution 86
direct cost 40
down pillows 163
downtime 49
druggets 75
dry cleaning 131
dust ruffle 163
dustettes 76
duty roster 57

Earth check 184
Ecobrite 128
eco-friendly 181
Ecolab 83, 124
EHK 27,31
ehthical sourcing of uniform 188
electrochemical solution 85
electrostatic sprayers 95
emergencies 147
EMS environmental management system 190
energy conservation 186
environmentally friendly 159
ergonomics 207
EU ecolabel 184
expenses 117

facility management 46
financial performance 44
fire safety 147
fixed budget 111
fixtures 163
flexible budget 111
floor supervisor 33
flooring 171
flower arrangement 176
flower care 176
flower room 22
food and beverage 18
forecasting 117
frequency schedules 55
front office 18

Green Globe 184
green hotels 182
Green Key 184
green leaders 184
green wash 193
guest bathroom 24
guest cycle 17
guest loan items 163

guest room 24

Hasawa 141
hazard 152
health & safety 168
HEPA filters 219
heritage hotel 12
hidden cost 40
HM software 215
hollywood twin 154
hospitality 1
hot water extraction 77
hotel 20
hotel uniform 131
housekeeping 12,23
    co-ordinator 21
    layout 20
hydrogen peroxide 94,95
hypo allergenic pillows 200

incentives 60
indirect cost 40
inovative cart 207
inspection 117
inventory 117
inventory control 112
IOT 217
ISO 184

job planning 54
job safety analyis 152

key performance indicator (KPI) 52

laminate floors 171
Lanai 154
laundry 21,41
laundry manager 35
laundry operations 121
leadtime 49
LEED 184

Index

leisure facilities 24
lighting 168
linen chute 137
linen management 135
linen par 137
linen room 22
long term budgeting 111
lost & found 12, 23, 148
LQA audits 62
luxury amenities 160

maintenance 18
    order form 19
manpower planning 55
manual equipment 74
marble flooring 172
mattress lift tool 207
mechanical box sweeper 75
mechanical equipment 76

occupancy 27
occupied room 97
operating budget 111
operational planning 51
OPL 27
organisation structure 25
OSH standards 152
OSHA 210
out of order rooms 97
outsourcing 39
    challenges 45

par level 133
partial outsourcing 40
performance 52
    standards 71
pest control 149
physical cleaning 93
pile lifters 76
pillow menu 200
PMS 214

porcelain flooring 172
pre-arrival 17
pre-opening budget 111
priodical cleaning 90
procurement 117
productivity 38
    standards 53, 55
pro-environmental behaviour 189
public area supervisor 34
purchase order 117
purchasing 30, 113

QMS 116
quad rooms 154

recruitment 30
recycling 183
reduce 183
refurbishment 27
repetitive task 71
resort 3
resource based view 44
reuse 183
revenue 117
RFID technology 121
RIDDOR 146
risk 144
    assessment 144
    management 144
robotic housekeeping 220
room status 96
rooms division manager(RDM) 15

safety 152
    data sheet 81
sales & marketing 20
satisfaction 44
scarifying machine 77
scrim clothes 75
Sebo Dart 77
security 19, 152

shampooing machine 77
sleep tourism 159
smart beds 201
smart hotels 222
sorting 122
spring cleaning 91
staff engegement 61
standard operating procedure 38
steam cleaning 96, 203
stock taking 137
strategic performance 44
studio room 154
suite rooms 154
supplier identification 49
supplier relationship management 49
supplier selection 49
sustainability 181,182
sustainable hospitality alliance 185
swab tests 96
Sybron 84

tailoring 22
technology 159
time and motion 37
TQM 114
training 30
transaction cost economics 44

trends 159
trolleys 75
TSA (textile services association)137
turndown 12
twin room 154

uniform design 132
uniform room 22
uniform supervisor 34
unique selling point (USP) 4
upcycle 183
upholstery 137
UV lights 94,96

vacant inspected 97
vacuum cleaners 76
villas 155
vinyl tiles 171

wall covering 172
wash cycle 122
waste management 185
water saving systems 187
wellness 196
WMSDS 141
woden flooring 172
work schedules 54